AIDS, South Africa, and the Politics of Knowledge

JEREMY R. YOUDE
Grinnell College, USA

ASHGATE

Published by
Ashgate Publishing Limited
Gower House
Croft Road
Aldershot
Hampshire GU11 3HR
England

Ashgate Publishing Company
Suite 420
101 Cherry Street
Burlington, VT 05401-4405
USA

Ashgate website: http://www.ashgate.com

British Library Cataloguing in Publication Data
Youde, Jeremy R.
    AIDS, South Africa, and the politics of knowledge. - (Global health)
    1. AIDS (Disease) - Prevention - Government policy - South
    Africa 2. HIV infections - Prevention - Government policy -
    South Africa 3. Medical policy - South Africa 4. AIDS
    (Disease) - South Africa 5. HIV infections - South Africa
    I. Title
    362.1'969792'00968

Library of Congress Cataloging-in-Publication Data
Youde, Jeremy R., 1976-
    AIDS, South Africa, and the politics of knowledge / by Jeremy R. Youde.
        p. cm. -- (Global health)
    Includes bibliographical references and index.
    ISBN 978-0-7546-7003-2
    1. AIDS (Disease)--South Africa. 2. AIDS (Disease)--Government policy--South
Africa. 3. AIDS (Disease)--Political aspects--South Africa. 4. Public health--South
Africa. 5. Knowledge, Theory of--Political aspects. 6. South Africa--Relations--Foreign
countries. I. Title.

    RA643.86.S6Y68 2007
    362.196'979200968--dc22

                                                                    2007009696

ISBN: 978-0-7546-7003-2

Printed and bound in Great Britain by MPG Books Ltd, Bodmin, Cornwall.

AIDS, SOUTH AFRICA, AND THE POLITICS OF KNOWLEDGE

Global Health

Series Editors: Nana K. Poku and Robert L. Ostergard, Jr.

The benefits of globalization are potentially enormous, as a result of the increased sharing of ideas, cultures, life-saving technologies and efficient production processes. Yet globalization is under trial, partly because these benefits are not yet reaching hundreds of millions of the world's poor and partly because globalization has introduced new kinds of international problems and conflicts. Turmoil in one part of the world now spreads rapidly to others, through terrorism, armed conflict, environmental degradation or disease.

This timely series provides a robust and multi-disciplinary assessment of the asymmetrical nature of globalization. Books in the series encompass a variety of areas, including global health and the politics of governance, poverty and insecurity, gender and health and the implications of global pandemics.

Contents

List of Tables

Acknowledgments

Serendipity works in strange ways. In my case, a seemingly casual conversation led me down my academic path.

During the summer of 2001, I received the Charles and Kathleen Manatt Democracy Studies Research Fellowship at the International Foundation for Election Systems in Washington, DC. This gave me six weeks to dive into independent research – but I was having some trouble focusing my ideas. One of my first days there, I had a conversation with John Mitchell, then the Senior Program Officer for Africa at IFES. Talking about my background, interests, and experiences, he casually asked, "What about the relationship between AIDS and democracy?" I had studied the impact of AIDS in Zimbabwe while studying abroad there as an undergraduate, but had never heard anyone talk about the impact of AIDS on the political system or thought it would be something to pursue. John's question embarked me on a research path that led to the creation of this book (and my academic career). I must thank IFES for providing me with a space to develop my research at such a crucial early stage of my graduate career – Tom Bayer, Margi Colson, Keenan Howell, Alex Knapp, Jerry Mindes, John Mitchell, Dan Murphy, Richard Soudriette, Dorin Tudoran, and many others.

From the beginning, many others helped me refine my ideas and pushed my intellectual development. Doug Dion introduced me to the work of William McNeill on disease's role in history. Rodney Bruce Hall encouraged me to push against the traditional boundaries of international relations, introduced me to the regime theory literature, and remains a friend and mentor to this day. Without his help (and the occasional kick in the pants), this project never would have come to fruition. Brian Lai asked critical, thought-provoking questions at critical points in my research and writing. Rod and Brian approach international relations and political science from very different perspectives, but they both pushed me to produce the best possible research. For that, they both have my undying gratitude. Bob Boynton, Shelly Campo, and Denise Powers read versions of all of these chapters, providing helpful criticisms and critiques.

My work is stronger for the input, support, and friendship of colleagues like Pieter Fourie, Yanzhong Huang, Audie Klotz, Bob Ostergard, Andrew Price-Smith, Per Strand, Matt Tubin, and Alan Whiteside.

My wonderful former colleagues at San Diego State University provided a stimulating intellectual environment for someone fresh out of graduate school. My heartfelt appreciation goes out to Farid Abdel-Nour, David Carruthers, Dawn Christensen, Jonathan Graubart, Lei Guang, Dipak Gupta, Richard Hofstetter, Carole Kennedy, Ron King, Kristen Hill Maher, Madhavi McCall, Julie Sullivan, Latha Varadarajan, and everyone else. I also thank the San Diego State University

Research Committee under the leadership of Carole Sweedler-Brown for providing me with Faculty Development Program (FDP) and Research, Scholarship, and Creative Activity (RSCA) grants. Without the financial and time support those provided, this book would have taken much longer to finish. At Grinnell College, I learned that you can indeed go home again. Bob Grey and Eliza Willis were not only my advisors during my undergraduate days, but they offered me the amazing opportunity to teach at my alma mater and further develop my research. Dionne Bensonsmith, Jimmy Clausen, Wayne Moyer, Ira Strauber, and Barb Trish all helped me to clarify my thoughts, and Karen Groves, Karla Landers, Linda Ludwig, and De Dudley helped keep me sane and going to the right place.

At Ashgate, Kirstin Howgate, Jacqui Cornish, and Margaret Younger have my unending gratitude for guiding me through the publishing process. I also extend my deepest appreciation to Bob Ostergard and Nana Poku, editors of the Global Health series, for selecting my book to be part of their series.

Some of the material in this book originally appeared in my article, 'The Development of a Counter-Epistemic Community: AIDS, South Africa, and International Regimes', in *International Relations* Vol. 19, No. 4, pp. 421–440 (© Sage Publications, 2005). This material is reprinted here by permission of Sage Publications Ltd., and I thank them for granting such permission.

Sara O'Brien has been one of my best friends since we met in junior high, and she continues to be an intellectual compatriot and kindred spirit. Her careful editing and well-developed arguments have made this book so much stronger. Brent Steele's encyclopedic knowledge of political science literature, incredible grasp of international relations theory, and hearty laugh have saved me from all sorts of problems. Jack Amoureux's insights and suggestions have always been spot-on. Tracy Slagter was my rock during graduate school and beyond. Her positive outlook and willingness to listen made writing my dissertation an almost-enjoyable experience. Megan Shannon, Andrew Bargen, and Dong-hun Kim provided encouragement and much-needed laughter at conferences.

My parents, Jerry and Cynthia Youde, deserve numerous accolades. I don't know that they fully understood what I was doing or why, but they always encouraged me in my pursuits. There's no motivation for finishing a project like hearing your mother and father tell you that they're anxious to read your book.

Most importantly, my partner, Ben Nauman, has stuck with me through this whole process. His love, encouragement, and support mean the world to me. He and our dog, Max, remind me that there's a world outside of research and writing – and for that, I am eternally grateful.

List of Abbreviations

AIDS	Acquired Immune Deficiency Syndrome
ANC	African National Congress
ARVs	Antiretroviral Drugs
AZT	Azidothymidine (zidovudine)
CD4	T Helper Cell
COSATU	Coalition of South African Trade Unions
DOH	Department of Health
GLBT	Gay/Lesbian/Bisexual/Transgendered
GRID	Gay-Related Immune Deficiency
HAART	Highly-active antiretroviral therapy
HEAL	Health Education AIDS Liaison
HIV	Human Immunodeficiency Virus
MCC	Medicines Control Council
MRC	Medical Research Council
NEPAD	New Partnership for African Development
NIAID	National Institutes of Allergy and Infectious Diseases
NIH	National Institutes of Health
NRA	National Resistance Army
NRM	National Resistance Movement
SAMA	South African Medical Association
SARS	Severe Acute Respiratory Syndrome
SSK	Sociology of scientific knowledge
TAC	Treatment Action Campaign
TB	Tuberculosis
TIG	Treatment Information Group
TRC	Truth and Reconciliation Commission
UNAIDS	Joint United Nations Program on HIV/AIDS
WHO	World Health Organization

Chapter 1

Introduction

When histories assess the democratic credentials of Thabo Mbeki's government in the future, it is likely that their most critical attentions will focus on its responses to the HIV/AIDS pandemic, surely the most formidable developmental challenge (Lodge 2002, 255).

South Africa's HIV/AIDS pandemic would overwhelm any government. With approximately 20 percent of its adult population HIV-positive, any state would face enormous challenges marshaling the human, social, and financial resources necessary to combat this scourge. Add to this the tremendous upheavals associated with dismantling a racist regime, and one can easily understand the scope the challenge South Africa faces.

South Africa has faced an additional challenge, one of its own (or at least, of members of its government's) making. Jacobs and Calland describe it bluntly: "Whenever one [from South Africa] traveled, the same – or similar – questions were put: 'Why has he [Mbeki] got such funny views on HIV/AIDS?' There has been no easy answer to this question" (Jacobs and Calland 2002, 3).

The country with the highest number of HIV-positive adults in the world, and one of the highest HIV prevalence rates, has seemingly embraced a policy one could describe as denialism. Instead of emphasizing the provision of HAART (highly active anti-retroviral therapy) and working with the mainstream international AIDS control regime, South African President Thabo Mbeki has openly questioned whether HIV actually causes AIDS. He and members of his Cabinet have called on AIDS dissidents, largely shunned by the international community and who deny the connection between HIV and AIDS, to serve as policy advisors. Dr. Manto Tshabalala-Msimang, the Minister of Health during Mbeki's second term, has called AIDS drugs toxic and encouraged the use of garlic, lemon juice, and olive oil to treat AIDS. Instead of working with the international AIDS control regime, the South African government has expressed reluctance, if not outright hostility, towards its fundamental beliefs. AIDS dissidents have managed to gain a foothold in South Africa and influence policy while nearly every other government has shunned them. Why is this the case?

The Paradox of AIDS Policies in South Africa

UNAIDS estimates that, as of the end of 2005, approximately 5.5 million South Africans are HIV-positive. The vast majority of that number is between the ages of 15 and 49, in the midst of what should be the most economically productive years of life (UNAIDS 2006a). The South African economy stands to lose billions of dollars, and the potential consequences for the political system are enormous. Even if South Africa managed to stop the spread of AIDS today, the country essentially faces the loss of an entire generation. Given such a grim scenario, we would expect the South African government to take the lead on treating those infected with the disease and preventing further infection. We would expect the South African government to take advantage of the resources offered by the international AIDS control regime to stem the tide of the epidemic. We would expect a group of international recognized experts on the disease to play a prominent role in formulating South Africa's AIDS policies. We would expect the South African government to be a leader in the fight against AIDS.

At best, one could describe South Africa's AIDS policies as schizophrenic. While President Mbeki and Health Minister Tshabalala-Mismang publicly express doubt about the efficacy of treating AIDS, other Cabinet members express support for the international mainstream consensus for addressing the disease. Members of the government advocate for nutritional interventions as the best way to treat AIDS, but the Department of Health continues to purchase millions of condoms and an increasing number of state-sponsored sites offer HAART, albeit on a limited scale. The national government's stance has often been at odds with individual provincial governments, especially those controlled by opposition political parties. Government officials express doubt about the epistemological bases of the AIDS policies that other parts of the national government have produced. In the post-apartheid era, it has been difficult for anyone to say with certainty what South Africa's national AIDS policies are. Leading policymakers have repeatedly challenged the mainstream scientific consensus on the cause of and treatment for AIDS. This in turn has undermined the effectiveness of AIDS prevention and treatment programs in South Africa. All the while, HIV infection rates and annual deaths due to AIDS continue to increase.

We find ourselves confronted by a paradox. Given the scope of South Africa's pandemic, we would rationally expect the South African government to actively collaborate with the international AIDS control regime and work with the recognized experts in the field to create the best possible policies. Instead, it has produced a jumbled mess of policies that reflect the influence of AIDS dissidents and challenge the fundamental bases of the international AIDS control regime and its epistemic community. Why would the country that seemingly has the most to gain from working with the international AIDS control regime and its epistemic community shun those experts and turn to a discredited group of AIDS dissidents? Some, including members of the South African government, argue that the cost of providing HAART is simply too expensive. While a national HAART program is indeed costly, it does not logically follow that an inability to afford the program would lead to a wholesale rejection by some prominent government officials of the fundamental tenets of AIDS science.

I posit that this situation has arisen because of the influence of a counter-epistemic community of experts who provide advice and policy recommendations from a fundamentally different basis than that of the mainstream international AIDS control regime. South Africa cannot incorporate the regime's messages without contradicting its own commitments. The mainstream epistemic community's messages, from South Africa's perspective, are inconsistent with, if not hostile to, the country's historical experiences with public health interventions and its identity commitments. This aversion to the mainstream epistemic community's messages comes from South Africa's negative experiences with outside public health campaigns and its expressed desire for an autonomous voice in international affairs as symbolized by the African Renaissance. The South African government's identity, especially in this post-apartheid era, is intertwined with avoiding the post-colonial paternalism that has often accompanied international policy toward Africa, while simultaneously promoting the need for African states to take an active role in African affairs. If we fail to understand the fundamental role that this clash of identities plays, we are left with simplistic, underdeveloped and unsatisfying answers.

Why would the South African government open itself up to international criticism by actively questioning the international consensus? The answer comes through an examination of the country's history with public health interventions and the state's identity commitments. Throughout South African history, government officials have invoked public health rationales to justify discriminatory, racist policies. For some current leaders, the international attention paid to South Africa's AIDS policies reek of an attempt to reassert control and domination over Africa. At the same time, the government actively promotes a post-apartheid national identity based on African Renaissance-inspired ideals. Finding African solutions for African problems is key to this identity, and proponents frequently reject the notion that Western experiences and suggestions can be superimposed on the African experience. (Curiously, though, nearly all of the AIDS dissidents are from Western countries, an odd juxtaposition to which I will return in Chapter 5.) President Mbeki and other members of his government have explicitly linked this African Renaissance-inspired identity commitment to the state's AIDS policies. This book will explore both of these factors in great detail.

Instead, it turned to a *counter-epistemic community* of AIDS dissidents. The counter-epistemic community of AIDS dissidents translates South Africa's history with public health interventions and its identity commitments translate into actual governmental policy. This counter-epistemic community of scientists and experts has an international membership and shapes the AIDS discourse in South Africa by offering advice and policy suggestions to the South African government. It serves as a counterweight to the epistemic community embraced by the international AIDS control regime. Just as any epistemic community does, the counter-epistemic community translates the amorphous notions of history and self-identity into policy outcomes, giving them real-world weight.

Peter Haas introduced international relations scholars to the idea of the epistemic community. An epistemic community is a network of scientists and experts to whom policymakers turn for guidance and unbiased information when a new issue emerges. Policymakers, in turn, take this information to craft appropriate governmental responses. Members of an epistemic community possess a significant amount power, as they frame the problem for the government and, often, the public. This power, according to Haas and other scholars, derives from the seemingly impartial nature of the information provided by members of the epistemic community. Because these scientists and experts are regarded as apolitical, policymakers are more willing to defer to them. Numerous scholars have adopted the epistemic communities framework to analyze issues like ozone depletion, Mediterranean Sea pollution, and the regulation of space satellites. The literature on epistemic communities and international regimes plays an increasingly important role in both academic and policy debates.

While the epistemic communities framework certainly represents an advance in our understanding of the role of scientific knowledge in international policymaking, it has one significant limitation: it assumes that only *one* epistemic community will emerge on any given issue. This is puzzling. First, claims of the impartiality of scientific knowledge are false. Scholars working within the sociology of scientific knowledge have demonstrated repeatedly that scientific knowledge often reflects a particular social, political, and historical context. That does not mean that this science is manipulated; rather, what counts as scientific *fact* reflects broader societal contexts. By the same token, they have demonstrated how policymakers have repeatedly cited the impartiality of science to justify policy action (or inaction) that accord with their own preferences. Second, it is epistemologically contradictory to argue on the one hand that policymakers will turn to a group of experts for policy advice when a new issue emerges, yet assert on the other that all these policymakers will turn to the *same* group of experts. The epistemic communities literature builds on knowledge-based theories of international regimes. These theories argue that normative and causal beliefs can have a direct impact on policy outcomes, and that changes in beliefs can lead to changes in policy. However, given its understanding of the power of normative beliefs on policy, it makes little sense to assert that only one causal belief will emerge. Haas notes that members of the epistemic community may disagree with one another on policy suggestions. He does not mention, though, what happens when competing groups of experts not only offer differing policy suggestions but also understand a given issue in fundamentally different ways. It is true that one explanation may eventually fall by the wayside as more information becomes available, but there is no a priori reason to assume this will always happens. How do these competing groups of experts impact international policymaking?

Through an in-depth, qualitative examination of the interactions between members of the South African government and the international AIDS control regime and its associated epistemic community, I examine not only the emergence of an epistemic community but also the development of a counter-epistemic community. Members of this counter-epistemic community are not simply crackpots; many of them have advanced degrees from prestigious universities and hold important positions in academia and industry. In essence, we find one group of highly-credentialed experts competing with another group of highly-credentialed experts, offering fundamentally divergent understandings of AIDS and radically different policy prescriptions. This is an important advance in understanding how and when epistemic communities operate which addresses both policy and academic concerns. It resolves the epistemological contradiction noted above, while also clearly demonstrating how differing causal and normative beliefs can have an important impact on policy outcomes.

This book is certainly more than the story of one man (Thabo Mbeki) and one woman (Manto Tshabalala-Msimang). These two people are highly prominent in the

South African government who have empowered a group of dissident advisors and help direct national AIDS policies. It is also the story of how scientific knowledge plays a role in the policymaking process, how governments empower different groups of actors, and how science can be a political tool and reflect a state's social, historical, and political contexts.

International relations theories traditionally assume that the state is a single unitary actor, speaking with one voice. Individuals exist within a government and may disagree with one another, but state actions ultimately present a single perspective. Within the neorealist vein, Waltz notes that, even as personalities and behaviors change within a state, the structures of that state endure. What's more, these structures place limitations on the actions of those personalities and channel state actions through the top leaders (Waltz 1979, 80–87). By this logic, then, we should rightfully understand that the state speaks with only one voice. Different voices may exist *within* the state, but policies eventually come from a single point with a single voice. Keohane, working within a neoliberal framework, agrees, as this assumption allows for more parsimonious theories and focuses attention on how structures constrain actors (Keohane 1984, 29).

If we start from this assumption, then it makes little sense to investigate the beliefs of Mbeki, Tshabalala-Msimang, and the AIDS dissidents. South African AIDS policies do not uniformly reflect a dissident stance. Even if Mbeki, Tshabalala-Msimang, and the AIDS dissidents wanted to unilaterally impose their ideas, they could not. They are simply parts of a much larger government, and the legislative process requires the assent of a wide variety of actors to make any idea policy.

However, the confusion and incoherence of the government's AIDS policies demonstrate the importance of disaggregating the state and investigating the beliefs of different groups. Milner notes: "When domestic actors share power over decision making and their policy preferences differ, treating the state as a unitary actor risks distorting our understanding of international relations" (Milner 1997, 33).

This is the situation that prevails in South Africa for its national AIDS policies. Mbeki and Tshabalala-Msimang's beliefs about AIDS may not be policy, but their doubts about the wisdom of conventional AIDS policies introduces a degree of doubt that undermines the effectiveness of those policies. AIDS dissidents may not make policy on their own, but they influence those policies, their implementation, and the public reception of those policies. The South African government is not speaking with one voice when it comes to national AIDS policies or communicating these policies to the outside world. Not every South African, or even every South African government official, values and supports the AIDS dissident position, but some highly-placed South Africans with a major impact on national policy (and the public reception of those policies) do.

The AIDS Epidemic in Perspective

We should put the AIDS epidemic in perspective. In its 2006 report on the worldwide AIDS epidemic, UNAIDS estimates that approximately 39.5 million people are

HIV-positive (UNAIDS 2006b, 1) – up from 34.3 million in 2000 (*Population and Development Review* 2000, 629). Nearly 95 percent, or 37.2 million, of these cases are in people over the age of 15. Over 4 million people contracted HIV during 2006, dwarfing the 2.9 million AIDS deaths during that same period (UNAIDS 2006b, 1). While some areas, like Zimbabwe, Tamil Nadu in India, and urban districts in Burkina Faso, have reported successes in decreasing their HIV prevalence rates, and research suggests that the worldwide HIV prevalence rate peaked in the late 1990s, the absolute number of HIV-positive persons continues to increase annually (UNAIDS 2006b, 6).

Women make up an increasing percentage of HIV infections. "Globally through 1997, women, children, and teenagers seemed to be on the periphery of the HIV/ AIDS pandemic. In 2002 however, they became the center" (Stine 2005, 332). In 2006, UNAIDS reported that women made up 44 percent of all HIV-positive persons (UNAIDS 2006b, 90). By 2005, over 50 percent of all *new* infections occurred among women (Stine 2005, 332). Not only are women more vulnerable to HIV infection for physiological reasons, but their lack of empowerment in many parts of the world puts them at risk. Women are also expected to care for those who get sick with AIDS, regardless of their own HIV status. UNAIDS suggests that women face greater stigma and discrimination when they reveal their HIV status than the male partners who infected them (UNAIDS 2006b, 90).

The situation is more dire in sub-Saharan Africa. UNAIDS reports that 24.7 million people in the region are living with HIV, an increase of nearly one million people since 2004. This means that nearly two out of every three HIV infections in the world in sub-Saharan Africa. While two million Africans died of AIDS during 2006, nearly three million new HIV infections occurred on the continent. The region's adult infection rate hovers around six percent. By comparison, the Caribbean is the second most-infected region at 1.2 percent, and the worldwide adult infection rate stands at one percent (UNAIDS 2006b, 2). Women comprise an increasing percentage of HIV infections in the region. By 2006, they made accounted for 57 percent of the HIV-positive adults in sub-Saharan Africa. The situation is especially acute for women aged 15 to 24, as they are 2 to 6 times more likely to be HIV-positive than sub-Saharan African men of the same age (UNAIDS 2006b, 88).

In the worst-affected region in the world, South Africa has one of the most severe epidemics. Over 5 million South African adults, approximately 18.8 percent of the adult population, are HIV-positive (UNAIDS 2006a). This figure gives South Africa not only one of the world's highest adult infection rates, but also one of the highest numbers of HIV-positive persons in the world.

The South African Department of Health published a comprehensive survey of HIV prevalence in 2006. It found that 30.2 percent of women attending antenatal clinics in 2005 were HIV-positive. Two years earlier, the national prevalence estimate was 27.9 percent. Infection rates were not uniformly distributed across the country, with KwaZulu-Natal (though its 2005 prevalence rate was lower than in 2004) and Mpumalanga recording the highest rates and Northern Cape and Western Cape the lowest (see Table 1.1). Women in their late 20s had the highest infection rates at 39.5 percent in 2005, followed closely by women in their early 30s at 36.4 percent (SADOH 2006, 9).

Table 1.1   South African Provincial HIV Prevalence Rates among Antenatal Clinic Attendees

Province	2003 prevalence rate	2004 prevalence rate	2005 prevalence rate
KwaZulu-Natal	37.5	40.7	39.1
Mpumalanga	32.6	30.8	34.8
Gauteng	29.6	33.1	32.4
North West	29.9	26.7	31.8
Free State	30.1	29.5	30.3
Eastern Cape	27.1	28.0	29.5
Limpopo	17.5	19.3	21.5
Northern Cape	16.7	17.6	18.5
Western Cape	13.1	15.4	15.7
National	27.9	29.5	30.2

Source: *SADOH* 2006, 11
Note: Figures reflect the midpoint within the 95 percent confidence interval.

The above figures only reflect pregnant women who attended antenatal clinics, not the entire population. Using mathematical models to extrapolate from these findings, the Department of Health estimates that approximately 5.54 million South Africans are HIV-positive, though they suggest this number is on the conservative end (SADOH 2006, 16). This translates to an adult HIV prevalence rate of 16.25 percent, with women comprising nearly 60 percent of this total (SADOH 2006, 17). While prevalence rates have declined for women under age 20, suggesting a decline in new cases, rates appear to be increasing for women aged 25 to 34.

A subsequent report by the Actuarial Society of South Africa, the Medical Research Council, and the University of Cape Town's Center for Actuarial Research reports similar findings, estimating that 5.3 million South Africans are HIV-positive over over 500,000 new infections would occur during the year (Dorrington et al. 2006, 8). This puts the overall prevalence rate in South Africa at 11.2 percent, with the adult (20–64) prevalence rate at 19.2 percent. Breaking it down by gender, adult women had a prevalence rate of 20.4 percent, compared with 17.8 percent for adult men. The prevalence rate for women peaked among those aged 25 to 29 at 32.5 percent. For men, the peak prevalence rate was 26.5 percent for those aged 30 to 34 (Dorrington et al. 2006, 10). Based on these numbers, the report found that 1.8 million South Africans had died of AIDS by 2006, and this total would reach 6 million in 2014 (Dorrington et al. 2006, 21).

Due to the high HIV infection rates, life expectancy rates in the country have plummeted. A man born in South Africa in 2002 could expect to live to 48, while a woman could expect only a 50-year lifespan. According to Alan Whiteside, director of the Health Economics and AIDS Research Division (HEARD) at the University KwaZulu-Natal, life expectancy in South Africa without AIDS would be around 62 years (Kaiser Network 2005). By 2006, UNAIDS decreased these life expectancy estimates for men and women to 47 and 49, respectively (UNAIDS 2006a).

The scope and scale of the AIDS epidemic in South Africa have dramatically increased in recent years. The first cases of HIV in South Africa were discovered in 1982 among White gay men. In 1990, the country recorded an adult infection rate of only 1 percent with approximately 36,000 HIV-positive persons in the entire country. By the country's first democratic multiracial elections in 1994, the epidemic had taken hold. That year, Dorrington et al. estimate that the country had more than 530,000 HIV-positive persons – a massive increase over a short period of time. Within two years, that number more than doubled again, with 1.3 million HIV-positive persons. By the time Thabo Mbeki assumed the presidency in 1999, over 3 million South Africans were HIV-positive. At the start of Mbeki's second term (and the ascension of Tshabalala-Msimang to Minister of Health), almost 5 million South Africans were infected, and the cumulative number of AIDS deaths in the country surpassed one million (Dorrington et al. 2006, 21).

According to the World Health Organization and UNAIDS, antiretroviral treatment remains out of reach for the vast majority of South Africans who need it. Nearly one million South African adults were judged to be in need to ARV treatment in 2004. As of December 2006, only 21 percent of those who need the drugs were receiving them (UNAIDS 2006a). WHO's 3×5 Initiative set a goal of putting 375,000 South Africans (approximately one-half of all who needed treatment as of 2003) on ARV treatment within two years. Its efforts did provide roughly 200,000 people with ARVs, but this still means that only twenty percent of the people today who need ARVs in South Africa are receiving them – and the number of those in need continues to go up every day (AVERT n.d.). Reports estimate that, as of June 2006, 140,000 of those on HAART received it through the public sector (Dorrington et al. 2006, 16). In an April 2006 interview, Nathan Geffen of the Treatment Action Campaign, which monitors ARV access in conjunction with the AIDS Law Project, noted that an additional 100,000 South African received HAART through private means (Pao 2006). The government pledged to roll out a large-scale national ARV treatment program in 2003, but many question the government's commitment. Its implementation has been very slow, and Tshabalala-Msimang has repeatedly criticized the international community and UNAIDS for "forcing" her to implement such a program. Many have called the program a cynical ploy by the government to fend off criticism prior to the 2004 elections.

The exact nature of the economic, political, and social impact of the disease on South African society is still somewhat unclear, but most analysts see definite negative consequences. Given the high rate of adult infection, South Africa essentially faces a lost generation. The very people who would be expected to work in and run the businesses, raise families, and take the reins of leadership are likely to be lost either to death or the demands of taking care of infected friends and family members. The economic impact has received a great deal of attention. Fredland argues, "While AIDS is one of many deterrents to development [in Africa], it has, in many affected countries, contributed significantly to undermining their future prospects" (Fredland 1998, 547–548). One macroeconomic analysis suggests that countries with a 20 percent prevalence rate (similar to South Africa's) experience a drop in per capita growth of 1.1 percent annually, resulting in a significant decrease over time (Lewis 2004, 114–115). Another analysis suggests that annual GDP growth is 0.3 to 0.4 percentage points lower than it would be in a scenario without AIDS (Fourie 2006, 2).

What happens to individual businesses? Looking at particular firms within various industries, another report indicates that firms face an 'AIDS tax' (the total annual cost of AIDS as a percentage of salaries and wages) of one to six percent (Lewis 2004, 106–107). This 'tax' cuts into profits, dissuades international entities from investing in the country, and retards job creation. More recently, Rosen et al. (2004) conducted an in-depth analysis of AIDS' costs to six formal sector enterprises in South Africa and Botswana, looking at the financial toll caused by sick leave, productivity loss, providing medical benefits, and training replacement workers. They found that the 'AIDS tax,' defined as the increase in a company's wage or operating costs due to the epidemic, ranges from 0.4 to 5.9 percent. The wide variation reflects the differing costs for skilled as opposed to unskilled workers and the epidemic's impacts in different sectors of the economy. They conclude, "By making labor more expensive and reducing corporate profits, AIDS limits the ability of African countries to attract industries that depend on low-cost labor and make investments in African businesses less desirable" (Rosen et al. 2004, 323).

A definitive analysis on the macroeconomic impact of AIDS on any society cannot be done, due to data limitations and methodological difficulties (Whiteside and de Waal 2004, 586–588; Zaba et al. 2004, S4). Nevertheless, the simple fact that HIV/AIDS generally affects people at the peak of their economically productive years does not bode well for the economies of heavily-infected states like South Africa.

Anecdotal evidence suggests that local and national political officials are dying of AIDS, even though that may not be listed as the cause of death on death certificates. Some reports suggest that the civil service, whose mission it is to implement the government's programs, is facing a major shortage of qualified workers and a loss of productivity due to AIDS. President Mbeki has dismissed such reports, casting doubt on the reliability and validity of such analyses (Seepe and Sibanda 2006).

AIDS Policies in South Africa

What is South Africa's AIDS policy? This seemingly simple question is difficult to answer definitively. The national government's policies and those of individual provinces have varied widely and occasionally been at odds with one another. Even if we restrict our attention to the national government (as we largely will in this book), it can be hard to pin the policy down. A cacophony of voices, often disagreeing with each other, offers different interpretations and confuses the public. On more than one occasion, the Minister of Health or President has publicly chastised the policies of national Health Ministry. The result is a patchwork of inconsistent policies that reflect the confusion within the South African government itself over the very nature of AIDS and how best to treat it.

In post-apartheid South Africa, Thabo Mbeki has been the dominant figure in crafting national AIDS policies and guiding the debate on these policies. As president, Nelson Mandela paid little attention to AIDS. "During his term of office, Nelson Mandela effectively ignored AIDS, avoiding the subject on the grounds that, in his culture, an elder did not publicly discuss sexual issues" (Gumede 2005, 152). Mandela himself has said that he saw his role as president largely in symbolic terms and left most of the day-to-day operation of the government to Mbeki, the deputy president (Sparks 2003, 251). He explained his silence on AIDS, saying, "I wanted to win [the 1994 election] and I didn't talk about AIDS." Afterwards, he said he "had not time to concentrate on the issue" during his presidency (Iliffe 2006, 67). In essence, then, post-apartheid South Africa's AIDS policies and the debate over those policies largely center on Mbeki and his advisors.[1]

When the African National Congress won the country's first multiracial elections in 1994, it endorsed an aggressive AIDS policy and designated it a "presidential lead project." This initial program pledged to move toward a human rights-based approach to treating AIDS. This meant couching AIDS care in broader social terms that encompassed the medical, legal, and economic needs of those affected by the disease (Fourie 2006, 107–108). It also sought to mobilize the entirety of South African society against HIV. The plan pledged to create a coordinated network of national and provincial technocrats with significant authority and autonomy to seamlessly implement policy while cutting across traditional bureaucratic lines (Schneider and Stein 2001, 725). Three key goals would guide all policy decisions: preventing the spread of HIV; reducing the disease's personal and social impact; and unifying local, national, and international resources (Fourie 2006, 109–110).

Despite the initial fanfare and promise that greeted this program, it failed to live up to its promise. The government overestimated the human and financial resources available to combat AIDS in the midst of a massive societal transformation, tensions arose between the national and provincial governments over implementing aspects of the program, and accounting irregularities over a planned AIDS-themed play consumed much time and attention (Butler 2005, 593–594). Around this same time, the government came under much criticism for its embrace of Virodene, a supposed AIDS cure developed in South Africa that turned out to be toxic (discussed in greater detail in Chapter Five). A 1997 review of the country's AIDS policies, led by then-Deputy President Thabo Mbeki, promised a reinvigorated effort to fight the disease's spread, but its promises largely remained unfulfilled and government attention soon waned.

With Mbeki's election to the presidency in 1999, many South Africans hoped that AIDS would finally receive the high-level attention necessary to promote an effective response. Mbeki had spearheaded the government's AIDS policy response during the Mandela administration, and his new Health Minister, Dr. Manto Tshabalala-Msimang, had helped draft the 1994 AIDS program. Instead, the national AIDS policies quickly fell victim to controversy. The *HIV/AIDS/STD*

---

1   Since leaving office, Mandela has found his voice on AIDS. He has publicly acknowledged his son's death from AIDS and has used his charitable foundation to support AIDS projects. He has also publicly chastised Mbeki for his policies.

Strategic Plan for South Africa 2000–2005 pledged to adopt a "multi-sectoral approach" (Tshabalala-Msimang 2003), but its recommendations were incredibly vague without concrete timelines, goals, or progress indicators. In addition, it largely side-stepped the issue of providing ARVs (Butler 2005, 595). The lack of attention to ARVs coincided with both President Mbeki and Minister Tshabalala-Msimang publicly questioning both their effectiveness and the validity of the HIV/AIDS hypothesis. When Mbeki convened a panel of experts to answer questions about AIDS and recommend appropriate responses, he included a significant number of AIDS dissidents who doubted the connection between HIV and AIDS. As a result, the panel's final report offered little guidance because panel members could not even agree on the basic facts about the disease. Instead, the report offered two competing sets of recommendations – one assuming HIV causes AIDS, and one denying that HIV causes AIDS (Presidential AIDS Advisory Panel 2001, 78–91). Members of the government expressed doubts about the wisdom of following the policy recommendations advocated by the international community and complained about being pressured to provide drugs they believed to be toxic. This led to widespread condemnation of Mbeki and unfavorable international attention. In late 2003, the government reluctantly unveiled a program to provide ARVs to HIV-positive persons in the face of court decisions, large protests by the Treatment Action Campaign, the upcoming 2004 elections, and internal divisions within the government. Many have decried the government for the slow pace in releasing and implementing such a plan (Hassan 2004; Willan 2004), and Tshabalala-Msimang continues to speak out about the inappropriateness of ARVs.

Trying to resolve the debates, Cabinet stepped into the fray in 2002. It released a statement on the country's HIV/AIDS campaign, stating, "In conducting this campaign, government's starting point is based on the premise that HIV causes AIDS" (Government of South Africa 2002). This is a remarkable statement, given that it came at the same time that members of that very Cabinet publicly challenged it – and continued to do so after its release. Nattrass cautions, though, that Cabinet's statement was very qualified and merely called for developing operational plans (Nattrass 2004: 55). Mbeki himself said he was withdrawing from the debates over whether HIV causes AIDS so as not to distract attention from implementing the policy, yet his continued public statements suggest that he still harbors doubts about the connection between the two and the extent of the epidemic within South Africa. For example, Mbeki has claimed in newspapers that he has "never known" anyone who has died of AIDS – even though both Nelson Mandela and Mangosuthu Buthelezi, two of South Africa's most prominent politicians, have lost children to AIDS and publicly cited these deaths as propelling their personal involvement in HIV/AIDS prevention work in South Africa (Timberg 2005).

Tshabala-Msimang has remained a target for AIDS activists as well. The 'Sack Manto' website (http://www.sackmanto.co.za) calls for the Minister's resignation and encourages visitors to sign a petition to force her out of office. Members of the Treatment Action Campaign (TAC), the South African Medical Association (SAMA), and six opposition political parties called on her to resign or be fired by President Mbeki during the summer of 2006 for allegedly breaking the country's medicines laws. According to SAMA, the Medicines Control Council (MCC) must vet any public claim of therapeutic treatment and benefit for any substance. Since Tshabalala-Msimang continues to publicly promote alternative treatments that the MCC has not verified, SAMA and TAC charge that she is in violation of South African law (*Mail and Guardian* 2006c). Tshabalala-Msimang has repeatedly insisted she will not resign, and President Mbeki has given no indication that he wants her removed (*Mail and Guardian* 2006b).

In early 2006, the government proposed a three-pronged strategy. Government officials argued that this strategy better reflected the unique contours of the epidemic as manifested in South Africa as opposed to Western Europe and North America (*ANC Today* 2006). First, it emphasized prevention. As no cure exists for AIDS, the best strategy is to avoid contracting the disease in the first place. Second, it encourages people to get tested and know their HIV status. Having this information is vital for protecting one's own health and the health of others. Finally, the government's program emphasizes four different treatment approaches. These four options reflect the degree to which AIDS dissidents have influenced the policy process in South Africa. The first approach, the Healthy Lifestyles program, emphasizes regular physical activity and avoiding health risks like smoking, alcohol, and unprotected sexual intercourse. The second advocates the use of vitamins and micronutrients to help the body fight infections. Developing and regulating effective traditional medicines is the third strategy for combating AIDS. Finally, and almost reluctantly, the government acknowledges that ARVs are "an option" for HIV-positive persons with CD4 cell counts below 200. Government officials proudly proclaim that these drugs are available free of charge in 231 health facilities in "72 percent of local municipalities," but refuses to set targets for how many people should have access to the drugs (*ANC Today* 2006). According to ANC officials, people may choose not to avail themselves of ARVs for a wide variety of reasons, so setting treatment targets would be both arbitrary and unresponsive to local needs. The government will provide limited access to ARVs, but it appears reluctant to promote their use. Activists and local and international health officials have criticized this approach for playing down the seriousness of the AIDS epidemic and for confusing the populace by relying on unproven and irrelevant treatments like micronutrients and traditional remedies.

As I write in early 2007, the South African national government has unveiled yet another new AIDS policy. This new policy aims to, by 2011, reduce new infections by 50 percent, increase access to sex education programs, and provide treatment for 80 percent of HIV-positive persons (*Mail and Guardian* 2006d). Perhaps more significantly, responsibility for implementing this new policy will move from President Mbeki and Health Minister Tshabalala-Msimang to Deputy President Phumzile Mlambo-Ngcuka and Deputy Health Minister Nozizwe Madlala-Routledge. Mlambo-Ngcuka has assumed greater responsibility for crafting national AIDS policies and received commendations from national and international sources for her work. Some have hailed the apparent sidelining of Tshabalala-Msimang as the best opportunity for the country to move forward with a coherent program and suggests that the government is finally moving away from its previous denialism (McGreal 2006). This is a hopeful sign for South Africa, and entirely consistent with my argument. As understandings and interpretations change, so too will the policies pursued. The counter-epistemic community that once held sway may finally be displaced, proving the dynamic role of knowledge within the policymaking process.

This brief overview cannot fully explain the changes in South Africa's national AIDS policies over the past 25 years (more fully detailed in Chapter 6), but it demonstrates the confusing, constantly changing nature of these policies. We can see the influence of the AIDS dissidents in the public statements made by government officials and the uneven response to internationally-recognized treatments.

Plan of the Book

To tell this story of AIDS dissidents, the South African government, and the role of science in policymaking, we must begin by placing the story within a broader theoretical framework. Chapters 2 and 3 discuss the theoretical foundations of both epistemic and counter-epistemic communities. Chapter 2 focuses on regime theory and epistemic communities and how these address the role of knowing in international policymaking. It provides an overview of the epistemic communities literature and its application since it came into wide use in the late 1980s. It describes how these communities operate, why policymakers rely on them, and how their functioning ultimately influences the policy process within the state. An epistemic community frames a problem in a particular manner, which then sets the course for future policy interventions. This chapter also points out some limitations and oversights inherent within the concept. In particular, it addresses a paradox: policymakers are thought to turn to the recognized experts within an epistemic community in response to a new and novel issue, yet the concept assumes that all policymakers will turn to the *same* group of experts to deal with this problem. If the problem is truly new and puzzling to policymakers, then it is counterintuitive to assume that all policymakers will recognize the same group of experts as having the authoritative knowledge necessary to adequately respond to the problem.

Chapter 3 picks up on this very point. In this chapter, I develop the concept of counter-epistemic communities. I describe how and why this alternative group of experts come about and gain significant influence over the policymaking process. This chapter also seeks to address potential objections to the notion of a counter-epistemic community and refute those objections. A counter-epistemic community also frames a given problem in a particular manner, but it starts from a fundamentally different premise than the mainstream epistemic community. Its frames embody and reflect a state's historical experiences and identity commitments. This chapter addresses why and how counter-epistemic communities have both theoretical and practical policy relevance.

Chapters 4 and 5 concentrate on the relevance of South Africa's history and identity commitments for understanding its AIDS policies. In Chapter 4, I examine the country's history with public health interventions. Throughout the country's history, public health and racism have been linked. The initial moves toward segregation found their legal basis in public health grounds, and apartheid justified the separation of races on the health needs of the different racial communities. With the emergence of AIDS, some White conservatives saw this as the solution to the anti-apartheid movement and praised the disease's spread among Black communities. Others resisted calls for greater racial integration on the grounds that doing so would expose 'low-risk' populations (read: Whites) to AIDS. This history has morphed into a mistrust of the intentions of outsiders who claim to be coming to ensure the health of the Black population.

Chapter 5 examines the role of identity. In the post-apartheid era, the South African government has sought to encourage a new national identity based on the tenets of the African Renaissance – finding African solutions to African problems. This includes promoting local culture and developing continent-wide political and economic accountability measures to prove to the rest of the world that Africa could take care of itself. The South African government has extended this to include AIDS policies. Its promotion of Virodene, a supposed miracle cure for AIDS discovered in South Africa and later found to be toxic, was largely based on promoting 'African science.' More recently, members of the Cabinet have advocated alternative remedies and treatments of dubious value precisely because they were more appropriate for the South African context. President Thabo Mbeki has publicly questioned much of the science and received wisdom about HIV and AIDS precisely on the grounds that the contours of the epidemic in Africa are so radically different from the West so as to be almost unrecognizable.

In Chapter 6, I turn my attention the AIDS counter-epistemic community itself. I examine who belongs to it, what they believe, and what sorts of policies they recommend. I also show how these beliefs have influenced the country's AIDS policies and how President Mbeki has turned to these individuals explicitly because their understanding of the disease embodies and reflects the nation's historical experiences and identity commitments.

Finally, in Chapter 7, I offer a conclusion and examine the implications of the counter-epistemic community on international policymaking. What does it mean for international cooperation when competing bodies of scientific knowledge hold sway over governments? Are there ways to find a compromise when a state's history and identity commitments are wrapped up in scientific knowledge and policy recommendations? I present some ideas and present two important avenues for future research. I also highlight the importance of counter-epistemic communities for the study of AIDS and of international relations as a whole.

Chapter 2

Knowledge and International Policymaking

How does scientific knowledge enter the international policy arena? For many scholars, the answer is, through epistemic communities. Epistemic communities bring scientists and experts together with policymakers, making their wisdom accessible to the government officials who, in turn, make the actual policies themselves. On its surface, AIDS is an ideal issue for promoting the emergence of an epistemic community – a new scientific problem requiring action by policymakers who themselves are not versed in the scientific complexities of the disease. Indeed, an epistemic community of AIDS researchers has emerged to provide advice and information to many members of the international community.

Shared knowledge for policymaking is essentially a form of international cooperation. States need to find ways to facilitate the exchange of knowledge if that information is to foster policy change. Much of the cooperation occurs through international regimes. What is a regime? Most scholars define it as a "set of implicit or explicit principles, norms, rules, or decision-making procedures around which actors' expectations converge in a given area of international relations" (Krasner 1983, 3). These regimes, organized around particular issues, bring states together, foster opportunities for states to communicate with one another, and have an impact on the international scene. They help set the rules of the game, and define what game is being played. They set out expectations for behavior, action, and policy. The question is, how does this regime formation occur? Do dominant states establish regimes for their own benefit, or do regimes allow states to interact on a relatively equal basis? What compels states to work through international regimes?

This chapter starts this chapter by examining the three main families of international regime theories: power-based, interest-based, and knowledge-based. These theories offer competing explanations for understanding the debates over South Africa's national AIDS policies. The next section looks more explicitly at epistemic communities themselves, addressing how they form and why they play an important role in policy debates on a wide range of issues. Epistemic communities do more than just provide scientific knowledge; they also reflect a society's history and identity commitment, and enter into the debates over the appropriate relationship between science and democracy. To see how, I explore these connections in the next two sections. In the final section, I point out some oversights in the epistemic communities approach – oversights that open the possibility of the emergence of a counter-epistemic community.

Table 2.1   Theories of International Regimes

	Power-based theories	Interest-based theories	Knowledge-based theories
Relevant actors	States as unitary actors	States as unitary actors	Diversity of actors; state not necessarily unitary
Basis of cooperation	Coercion	Mutual interests	Shared understandings
Role of knowledge	Replicates existing power relationships	Allows states to achieve goals	Allows states to define themselves and others

The differences among the three dominant theories revolve around three main issues: the relevant actors, the basis of cooperation, and the role of knowledge. Table 2.1 offers a quick comparison of the theories along these bases, and shows that these theories take very different views of who matters, why states cooperate, and whether knowledge plays a significant role.

Knowledge as Strength: Power-based Theories

Power-based theories, closely aligned with neorealist theories of international relations, focus on the distribution of power within the international community among states as unitary actors. Regimes and epistemic communities merely reproduce existing power relations in the international sphere. Mearsheimer writes, "Institutions are basically a reflection of the distribution of power in the world. They are based on the self-interested calculations of the great powers, and they have no independent effect on state behavior … they matter only at the margins" (1994/95, 7). If you want to understand how a regime operates or in whose interest it operates, you merely need to look at who holds the most power. Scientific knowledge is not a tool for changing the international system; it further bolsters the power of the most dominant states. Knowledge is one more tool in the powerful state's arsenal to maintain its power.

Power-based theories are the most pessimistic about achieving international cooperation through regimes (or any other means, for that matter). States fear each other, and are suspicious of others' ulterior motives (Mearsheimer 1994/95, 11). The international arena is an anarchic, Hobbesian state of chaos with no overarching power, so each state must constantly be on guard to protect itself. This fear forms a substantial impediment to forming an international regime. States worry that others will use the knowledge created by an international regime against them. If I join an international regime, I will have to share some of my knowledge and information with you – information which you could use later against me. Instead of promoting cooperation and peace, a regime could actually sow the seeds of my own destruction. Scientific knowledge thus becomes another potential weapon that states can use, so it is often in a state's interest *not* to collaborate with others.

Despite these fears, regimes and epistemic communities do exist. Why? For the power-based theories, regimes come about only when the most powerful states create and maintain them. Initially, this idea is counterintuitive. If states are hesitant to share information because they fear it could be used against them, then why would the most powerful states, who presumably have the most to lose, facilitate sharing knowledge through regimes?

Because they can use these regime to reinforce their dominant position within the international community. They do not create and maintain regimes for altruistic reasons. They create them to gain everyone else's knowledge, and they often structure the regime to force other states to shoulder the costs of the regime (Gilpin 1981; Snidal 1985). The regime is a tool for the powerful state to get as much information and knowledge from everyone else, while giving away as little of their own as possible, to get even more powerful. Knowledge in and of itself has little independent power; it will not reorder the international system, and a state cannot use this knowledge to overthrow the dominant state. By controlling the spread of knowledge, though, the dominant state can dictate who gets what information and under what circumstances. They force compliance and provide information solely to cement their own strong position and deter any challengers.

If the regime is so unequal, why would other states participate? The dominant state may force other states to join (e.g., if you want to trade with us, you must participate in the regime). The dominant state could also compel others to join by solving the collective action problem (e.g., we'll provide this regime that we all want if you'll pay for it). The powerful state will basically structure the regime so that, while participating in the regime may reinforce its dominance over smaller states, *not* participating will be even more harmful to those smaller states. The regime becomes an almost Faustian bargain.

How might a regime operating according to the power-based theories look? Some have argued that the free trade regime operates in this way. Free trade, in this analysis, works to strengthen the economic power of the developed states and co-opts developing states into supporting a system that works against their interests (Cox 1996; Phillips 2005). By requiring states to open their markets to outside competition and restricting the use of subsidies and other preferential arrangements, developing states lose access to powerful tools that could promote economic growth – tools that developed states have used and continue to use today. Because the developed states are so dominant, though, developing states cannot effectively challenge the system. Doing so would risk losing access to markets or having high tariffs imposed on their goods.

To figure out how compelling power-based theories are, we first need to establish whether the dominant states are the primary supporters of the international AIDS control regime. It is clear that some sort of international AIDS control regime exists. International expectations exist around appropriate treatments, the responsibility of governments to care for their HIV-positive citizens, and the need to implement a variety of AIDS prevention programs. It is also clear that the contributions of the dominant international actors sustain much of this regime's activity. The Joint United Nations Program on HIV/AIDS, or UNAIDS, combines the efforts and resources of ten different international agencies, all of which are sponsored primarily by the most powerful states in the international system. Thirty nations provide US$118 million directly to UNAIDS to support its work. The top three contributors, which provide over 60 percent of that total, are the Netherlands, the United States, and Norway (UNAIDS 2004). These same three countries have provided US$306 million to support UNAIDS' core budget since its founding in 1995 (UNAIDS 2004). The Global Fund to Fight AIDS, Tuberculosis, and Malaria, which bills itself as "an innovative approach to international health funding" (Global Fund n.d.), has received similar financial and logistical support from the dominant states in the international system. The Global Fund emphasizes that contributions by states or other actors are completely voluntary, yet the Fund received pledges of US$9.0 billion between its inception in 2001 and 2008, with US$5.1 billion paid into the Fund by the end of 2005. Nearly half of this amount comes from the United States and the European Union (Global Fund 2004a). PEPFAR, the President's Emergency Plan for AIDS Relief, is a five-year initiative to provide US$15 billion in AIDS funding in over 100 countries worldwide. This outlay is the largest financial pledge by a single government to a single public health crisis in history (Bush 2003). The powerful states within the international community are subsidizing the international AIDS control regime, with the United States, the dominant international power, shouldering the heaviest burden.[1]

Since the majority of AIDS researchers work in the United States and/or depend on US government funding for their research, some might interpret this regime as a tool of dominance. The United States subsidizes the creation of knowledge about this disease and also provides the bulk of international aid for AIDS. The US essentially holds both the intellectual and financial capital to force compliance with its ideas and dictates. If states want access to this life-saving knowledge, then they must follow the rules laid out by the United States.

Using this framework, then, South Africa's action may represent an attempt to break the power of the dominant actors. It is attempting to fight back against the hegemony of the United States. By refusing the knowledge created by the US-sponsored regime, South Africa frees itself from the powerful grip of the United States and its allies. It retains its autonomy in the face of overwhelming pressure to the contrary. It frees itself from the intellectual dominance of the West, and takes its own place at the international community's table.

While this may be an appealing notion and could even be what South Africa is doing, it shows the limits of power-based theories. Even if all South Africans embraced the AIDS dissidents and wanted to use their knowledge to challenge the international AIDS control regime, power-based theories could not explain this. Why not?

The above explanation affords knowledge a measure of autonomous power within the international system. It may indeed be true that the South African government

---

1 I do not want to imply that the international AIDS control regime is UNAIDS, the Global Fund, PEPFAR, or any other single organization, nor that institutional manifestations are the only means by which we can examine a regime. As the two most prominent and well-known organizations devoted to AIDS, though, they provide a useful example of one aspct of this regime.

predicates its rejection of the mainstream AIDS epistemic community on rejecting the intellectual hegemony of the West, and that it seeks to foster the creation and recognition of locally-based knowledge. In that case, then, knowledge gains a measure of independent power that power-based theories do not provide. Power-based theories lack a mechanism whereby a state can employ scientific knowledge to establish an independent role and challenge the dominant positions. Knowledge, for the power-based theories, is a tool for *maintaining* dominance, not challenging someone else's dominance. For a power-based explanation to work here, it would need to recognize an independent role of knowledge as a source of power *for non-dominant actors*. Without that recognition, a power-based theory cannot take us very far in understanding the role of AIDS dissidents in South Africa.

Knowledge through Incentives: Interest-based Theories

Interest-based theories of international regimes fall within the neoliberal tradition, and are generally considered the 'mainstream' school of international regime theory (Hasenclever et al. 1997, 23). Interest-based theories see states as unitary actors and self-interested utility maximizers with stable and exogenously-knowable interests. In other words, states know what they want, and others can know that, too. International regimes allow states to satisfy their interests by facilitating cooperation with others (Keohane 1984, 6). Regimes alter incentives for states to make cooperation rational for states so as to satisfy their interests without altering those interests or identities (Keohane 1984, 26).

States cannot get everything they want by themselves, so they need to work with other states to achieve their goals. Regimes make it easier for states to work together. They regularize interactions, they establish some ground rules, and they benefit all parties involved. Regimes do not change what states want; they instead offer the tools to achieve what states want. The regime makes it easier for states to exchange information and knowledge that will, in turn, benefit all members of the regime. It is easier and cheaper to do this through a regime than outside of it. In essence, the regime is a logical, rational tool for achieving a state's goals on a particular issue.

To return to our earlier example of free trade, states may come together in a free trade regime because it will help all of their interests. States recognize that promoting trade will foster their economic development, and they seek trade arrangements that will maximize their benefits and minimize their losses. To do this effectively, states need to work together to coordinate policies. No single state can improve its economic status alone, but the combined strength of the states in the regime could benefit everyone (Miyagawa 2005). The regime will not necessarily only benefit one states or a small group of states; instead, it is designed to help all states participating in the regime.

Given their centrality to the study of international regimes, we might naturally expect interest-based theories to offer insights into the interactions of the South African government and the international AIDS control regime. After all, the South African government obviously has an interest in stemming the spread of AIDS among its population. The disease has depressed South Africa's economic growth, costs the government millions of dollars annually to treat AIDS patients, and deprives the state of its future leaders, educators, and businesspeople. Further, the South African government has acknowledged that it lacks the financial resources necessary to combat the disease on its own. Health Minster Tshabalala-Msimang, addressing the financial strain antiretroviral drugs place on the South African health budget, stated "The budget I have for medicines is R2 billion [approximately US$233 million at the time]. If I were to buy antiretrovirals, I would have to forget about everything else" (Associated Press 2001). If regimes are rational tools for exchanging information to further mutual interests, then can they explain why AIDS dissidents have advised members of the South African government?

Not really. Applying interest-based theories lead to two distinct conclusions, neither of which makes any sense. The first would assert that the South African government has *no* interest in treating AIDS patients or stopping the disease's spread. Remember, interest-based theories argue that states specifically choose to participate in regimes when those regimes allow them to satisfy their interests. The result in this case then would be that the South African government has challenged the international AIDS control regime and its epistemic community because it has no interest in stopping AIDS. Such a view presents a rather callous, if not evil, image of the South African government. Further, it is demonstrably false. While it is certainly true that the South African government has made dubious claims about the connections between HIV and AIDS, it has not ignored the disease. The government's running disagreements with the international AIDS control regime show that it *is* concerned about AIDS. Why would the government expend so much time and effort discussing AIDS if it did not consider it to be a vital issue? President Mbeki has made explicit references to the challenges AIDS poses to South Africa in his State of the Nation Addresses in 2000, 2001, 2002, 2003, 2004, 2005, and 2006 (Mbeki 2000a, 2001b, 2002, 2003, 2004b, 2005, 2006), though he rarely devoted more than a few sentences to it. During his much-maligned opening address at the 13th Annual International AIDS Conference held in Durban in 2000, Mbeki stated, "I welcome you all…convinced that you would not have come here, unless you were to us, messengers of hope, deployed against the spectre of the deaths of millions from disease" (Mbeki 2000b). At the end of 2003, the South African government unveiled its comprehensive plan for treating HIV/AIDS in South Africa. During the announcement of the plan, Tshabalala-Msimang noted, "Government is once more strengthening the hand of the nation in the fight against HIV and AIDS, in keeping with its mandate to build a better life for all" (Tshabalala-Msimang 2003). The South African government considers HIV/AIDS to be one of its "key issues," along with the budget, regional security, and the much-hailed New Partnership for African Development, or NEPAD (Government of South Africa 2004). Since interest-based theories assert that a state's interests are exogenously knowable, and the South African government has made it clear that it perceives HIV/AIDS as a problem that must be addressed, it is difficult to maintain the assertion that controlling the spread of HIV/AIDS is not in the interest of the South African government.

Second, interest-based theories assume that states find regimes and epistemic communities useful for satisfying their interests. The international AIDS control regime offers large amounts of funding and resources dedicated to combating the

AIDS epidemic. It provides the technical and scientific know-how that some states may lack. In essence, the regime offers member-states all the materials and information necessary to effectively combat this epidemic, regardless of the state's own resources. The South African government has demonstrated its interest in stopping the spread of AIDS. Therefore, interest-based theories would conclude that the South African government does not need the resources, support, and knowledge of the regime to realize its interests. This claim fails to comport with reality. The South African government has demonstrated its fundamental inability to adequately respond to the challenges posed by HIV/AIDS with only its resources. Tshabalala-Msimang herself pointed out that the government's available budget for drugs was inadequate to cover the costs of providing antiretroviral drugs to AIDS patients. Schneider and Stein note that South Africa's greatest problem relating to implementing a comprehensive AIDS strategy has been its lack of the necessary resources to carry out the program on the ground (Schneider and Stein 2001, 729). Willan finds that the lack of necessary drugs, staff, training, and money has prevented the implementation of national AIDS policies at the local level (Willan 2004, 110–111). While research by the Institute for Democracy in South Africa's (IDASA) AIDS Budget Unit demonstrates that the South African national government often underspends its AIDS prevention and treatment budget (Guthrie and Hickey 2004), the government has publicly argued that it lacks the resources to provide nevirapine to HIV-positive pregnant women or a large-scale HAART program.[2]

Interest-based theories assume that states come together to share knowledge when this will allow them to achieve their goals. The South African government has repeatedly stated that it seeks to stop the spread of AIDS and that it considers AIDS a serious challenge. It does not then follow that the government would shun the knowledge of the international AIDS control regime and its epistemic community. Interest-based theories cannot explain why a state with an interest in stopping a disease's spread would challenge a regime devoted to that very issue.

Is AIDS in the Government's Interest?

Interest-based theories assume that states come together in regimes when they share mutual interests in addressing a particular issue. Not participating in a regime may show that a state does not have an interest in a particular issue. The domestic political sphere may encourage (or discourage) governments from pursuing certain interests. Strong electoral incentives could persuade the government to oppose the international AIDS control regime, or the government may simply lack the political will to tackle the issue. By the same token, organized interest groups within South Africa promoting the ideas of the AIDS dissidents could influence the government to pay attention to these groups. If powerful interest groups discourage the acceptance of the international AIDS control regime's knowledge or electoral incentives work

---

2   Government officials have often argued that they emphasize spending resources on prevention because it is more cost-effective. Numerous studies dispute this, and show that treatment programs not only reduce government health outlays in the long-term, but that they also strengthen prevention programs (Nattrass 2004).

against international cooperation on this issue, then it makes sense that AIDS dissidents have managed to play an important role in the debates over the country's AIDS policies.

This reasoning fails to prove convincing for three reasons. First, quixotic AIDS policies are not an effective means for increasing support. If instrumental political motives currently drive the government's AIDS policies, its choice of policy area is curious at best. No evidence exists that the government's AIDS policies are generating additional support amongst voters. A survey taken in July and August of 2000 found that 57 percent of South Africans rated the government's response to AIDS as "not very well" or "not well at all" (Whiteside et al. 2002, 28). This dissatisfaction comes at the same time that an increasing number of South Africans seeing AIDS as a priority for the national government. During the country's first post-apartheid election in 1994, only 1 percent of South Africans identified AIDS as the government's top priority. In 2000, the number shot up to 13 percent. By 2002, this figure had doubled to 26 percent (Afrobarometer 2004, 4). More recent survey data indicate a strong and significant correlation between prioritizing HIV/AIDS policies and dissatisfaction with current government policies. Those who believe HIV/AIDS should be one of the government's top priorities are more likely to evaluate the government's AIDS policies negatively (Strand et al. 2005). Furthermore, a majority of voters believe that the government's AIDS policies are inadequate. Less than half of the population believes that the government has allocated sufficient resources to combating the AIDS epidemic in South Africa (Human Sciences Research Council 2002, 90). Increasing recognition of the AIDS crisis and the government's role in addressing the issue thus seems to be correlated with *lower* levels of satisfaction with the government's AIDS policies.

Opposition parties in South Africa have attempted to make the ANC's AIDS policies a major political issue, but their efforts have largely failed to resonate. Butler describes the political parties in South Africa as largely separated along 'historical' lines, which imbues their political appeals with racial and ethnic undertones (Butler 2003, 99). Therefore, when the (primarily White) opposition Democratic Alliance chastises the government for its failure to adequately care for AIDS patients (Democratic Alliance 2004), its criticisms are interpreted in racial terms. Looking at the 2004 parliamentary elections, Schlemmer (2004) notes that the Democratic Alliance's criticisms of the government's AIDS policies failed to make much of an impact because the party has had little success in broadening its support base to include Blacks. Election results may then reflect the inability of opposition parties to effectively marshal support, as opposed to support for those policies.

Most tellingly, Mbeki's AIDS policies have drawn widespread domestic criticism. Nelson Mandela has publicly criticized Mbeki for this inattention to AIDS and his flirtation with AIDS dissidents. During the International AIDS Conference in Thailand in 2004, Mandela addressed the assembled delegates:

> Leadership involves personal commitment and concrete actions. Leaders must mobilize and inspire people to respond to the [AIDS] crisis. They must lead the response with clear vision and imaginative action. Our inability to act decisively on this challenge is a direct reflection of our disregard for our common humanity (cited in Bridgland 2004).

Media sources widely interpreted these remarks as a repudiation of Mbeki's AIDS policies. Mandela's criticisms of Mbeki's AIDS policies have even led to tensions between the former president and current government officials (Munusamy 2002). It seems incredibly unlikely that Mbeki would be able to gain much political headway with South Africans when the country's preeminent political figure has publicly chastised him and his policies.

Others have also criticized Mbeki's AIDS policies, distancing themselves from policies they believe are disastrous. Archbishop Desmond Tutu, long considered the 'moral father' of the anti-apartheid movement and a Nobel Peace Prize winner, has publicly come out against Mbeki's approach to AIDS. The Coalition of South African Trade Unions (COSATU), long one of the ANC's staunchest allies and part of its Tripartite Alliance, called on the government to stop entertaining dissident notions and provide AIDS drugs (McGreal 2000, 19). With such powerful domestic forces aligning against these policies, no political gain comes from supporting the AIDS dissidents.

Debates over Mbeki's and Tshabalala-Msimang's consultations with AIDS dissidents have roiled the ANC itself. Divisions within the Cabinet have surfaced, with reports suggesting that the majority of Cabinet members disagree with Mbeki's stance but are unwilling to challenge him on it. Cabinet released a statement in August 2003 offering qualified, cautious support for developing an operational plan to roll out HAART (Nattrass 2004, 55). This followed their somewhat qualified statement the previous year, emphasizing "[G]overnment's starting point is based on the premise that HIV causes AIDS" (Government of South Africa 2002). At the same time, though, Cabinet has rejected calls to oust Tshabalala-Msimang for her controversial statements on AIDS (Leonard 2006).

Second, most of the strong, well-organized AIDS civil society groups are explicitly pro-mainstream AIDS epistemic community and anti-government AIDS policies. The Treatment Action Campaign (TAC), the most prominent AIDS group in South Africa, has taken the government to court on numerous occasions for denying AIDS drugs to patients and failing to live up to its constitutional responsibilities to provide proper health care for the citizenry. TAC and its national chairperson, Zackie Achmat, have received worldwide adulation and praise for their efforts to call attention to the failures of the South African government's AIDS policies. Achmat and TAC were even contenders for the 2004 Nobel Peace Prize (Gmax.org.za 2004).

On the other side, few pro-AIDS dissident civil society groups actively operate in South Africa. HEAL, one of the largest pro-dissident groups in the world, has no chapters in South Africa and few outside of the United States. The Treatment Information Group (TIG), a South African organization that campaigns against antiretroviral drugs, bills itself as a "research-based" alternative to the Treatment Action Campaign, but it appears to have few (if any) members and is solely subsidized by the Dr. Rath Foundation South Africa. Since the Dr. Rath Foundation sells vitamins that it claims can treat AIDS, TIG is essentially an 'Astroturf' lobbying group.[3] None of the

---

3   Astroturf lobbying groups are seemingly grassroots organizations or coalitions that are actually created by corporations or public relations firms to advance particular interests.

prominent pro-dissident groups appear to have links to any similar organizations operating within South Africa, though these groups do express a high degree of sympathy for and solidarity with Mbeki. Because the primary interest groups dealing with AIDS in South Africa *oppose* the government's AIDS policies, it is unlikely that pro-dissident interest groups have "captured" Mbeki and his allies.

Third, this issue is larger than Mbeki. Arguments about domestic political considerations implicitly assume that these policies are due exclusively to Mbeki and his presence in the government. When Mbeki leaves office, goes the argument, so too will these quixotic policies. This argument proves too simplistic. Mbeki is certainly an important patron for AIDS dissidents, and his support has provided them with a high degree of influence, but the issue goes further than that. Others have taken up the cause, and done so very publicly. Tshabalala-Msimang has made numerous public, provocative statements about the connections between HIV and AIDS, like suggesting that garlic and beet juice can cure AIDS (LaFraniere 2004, 12). Peter Mokaba, the former head of the ANC's Youth League, wrote a 114-page treatise lambasting antiretroviral drugs, the pharmaceutical companies that produce them, and the belief that HIV causes AIDS. Mokaba claimed that Africa's enemies created the disease, that theories of an African origin of AIDS were "insulting," and that Western AIDS research simply views Africans as promiscuous and diseased (Butler 2003, 110). Mokaba's document received wide circulation after Mbeki emailed it to many of his colleagues (Power 2003).[4]

More problematically, focusing exclusively on Mbeki serves only to demonize the president without properly examining *why* he has followed such a controversial path. Mbeki is not a stupid man or a simple rejectionist, yet his decisions have indeed imperiled the lives of millions of his compatriots and needlessly exposed more to a deadly virus. If analyses simply chastise Mbeki for being a 'bad guy,' then we learn nothing about why he has given space to dissidents on this issue but not others. Neither international relations, nor AIDS policymaking, advances if we fail to interrogate and understand what is behind these actions.

It is plausible that domestic political pressures offer few incentives for the South African government to address AIDS. "Given the immense hardships African countries have endured during severe austerity programs, government officials have been reluctant to draw attention to an incurable disease out of concern for their own political survival" (Boone and Batsell 2001, 10–11). Addressing AIDS could not only call attention to the government's inability to prevent the epidemic, but also offer politicians few rewards. A pragmatic politician is unlikely to spend time and political capital educating the public about a disease "that can only be prevented by wholesale behavioral changes … [which are] unlikely to reach fruition during any given leader's tenure in office" (Fredland 1998, 562). The short horizon of upcoming

These groups give the appearance of broad-based support, but rarely have individual members (Silverstein 1997).

4   Mokaba himself is widely believed to have died of AIDS in 2002 at the age of 43, though the official cause of his death was "acute pneumonia, linked to a respiratory problem" (Shaw 2002).

elections may dissuade politicians from expending energy on a problem that cannot be solved in the short-term.

This argument makes some sense, but ignores the larger realities of the South African government's response to AIDS for two reasons. One, other African governments, like those in Senegal and Uganda, *have* benefited from placing AIDS at the top of their national agendas. Uganda faced a high rate of adult infections in the mid-1980s, while Senegal sought to preempt an AIDS epidemic within its borders. Both countries took bold, public actions designed to address the issue. Government officials made speeches about the importance of condoms. Church leaders worked with the government in their outreach efforts. Public education campaigns spread throughout the country. Their actions were successful; Uganda's adult HIV prevalence rate has declined appreciably, and Senegal has managed to avoid a widespread AIDS epidemic. This contradicts the idea that governments will not see the results of their efforts. It also reinforces the idea that active government involvement at all levels is vitally important for prevention programs to succeed (Boone and Batsell 2001, 11).

Two, this argument does not explain why prominent members of the South African government have actively challenged the bases of the international AIDS control regime and the mainstream AIDS epistemic community. Let us assume that the above logic is correct; that South African government officials simply see little political payoff from getting involved in AIDS prevention work, and therefore do not engage in it. In that case, we would assume silence from the government. AIDS would be a non-issue. Instead, some members of the South African government have openly questioned the link between HIV and AIDS. President Mbeki invited AIDS dissident scientists to sit on his 2001 advisory panel and has become embroiled in international diplomatic controversies over his interpretations of AIDS' societal impacts. This is hardly the model of government officials ignoring AIDS to avoid political fallout. This is instead the model of government officials that approach the disease from a fundamentally different basis.

Understanding Self and Other: Knowledge-based Theories

Knowledge-based theories of international regimes start from a different basis than the other two. They shed the assumption that states are unitary actors, and deny that we can intuit a state's interests (Hasenclever et al. 1997, 136). We cannot simply assume that states are participating in a given regime because it is in their interest to do so. Instead, regimes shape and are shaped by normative and causal beliefs. Regimes are social (Evans and Wilson 1992, 332), and participation in a regime can allow state actors to understand themselves, their interests, and their policies in different ways. Regimes influence not just how states respond to issues, but also how they *understand* those issues (Dimitrov 2003, 124). Knowledge-based theories see regimes as influencing and shaping the identities and interests of their members (Young 1999, 204–205). If we want to understand how regimes operate and influence policy outcomes, then we must examine how regimes foster the development of shared understandings of issues.

Unique among regime theories, knowledge-based theories pay attention to the role of identities within these regimes and epistemic communities. Identities are of crucial importance because they inform states not only who they are, but they let others know who they are. Even more importantly, a state's identity strongly implies a certain set of preferences and interests (Hopf 1998, 175). This strong relationship between state identity and state interest structures how states perceive their options when they take action on a particular issue (Farrell 2002, 50). Being part of an international regime or epistemic community is a sign of how a state sees itself and wants others to perceive it.

Regimes, in the knowledge-based theories, provide new space for discourse. They are not neutral, apolitical spaces, but rather shape and are shaped by shared understandings and identities (Ellis 2002, 279–280). This social aspect of international regimes and epistemic communities allows space for change to occur (Arts 2000, 527). The regime is a venue both for pursuing interests and for defining those interests in the first place. This means that a state's identity (or identities) is not static. As identities change, so too may the policy choices that states make.

What does this mean in practical terms? Let's consider a real world example. A number of Eastern European countries have sought (and in some instances, gained) admittance to the European Union and NATO. While membership in these groups certainly offers some tangible benefits (such as agricultural subsidies or increased defense), they also signify being a member of the community of democracies (Daalder and Goldgeier 2006). States gain a certain status by being part of these groups, and these groups also help shape how those states perceive their responsibilities to their citizens and the international community. At the same time, the addition of these new states changes how the European Union and NATO deliberate over particular actions. The regime thus shapes the state's interests and actions, and the regime's own interests and actions are shaped by the members involved in the regime.

The norms that regimes advance can encourage or guide behavior, but they do not "cause" that behavior per se. Instead, they make it possible for states to pursue certain behaviors. The norms that exist within international society represent generalized behavioral patterns and expressions of moral standards. As Dunn notes, "Discourses are not simply ideas, but are also the actions, thoughts, and practices that make that idea a 'reality' by structuring and delineating that reality, thereby making it knowable" (2001, 56). Culture and identity serve as heuristic filters, shaping how states see their environment (Legro 1997, 36). Regimes allow states to make sense of themselves, their interests, and the international community as a whole.

Why cooperate with a particular regime under this knowledge-based framework? States work within a particular regime because its discourse resonates with the state and its understandings of itself and others. States join and participate in a regime because they agree with its outlook and vision. Regimes provide a sense of legitimacy for taking certain actions (Bull 1977), a discourse for talking about an issue (Kratochwil 1989), an understanding of history's importance (Cox 1996), and an identity for their members (Wendt 1999).

These theories offer promise for understanding why the South African government would embrace AIDS dissidents who had been shunned by the rest of the international community. The failures of the power-based and interest-based theories largely rest on their inabilities to accurately conceive of how the South African government sees itself and the international community in the face of the demands of treating a large number of AIDS patients. Knowledge-based theories point to the need to understand how South Africa sees itself in relations to both the AIDS epidemic writ large and the international AIDS control regime and its epistemic community. They also highlight the importance of accounting for the interactions between the international AIDS control regime and the South African government. Knowledge-based theories appear well-positioned for this sort of endeavor.

To be truly useful in this case, though, we must augment two deficiencies within the knowledge-based theories. First, they provide little guidance about the circumstances under which regimes fail to take hold within particular states. Through communication, the spread of shared scientific understandings, and the advocacy efforts of relevant epistemic communities, regimes will form as problems arise in the international system. Little attention is paid, though, to why states would receive this knowledge and communication, yet still challenge the mainstream consensus. The South African government is not some pariah state oblivious to various international discussions and debates about HIV and AIDS. The state is fully integrated into the international community, and in many ways is the leading state in sub-Saharan Africa. No other state in the region can lay claim to middle-power status like South Africa (Hamill and Lee 2001), and South Africa has the largest and best-equipped scientific research facilities on the continent (Furlong and Ball 1999). It would be difficult to make a convincing case that South Africa's failure to conform to the international community's about AIDS reflects the state's isolation from the international intellectual engagement over the issue.

Second, knowledge-based theories tend to ignore how history and identity actually get translated into action. What good is it to say that knowledge-based regime theories emphasize identity, history, communication, and legitimacy if one cannot show how those factors actually get translated into policy? The history and identity of the United States have very different implications for its willingness to engage in an international regime dealing with AIDS than South Africa's. Most knowledge-based theories, though, fail to explain *how* or *why* they matter. How do the differing histories and identities of the United States and South Africa impact how these states approach and react to an international regime? Are these processes different when we look at a regime dealing with AIDS rather than something like ozone depletion? Knowledge-based theories are not explicit enough in their answers to these questions. Some answers, though, can be found by turning attention to research on epistemic communities.

Epistemic Communities

Epistemic communities facilitate the dissemination of information and the framing of transnational problems. They play a crucial role in distributing and sharing information among states. Peter Haas defines an epistemic community as:

> A network of professionals with recognized expertise and competence in a particular domain and an authoritative claim to policy-relevant knowledge within that domain or issue-area. Although an epistemic community may consist of professionals from a variety

of disciplines and backgrounds, they have (1) a shared set or normative and principled beliefs, which provide a value-based rationales for the social actions of community members; (2) shared causal beliefs, which are derived from their analysis of practices leading or contributing to a central set of problems in their domain and which then serve as the basis for elucidating the multiple linkages between possible policy actions and desired outcomes; (3) shared notions of validity – that is, intersubjective, internally defined criteria for weighing and validating knowledge in the domain of their expertise; and (4) a common policy enterprise – that is, a set of common practices associated with a set of problems to which their professional competence is directed, presumably out of the conviction that human welfare will be enhanced as a consequence (Haas 1992, 3).

When the members of an epistemic community both possess consensual knowledge and are recognized by others for their knowledge, they are in a unique position to share and distribute the information needed by states (McFadden 1995, 15–18). This role is particularly important when policymakers are uncertain about their next step, and scientists are in general agreement about the information (Adler and Haas 1992; Haas 1989, 1992). Epistemic communities can also alter how states perceive their roles within the international community. For example, through the work of epistemic communities addressing environmental issues since the 1970s, protecting the environment has now largely become part of what it means to be a nation-state (Frank 1999, 529). Environmental science framed the issue and provided key pieces of information to policymakers. They convinced government officials around the world that environmental protection is an important issue and that state policies can play a significant role in ensuring that protection. This, in turn, altered how states viewed their obligations to the environment and each other. To take one famous example, Mediterranean states did not come together to stop discharging pollution into the Mediterranean Sea out of some sense of altruism; rather, it took environmental scientists to provide evidence and convince these governments that they could and should do something about the issue (Haas 1989).

Knowledge can impact policymakers – but it must be widely shared to do so. The learning process, if it is to alter regime formation and international politics, must occur internationally; one state's learning does not change things unless other states also learn (Knopf 2003). Policymakers must come to understand problems in a common way, and share some similar perceptions of the most appropriate manner in which the state can respond to the problem at hand. Without a shared framing of the problems of ozone depletion, for example, states could hardly begin the negotiation processes to decide how best to combat the problem. Therefore, policymakers require high-quality information to frame the problem and set the stage for subsequent negotiations. Shared knowledge helps states understand the world around them, thus structuring their preferences and allowing states to arrive at the necessary collective understandings. Epistemic communities provide the social conditions that develop this knowledge and allow it to influence policymakers (Haas and Haas 2002).

This is where epistemic communities play their role. Policymakers do not necessarily recognize the usefulness or relevance of a given body of knowledge. Institutional processes can facilitate or impede the ability of an epistemic community to have influence on a particular issue-area (Zito 2001). Haas identifies three crucial requirements for an epistemic community's expertise to have an impact on international policymaking. First, there must exist a high degree of *uncertainty* among policymakers about how to approach an issue. Government officials may not know how to conceptualize new or highly complex issues and the appropriate responses to them. Epistemic communities provide the information and conceptual framework that allows these policymakers to ground their thinking. Second, members of the epistemic community must reach a *high level of consensus* among themselves. If members of a particular expert group do not agree, it is difficult to speak of an epistemic community in the first place, let alone one that has a high degree of influence. This does not mean that the community members must be in unanimous agreements about all issues or policies, but they do need to share a similar framework and understanding of the issue. Third, a high degree of *institutionalization* of scientific knowledge must exist. The epistemic community must have access to policymakers. Without access to policymakers, all the consensual information in the world will not have a significant influence (Haas 1992, 14–27). Access to policymakers makes the members of the epistemic community players in the policy debate. Once these communities gain influence, they become important players and have a seat at the table. Gough and Shackley write, "Scientific knowledge is the 'glue' that helps keep policy actors committed and can be used as a trump card against opponents to the epistemic coalition" (2001, 332).

To be truly influential, an epistemic community needs a patron (or patrons) within the government. Someone must be willing to take up their cause and invite them to the table. Without this, governments are unlikely to afford the epistemic community much influence or access (Haas 2000, 561– 565). This is an important insight which studies on the sociology of scientific knowledge (SSK) stress. Scholars working within this tradition fault most studies of epistemic communities for focusing too much on the *content* of scientific knowledge without paying sufficient attention to the social and policy *interactions* that gives that scientific knowledge its *meaning* (Lidskog and Sundqvist 2002, 85). If scientific knowledge embodies and reflects the social and cultural milieu that support, creates, and disseminates that knowledge (Wynne 1991, 1996), then we must understands how and why these interactions occur.

This idea is not universally accepted, and critics accuse it of being overly relativistic. If scientific knowledge depends on particular social and cultural contexts, these critics argue, then we lose the whole notion of truth. Scientific facts are real because they answer questions. Dawkins writes, "Science boosts its claims to truth by its spectacular ability to make matter and energy jump through hoops on command, and to predict what will happen and when" (2003, 15). He goes on to say, "Scientific truth … regularly persuades converts of its superiority" (Dawkins 2003, 15). Dawkins and his allies are indeed correct, but they miss the point. Epistemic communities do not create particular truths or fudge the facts to fit a particular paradigm, but they do shape our reception of those facts. They provide a framework for thinking about an issue and how governments should respond to that issue. I could not say that 3 plus 4 equals 7 only in the United States. However, that fact only has meaning within a certain context – in this case, the context is a base-10 counting system. In a base-6 system, though, 3 plus 4 would equal 11, while a binary system would not even conceive of 3 and 4 as written (though it would recognize that 11 plus 100 equals 111). The context does not necessarily *change* the truth, but it gives that truth meaning and relevance.

SSK studies begin from the premise that not all knowledge is valued in the same way and to the same degree. From this base, the sociology of scientific knowledge advances three main arguments. First, it emphasizes that scientific knowledge must be "carried by social arrangements in order to be distributed in society" (Lidskog and Sundqvist 2002, 84). Knowledge only moves freely, or at least appears to move freely, when supportive networks for disseminating this knowledge exist. Some mechanisms must exist to move knowledge from the knowledge-makers to the policymakers. Second, the *content* of scientific knowledge does not determine the *value* of that knowledge (Lidskog and Sundqvist 2002, 84). The value of such information comes through the processes of negotiating the boundaries of what is 'scientific.' This is why understanding and appreciating context is so important. Finally, science and policy shape each other and are co-produced (Lidskog and Sundqvist 2002, 84–85). Scientific knowledge will influence policy, which will in turn influence the production of future scientific knowledge. If I believe God's displeasure causes disease, that will influence how I treat my ailments, and my future actions will be influenced by that belief. Over time, my beliefs could change, and those new beliefs will now influence my future actions. Lidskog and Sundqvist use the sociology of scientific knowledge framework to argue that knowledge becomes relevant to policymakers when it supports politically-accepted discourses and reasoning, is ratified by a privileged policy community, finds support from convergent business and government interests, and is a part of the general technological culture (2002, 86). It iss not scientific knowledge on its own that influences policy; it is the interaction between that knowledge and the broader cultural contexts in which that knowledge exists.

Science, Democracy, and Policy-relevant Knowledge

Science is a tool for addressing the world's problems. Many assume that scientific knowledge consists of objective truths, free from political manipulation, making it an authoritative, neutral source of information and guidance. These assumptions are central to why policymakers turn toward an epistemic community to provide policy solutions to new and novel problems. Policymakers believe that the members of an epistemic community will simply report 'the facts,' and science will avoid the pitfalls and manipulations that often befall the policymaking process. Political actors of all stripes try to marshal scientific evidence to bolster their claims. Jasanoff writes:

> Although science no longer seems to deliver the grand, unifying narrative of progress that animated the founders of the American republic, the promise of science still draws adherents from right across the social and political spectrum ... In all these disparate projects of self-realization, science remains an instrument of choice (2004c, 153).

The idea of science as objective and neutral is powerful, but one that has come under increasing attack. Leading social science luminaries like Max Weber struggled with how to present and interpret scientific information in a value-neutral manner. More recently, the fields of science studies and the sociology of scientific knowledge have emerged to challenge whether such a distinction is possible. Because science exists within a social environment, as does politics, and scientific knowledge is frequently called upon to address political conflicts, science studies scholars largely argue that science is inherently political. The question then becomes, how does the political process impact the use and reception of scientific knowledge? What implications does science have for democratic political processes?

Epstein (1996, 14–17) delineates two main schools of thought about the intersection of science and politics. The first sees science as, to paraphrase Clausewitz' famous dictum about war, politics by other means. Scientific knowledge is simply another tool in a politician's arsenal. To use it successfully, the politician must convince others to accept that his or her scientific knowledge is impartial. The struggle to gain acceptance of a fact essentially comes down to who has more power. In this case, power can mean befriending influential allies and patrons, getting published in the 'right' journals, or creating 'essential' technologies that other researchers must use for their own projects (Latour 1987). This power creates 'passage points,' through which others must pass and which reinforce the knowledge embedded within them. Essentially, these passage points serve as the ideas upon which subsequent research will be based, therefore informing future claims to scientific truth. In time, it becomes common sense. "The more well traveled such passage points, the more fully institutionalized the knowledge claims become" (Epstein 1996, 15). Scientific facts, then, are those that have friends in the right places and muscle competing ideas out of the way. They are accepted as fact because they won the political game. This does not mean that a nefarious and powerful politician could change Earth's rotation around the sun, but it does mean that this power can dictate research agendas and our collective ideas about what it is (or should be) scientifically researchable and valid.

The second school focuses on issues of trust. Without trust, there is no scientific knowledge (Barnes 1985). Accepting any scientific claim requires some measure of trust in the person producing that knowledge. Experiments can never be exactly replicated, and it is impossible for even the most ambitious scientist to directly conduct research in all fields. Therefore, if we are to accept a claim of scientific truth, we must be willing to trust that the methods and outcome of an experiment. "At any given moment, *some* knowledge must be taken on faith, if science is to proceed as a social institution" (Epstein 1996, 17; emphasis in the original). This trust necessarily runs two ways, for *distrusting* one particular truth claim requires *trusting* other truth claims (Shapin 1994). In essence, we (the general public) must place our faith in the process of science and those employing the scientific method. We must trust that the scientific enterprise will police its own and allow the correct ideas to come to the forefront through a meritocratic process.

Both schools of thought highlight the fact that scientific knowledge is, at heart, a social and political process. Scientists may make fascinating discoveries in their labs, but the acceptance of those discoveries only occurs by engaging the wider community. Without such engagement, we cannot rightfully speak of the accumulation of scientific knowledge. Scientists become political actors, and their discoveries are necessarily understood and interpreted through existing social frames. Scientific knowledge is co-produced, meaning that "the ways in which we know and represent the world (both nature and society) are inseparable from the ways in which we choose to live in it" (Jasanoff 2004a, 2). As Irwin and Wynne explain:

[S]cience ... offers a framework which is unavoidably *social* as well as technical since in public domains scientific knowledge embodies implicit models or assumptions about the social world. In addition, as an intervention in public life, scientific knowledge involves rhetorical claims to the superiority of the scientific worldview but it also builds upon social processes of trust and reflect social interests and social assumptions (1996a, 2–3; emphasis in the original).

Science is a part of the social world and impacts the wider community, so it invariably becomes political. In so doing, it becomes prone to many of the same processes which impact all other political policymaking decisions.

Political actors can use scientific knowledge to advance certain ideas or reinforce their own power. This is not to say that these actors intentionally manipulate scientific knowledge or misrepresent findings.[5] Instead, it acknowledges that science and scientific knowledge can be an important tool for control by recognizing certain expertise. "Science, particularly when linked to international networks, offers authority through the enlistment of accredited experts, the production of formal publications, and the use of statistics. This is reinforces by the location of such expertise in state (and international) bureaucracies" (Keeley and Scoones 2003, 4–5). Affording credibility to certain scientific claims over others, and integrating those claims into state structures, becomes an incredibly powerful political tool. Such a tool can, in turn, shape and control people, resources, and agendas (Keeley and Scoones 2003, 21).

Not only can the state legitimate scientific knowledge, but scientific knowledge itself is crucial in creating and sustaining the state. Science offers a "cultural resource in the 'construction' of the political order" (Ezrahi 1990, 10). Even more than providing the instrumental tools the state needs to achieve its ends, scientific knowledge validates and legitimates actions taken to achieve those ends (Ezrahi 1990, 11). Policymakers can point to scientific knowledge to give credence to their actions, which in turn boosts their own credibility. The validity of the state and its actions are backed by "scientific fact." Jasanoff expands upon this point:

It is no longer possible to deal with such staples of democratic theory as citizenship or deliberation or accountability without delving into their interactions with the dynamics of knowledge creation and use (2005, 6–7).

If we are to understand how the public relates to the state, and vice versa, then we must understand the role that scientific knowledge and its creation play.

These attempts to harness the power of scientific knowledge to legitimate the state can backfire, though. Trying to import inapplicable knowledge wholesale from a different context or failing to consider how local conditions may certain claims can undermine trust in both scientific knowledge and the institutions that legitimated that

---

5   Politicians may manipulate scientific findings to bolster their own policy preferences (Mooney 2005), but such scientific fraud is a distinct issue from scientific interpretation.

knowledge. Further, states may employ scientific knowledge to impose problematic versions of social identities (Wynne 1996, 20–25). Think of the 'science' that supported racial segregation and the social identities that it imposed to understand this latter point (for an excellent discussion of racial science in South Africa, see Dubow 1995). We may discount the 'science' of eugenics today, but the important point is that it *was* recognized as science at the time because it fit within a particular social, political, and historical context.

The standards for interpreting scientific knowledge may vary from place to place. Jasanoff speaks of a civic epistemology, or the criteria for evaluating public knowledge, and notes that these criteria will change depending on a locality's (or group's) cultural, political, and historical space (Jasanoff 2004c, 155). For example, Carolan (2006) examines why farmers in Iowa resist adopting sustainable agricultural practices, despite positive benefits like lower rates of soil and nutrient loss, increased soil health, and fewer chemicals entering water tables. He finds that this is largely due to "epistemic distance." The cultural and economic infrastructure surrounding modern farming operations externalize many of the costs to the public as a whole and are largely invisible. These keep farmers removed from these processes, and make it difficult for them to change their practices or even, in some cases, accept the scientific truths about the dangers of conventional agricultural practices. Thus, the societal expectations and understandings preclude the farmers from accepting and implementing the scientific knowledge about sustainable agriculture.

As science becomes part of the political process, it can have important implications for democratic practices. Salomon highlights an interesting paradox here. In many ways, science and scientific institutions are undemocratic systems. By their very nature, they create a certain elite and are often removed from the general discourse. On the other hand, though, science is perhaps the *most* democratic social system because all who belong to the system can engage it, contribute to its collective knowledge, and challenge others (Salomon 2000, 33). Science and scientific knowledge allow for large-scale debates and discussions – a hallmark of democracy – but only within a select group. The challenge, then, is to delineate who can rightfully participate within the group and find an appropriate way to share this knowledge with the larger public. The social negotiation that occurs between scientists and the lay public can be crucial for the eventual reception and acceptance of the scientific knowledge (Jasanoff 1990, 234).

At the same time, contending groups within a democratic political system will attempt to use "their" science to counter the claims of others. Experts will argue with one another. Studies will disagree about conclusions. Groups will cast doubt on the credentials and authority of scientists who disagree with them. Opposing sides will even call upon the insights of science studies and the sociology of scientific knowledge to challenge others. In an attempt to undercut their opponents' expertise and deprive them from using science as a political resource, groups may highlight the contextual elements that encouraged the adoption of some scientific knowledge (Jasanoff 1996, 399). If a group can cast enough doubt on another's scientific knowledge, then they can hope to prevail. Science becomes another weapon in political battles. Even the attempts to *depoliticize* science and remove it from the political realm may be interpreted as a political move (Ezrahi 1990, 51–53).

Colgrove (2005) offers a fascinating case study of how a state's attempt to use scientific knowledge to bolster its credibility can actually undermine that trust. In early 20ᵗʰ Century America, advances in preventing smallpox led a number of states and municipalities to require smallpox vaccination for children. These new regulations provoked an outcry of dissent among many. Vaccination did carry a small risk, and a very small number of children did suffer ill effects or even died, but the number was incredibly small when compared the vast majority who were spared from contracting an often fatal disease. Interestingly, the objections to compulsory vaccination came in many different forms. It was not a divide between political parties or among religious groups; the anti-vaccination groups exhibited a remarkable diversity. Some protested that it was essentially a socialist policy, with the government unilaterally imposing a law on the citizenry without public discussion. Others expressed doubts about the safety of the vaccine. One group complained that the government was overriding a parent's right to direct medical care for her or his child. Government officials and prominent academics countered these criticisms and highlighted the scientific evidence that vaccination conferred an immense benefit – yet this just further animated the opponents and made them even more determined to repeal compulsory vaccination laws. They attempted to counter the 'official' science with their own scientific evidence and statistics, trying to meet the scientific and government officials on their own grounds. Though it had little success actually changing laws, a large-scale anti-vaccination movement remained a potent political force in the United States through the 1920s.

What animated such a broad spectrum of Americans to oppose a medical intervention that the government believed and scientific evidence strongly indicated would provide an immense public health benefit? Colgrove notes that the advances in vaccination technology and the compulsory smallpox vaccination laws coincided with broader changes in American politics and society that altered the relationship between citizens and the state. New administrative institutions were playing an increasingly large role (Colgrove 2005, 171–172). Traditional structures were changing, leaving many feeling unsettled and uncertain of their status within the polity. Urbanization, immigration, and changes in the national economy fundamentally altered the place of many people within the broader society, and many people felt insecure with their new position. In essence, government officials' use of scientific knowledge to validate new policies led many citizens to believe that they were now subject to a new social identity – one which afforded them less autonomy and one which they found problematic. They did not trust the officials validating this scientific 'truth,' so they attempted to create and promote their own. They saw science being used to change the government's relationship to the public in a negative way, and they rebelled against those changes. Members of the public rejected the government's attempts to legitimate and validate its actions through scientific knowledge. The social context influenced whether people accepted the scientific fact.

All is not doom and gloom when science and democracy intersect. Many have argued that science can play a unique role in embedding democratic practices within a state and ensuring that the citizenry maintains vigilance over its government. By encouraging the mass public to take an active role in the scientific process, people are empowered to contribute to the improvement of their own lives. This, in turn, leads to improvements in society as a whole. Mass involvement in the creation and dissemination of scientific knowledge will allow the public to overcome the power and privilege of favored minority groups and elites (Ventura 2001, 83). Science offers a way to place a check on society's elites and ensures that state policies will reflect the needs and concerns of the general population. "Essentially, a wider spectrum of citizens must become more cognitive and analytical, if democracy is to mature and realize its potential ... the questions being posed and tackled by scientists cannot in a democratic dispensation, be left to the scientists themselves" (Ventura 2001, 81). In South Africa, Mbeki and his supporters have invoked this very argument to justify their involvement in scientific debates about AIDS. "In the face of relentless criticism of the president's pro-dissident stance, his spokespersons and supporters argued against the guild-like exclusivism of the scientific community and insisted upon the democratic right of the President to participate in debates on AIDS science" (Robins 2005, 116).

As part of a democratic society, all members of the society have a right to engage in scientific debates and the processes whereby scientific knowledge is legitimated – just as they have in other realms of the political culture. This argument has fostered calls for a 'civic science.'

Civic Science

Science should serve the interests of the people. This basic notion lies at the heart of civic science – "the process of linking experts and stakeholders in planning social, economic, and environmental improvements" (Schmandt 1998, 62). If lay people are involved in the scientific process, then they will more readily accept the outcomes of that process because their involvement shaped those very outcomes. For civic science advocates, this involvement is a sign of a truly democratic polity.

If scientific knowledge is fact, then why is citizen involvement important? Citizen participation is important for encouraging acceptance of policy outcomes. "[P]olicies that are consistent with the visions, beliefs, and aspirations of citizens will have more chance of success in the twenty-first century than policies imposed without consideration of citizen opinion" (Kasemir et al. 2003, 7).

Bäckstrand (2003) emphasizes the importance of public involvement and understanding, making explicit links to democratic practice. Calls for civic science, she notes, emerge in response to crises of legitimacy within science. Why would science face a legitimacy crisis? Civic science advocates argue that scientific processes, methodologies, and outcomes are perceived as too opaque and too far removed from the concerns of the general public. Though international policymakers increasingly display a rhetorical allegiance to democratic practices in policymaking, knowledge is increasingly relegated solely to the arena of scientific expertise, which limits those who can claim to have knowledge (Gough et al. 2003, 39).

Civic science resonates with pragmatic democratic theory, which emphasizes open debate and organized deliberation to achieve optimal policy outcomes – processes that include science. Failure to create an open process leads to a lack of trust. "If expert authority is a problem, it is because the political institutions in which it is embedded are no longer open to the publics affected by them," writes Bohman (1999, 598). Thus, civic science is crucially linked with democratic theory and practice. The civic science movement also relates to Barber's notion of 'strong democracy.' Strong democracy "rests on the idea of a self-governing community of citizens who are united … by civic education and who are made capable of common purpose and mutual action by virtue of their civic attitudes and participatory institutions" (Barber 1984, 117). It empowers communities to work together to advance their mutual interests and understand their commonality by providing the tools, training, and civic institutions to allow for meaningful participation in all spheres of civic life – and this includes the scientific process and understanding how scientific knowledge impacts a community. Involvement of affected publics is a hallmark of a democratic society, as it ensures that the public's voice is heard throughout policy debates. Civic science extends this notion to include the scientific process.

Durodie cautions us, though, that civic science's advocates may be conflating two unrelated social phenomena. Public participation in the policy process may indeed be on the wane, but that does not necessarily mean that science is too closed off from the public. Calls for the inclusion of public dialogue in the scientific process confuse the demise of public political participation with growing societal disillusionment with science in general. The solution is not to expand science to incorporate everyone and every possible idea, but rather to restore integrity to the political process through a reinvigoration of public dialogue. He admonishes: "By having to make science more 'accessible' in order to be 'inclusive,' this ends up by diluting the detail, eroding the evidence, and trivializing the theory. This is not access to science but access to science as simplistic morality tales for a nervous society" (Durodie 2003, 85).

Some authors see the debates over teaching evolution and creationism in the public schools as the clearest example of the dangers of throwing science open. Including a diversity of views simply for the sake of appearing balanced can imply a lack of consensus within the scientific community, even on seemingly settled issues. Since few members of the public have the necessary scientific knowledge to critically evaluate the competing claims and evidence, this false sense of balance creates more confusion (Mooney 2004).

Civic Science and AIDS

Unique among public health issues, the AIDS epidemic has featured numerous struggles and debates over credibility and claims to expertise. Public activism around AIDS in the 1980s and 1990s in the United States largely centered on who has the right to speak for AIDS patients and determine research agendas. This was essentially a debate over the role of civic science – what is the relationship between the scientific community and the public, and what *should* that relationship be?

The controversy started almost immediately after the discovery of HIV. Medical researchers argued that the spread of AIDS was linked to the sexual transmission of a new virus. Members of the GLBT community vociferously rejected this finding, arguing that it was a moral condemnation of sexual freedom under the guise of scientific fact (Epstein 1996, 64). When dissenting opinions about the cause(s) of

AIDS emerged, the mainstream scientific community initially ignored them in hopes they would disappear. Instead, this response (or lack thereof) gave ammunition to the AIDS dissidents and made the scientific community appear unwilling to engage in public discussion (Epstein 1996, 109). The seeming lack of democracy and unwillingness to incorporate the voices of those affected by the disease in the scientific process undermined the credibility of the scientific community in the eyes of many AIDS patients and activists. This process continued as AIDS patients saw few tangible benefits from mainstream science. Epstein notes that profound desperation and mainstream science's failure to deliver any effective treatments led many to embrace alternative theories about AIDS and its treatment, with strong condemnation of mainstream science for not taking these ideas seriously (Epstein 1996, 116–117).

Dissident theories, publications, and conferences often cloaked themselves in the language of democracy, freedom of expression, and heroic challenges to an uncaring establishment. At the same time, an increasing number of AIDS activists began conducting their own research projects and learning the mainstream scientific literature on the disease. These activists argued that scientists were too close to the data and funding sources to properly analyze the results and discuss the conclusions. Further, they translated scientific conclusions into easily accessible language in order to allow AIDS patients to speak for themselves and educate their care providers (Epstein 1996, 195–206).

Using the tools of civic science, AIDS activists had a substantial impact on clinical drug trials by advocating for the use of surrogate markers in the evaluation of new anti-AIDS drugs. Surrogate markers are laboratory measurements that indirectly indicate a treatment's effect on a disease. Though they introduce greater uncertainty, they are often used with life-threatening diseases to speed up the approval process of new drugs (Epstein 1997). The Food and Drug Administration initially rebuffed the activists' demands, but it eventually agreed to use CD4 cell depletion as a surrogate marker. Epstein traces the FDA's change of heart to the changing tactics of the activists. Prominent activists became "credible speakers *about science*" by adopting the "language of biomedicine" (Epstein 1997, 717; italics in original). By demonstrating that they could interpret scientific research and speak knowledgably about it, AIDS activists could collaborate with scientists and regulators to create an appropriate measure. "Without the AIDS activists, CD4 counts would not have been accepted as a surrogate marker in 1991" (Epstein 1997, 717). This is the hallmark of Schmandt's civic science – stakeholders (AIDS activists) and experts (scientists) linked together to plan social improvements.

What's more, AIDS activists used civic science to wrest power away from the established scientific experts. They raised questions about the use, content, processes, and control over the science of AIDS. They countered the claims of scientists regarding appropriate markers and the proper means for testing medications for an incurable disease. They challenged the interpretations of scientific studies conducted by established scientists (Epstein 1991). In short, they brought their own knowledge and expertise to the table. Through their knowledge, they sought to have their science and expertise recognized as credible in order to alter the policy agenda and direct resources toward projects they believed mainstream science overlooked.

History, Identity, and Epistemic Communities

History and identity are crucial elements for understanding the political organization of any society. At its most fundamental levels: "[I]dentity, at any level of collectivity, shapes preferences about most everything, certainly shapes the probability and character of many varieties of conflict, and stimulates group rights claims and assertions of self-determination" (Green 2002, 31).

Identities, which are shaped by history, necessarily impact how we respond to issues that emerge within the polity without doing so overtly. Hall (1999) convincingly demonstrates how major political transitions in European history corresponded with radical changes in societal collective identities. As people redefine how they see themselves, their relationship to each other, and their relationship to the political leadership, government structures change to embody and reflect these new identities. Identities impact government policies and institutions at all levels.

This same process applies to epistemic communities. History and identity commitments play an important, if subtle, role in epistemic communities. The epistemic community, its beliefs, and its role within society reflect broader concerns and understandings of the state. Though they are not state structures per se, they influence, and are influenced by, broader societal arrangements. They assist in "developing and circulating causal beliefs and some associated normative beliefs," "shap[e] how conflicts of interest will be resolved," and serve as "the cognitive baggage handlers of constructivist analyses of politics and ideas" (Haas 2001, 11579). A society's history and identity commitments inform these beliefs and conflicts that the epistemic community addresses and attempts to resolve. States do not consciously promote an epistemic community because it reflects a particular understanding of history and identity; it is obviously a far more subtle process than that. Instead, government officials *unconsciously* turn to epistemic communities that "think like them" with experts who share and reflect the society's interests and experiences.

This does not mean that government policymakers simply look for scientists and experts who will tell them what they want to hear. When policymakers turn to an epistemic community, it implies that policymakers do not even *know* what they want to hear. Members of the epistemic community frame the debate and the policy options, and their understandings and approaches are likely to reflect the society's broader understandings of itself. Scientists are "part of a broader cultural discourse … [and] reflect the broader culture of the society from which they emerge" (Haas 2004, 572). An epistemic community can, in turn, transform societal identities and interests (Adler 1997, 344). It is part of the co-constitution of societal identities.

Why would history and identity play a role in a seemingly objective setting like scientific knowledge? As Carolan and Bell succinctly highlight: "Truth depends essentially on social relations … [C]hallenges to what constitutes the 'truth' are equally challenges to identities and the social networks of trust in which that truth is embedded" (2003, 225).

Truth is a reflection of trust; we tend to believe those we trust. Because the issues at stake in scientific knowledge are generally larger than any one individual, we rely on our social networks to help us make sense of the world. It is certainly true that a disease infects an individual, but a disease epidemic is largely than any individual. When we move to the point where the state is involved in formulating a response, the issue has moved beyond the individual. The issue is complex. It is hard to understand. Relying on our social networks – on people we trust – offers a cognitive shortcut to make sense of the issue. We trust people who can speak to our experiences and understandings. A group of experts that reflects a society's experiences and understandings is more likely to find favor than one that does not share this background.

Trust and truth also depend on context. This is not a postmodern argument, denying the plausibility of objective truths. Instead, context conditions how we inquire about something, what we consider important to research, and how we present the results of that research. Members of an epistemic community not only share causal beliefs and frames, but they also share common norms about how good research should be done (Miller and Fox 2001, 681). Again, this does not mean that objective truths do not or cannot exist. It does mean, though, that *how* we value knowledge and its production depends upon the context within which it is produced. Barker and Peters offer clear insights on how this process operates without dismissing the notion of objective knowledge. "Most facts are, in reality, determined by theory and by the particular measurements of the observer ... Even very simple 'facts' depend upon concepts and measurement. Water boils at 100 C, but this depends upon a concept (temperature) and a measuring scale (centigrade)" (1993a, 5).

Let me clarify this point with an example. Few, if any, modern scientists in Western nations would legitimately claim that a disease epidemic is evidence of God's displeasure with humanity. That simply is not part of the modern consensus of what deserves research attention or how good research is done. That does not mean it was always so. During the bubonic plague epidemic in Europe in the 1300s, though, most people turned to physician-clerics for medical advice. These physician-clerics interpreted and researched the epidemic's outbreak within a particular religious context which resonated with European beliefs about religion, health, and the relationship to the state (Tesh 1988). We can look back now and highlight the errors in such an approach. We may even laugh at the notion that a priest could cure a disease. However, that does not negate the importance of the research, flawed though it may have been, within this particular context. The knowledge that was being produced by the physician-clerics of the 14th Century reflected society's history and identity commitments. It did not create that history or those identity commitments, nor did the physician-clerics simply 'make up' something that they thought people wanted to hear. They applied their socially-resonant methods to address a new issue. Today, those same historical and identity commitments may lead us to seek someone in a white lab coat, a traditional healer, or a practitioner of 'alternative' medicine when we feel ill.[6]

---

6   By the same token, some people will continue to seek out priests or other religious figures to treat their illnesses today.

Oversights in the Epistemic Communities Approach

The insights gathered from research on epistemic communities initially seem promising for understanding the divergence between the international AIDS control regime and the South African government. One could argue that the South African government does not recognize the expertise of the AIDS epistemic community, that the regime is not institutionalized enough within South Africa, and that reinforcing norms do not exist to embed the epistemic community within South Africa. These explanations open up more questions than they answer. First, South Africa's scientific infrastructure is far and beyond that possessed by any other sub-Saharan African state (Furlong and Ball 1999). It would be odd, then, to argue that the country with the strongest scientific community cannot institutionalize an epistemic community accepted by states with weaker scientific communities. Second, if the South African government does not recognize the expertise of the transnational AIDS epistemic community, we cannot readily tell from this explanation why that is. Leaving the answer there cannot give us any clues into the processes that prevent that community from gaining the same influence in South Africa that it has acquired in nearly every other state. Third, these explanations would encourage us to view South Africa as outside the larger international society. South Africa does recognize the expertise of other international epistemic communities, as evidenced by its active participation in many international regimes. Asserting that South Africa does not recognize the authority and expertise of this epistemic community begs the question of what is different about this particular regime.

These shortcomings point to three larger oversights within the literature on epistemic communities. First, the literature on epistemic communities takes a largely functionalist view of international relations. Functionalism, which has long been central to studies of international integration and international relations as a whole (Rosamond 2000, 31), argues that form follows function through an almost Darwinian evolutionary process. Solutions to problems evolve through organic processes. In the present context, functionalism posits that epistemic communities develop and evolve through natural processes and are naturally recognized for their expertise. Unfortunately, this is not the case. Studies of the sociology of scientific knowledge part ways with the literature on epistemic communities precisely over this point (Lidskog and Sundqvist 2002, 85). The literature on epistemic communities tends to examine the conditions under which communities gain more influence, but it takes it as a given that the community's expertise will be recognized.

Second, the epistemic communities literature largely ignores the role of discourse. Litfin notes that an epistemic community's advice is "informed by its own broader worldview" (Haas 1992, 4), but the literature is largely silent about how that broader worldview is created. Understanding the latter is of crucial importance, because the sorts of transnational problems addressed by epistemic communities are not simply physical events. Instead, one needs to understand them as struggles over contested knowledge claims (Litfin 1995, 254). The worldwide AIDS epidemic is not simply an outbreak of an infectious disease; it also embodies intense battles over how best to address the epidemic, why the disease is spread, and what responsibilities states have to their citizens infected with AIDS. The outcomes of these debates often depend upon the discursive narratives employed. Framing the rise in obesity rates, for example, as an issue of genetics versus one of personal responsibility will lead to very different outcomes. The epistemic community literature acknowledges that these debates exist, but pays little attention to how these debates come to be in the first place. Discourse is inhibited when different groups assign different meanings to core terms of the debate (Haas and Haas 2002, 582). The sociology of scientific knowledge provides some insights about the role of discourse, but it largely focuses its analytical gaze at the social and political interactions that endow scientific knowledge with its value. Social and political interactions certainly include discourse, but the sociology of scientific knowledge pays less attention to discourse and more to existent power relationships. Discourse obviously figures into power relationships, but the sociology of scientific knowledge does not significantly develop this point.

Finally, the literature on epistemic communities assumes that only one epistemic community exists on any given issue. From this starting point, it then goes on to delineate the conditions under which this one epistemic community gains influence. The debate is over how much influence a particular epistemic community has without examining the possibility that the level of influence attained by one epistemic community may be related to a competing epistemic community's degree of influence. The epistemic communities literature ignores the possibility of a counter-epistemic community. This omission is puzzling. If one accepts the notion that context significantly impacts the reception of scientific knowledge, a central tenet of knowledge-based regime theories and epistemic communities, then why assume that only *one* epistemic community would emerge on a given issue? Remember, it is the complexity of modern transnational problems that allows epistemic communities to have their influence in the first place. If these problems are truly complex, then it is inconsistent to presume that all scientists and policymakers would understand these complex problems in the same way. The very definition of an epistemic community asserts that these groups share principled beliefs, causal beliefs, notions of validity, and common policy enterprises. Why, then, should we assume that only one such group would emerge?

Chapter 3

Counter-epistemic Communities

Scientific knowledge plays an important role in international politics, but current attempts to appreciate how and why scientific knowledge matters leave much to be desired. By assuming that only one group of experts will emerge on a given issue and that all policymakers will recognize that group as authoritative overlooks the socially constructed nature of knowledge creation. The burgeoning literature on the politicization of science (not to mention the scientization of politics) amply proves that science and politics have a tense relationship, and that this relationship often depends on the nature of the policy objectives pursued.

Epistemic communities translate scientific knowledge. They make knowledge understandable within a framework circumscribed by history and identity. Since different groups and states have different histories and identity commitments, different epistemic communities may emerge on the same issue. Recognized scientific experts may offer radically different policy proposals because they understand and interpret the scientific knowledge on that issue in fundamentally divergent manners. When competing epistemic communities emerge, one can speak of the existence of a counter-epistemic community.

Let me emphasize that this argument about competing epistemic communities in no way implies that no objective reality exists. Instead, different groups understand and interpret that reality in different manners based on their historical experiences and identity commitments. If a dog barks at me, my historical experiences with dogs (a dog bit me when I was a child, or I grew up with a beloved dog) and my identity commitments regarding dogs (I consider myself a cat person, for instance) will guide how I respond. My understanding of how and why the dog barks might differ from others' reactions, but that does not change the fact that a dog did bark.

What is a Counter-epistemic Community?

How do a state's history and identity translate into actual policies? We could simply posit that history and identity matter, and leave it there. This would tell us very little, though. How do they matter? Through what means do a state's history and identity translate themselves into policy outcomes? How do we generate real-world consequences from these rather abstract, nebulous ideas? This is where epistemic communities enter the picture.

Bear in mind that one of the key functions of an epistemic community is to frame a problem and provide relevant policy suggestions. Framing is immensely powerful. It sets the terms of the debate, and dictates how others view the problem. It lays the groundwork for privileging certain ideas and approaches. This process is not value-neutral, though. Along with framing come the framer's ideas, prejudices, and outlooks. Framing also shapes the role of experts, decisions on who qualifies as an expert, and the kind of knowledge necessary to address the problem (Radaelli 1995, 178). It immediately imbues a certain moral and ethical context to the problem that encompasses a state's history and identity. Calling the early outbreaks of Kaposi's sarcoma and Pneumocycstis pneumonia gay-related immune deficiency (GRID) fomented a different sort of response than when the Centers for Disease Control rechristened the disease acquired immune deficiency syndrome (AIDS) in 1982 (Shilts 1987, 121). The name GRID brought with it different expectations about who was at risk, who should treat the disease, and what obligation the national government had to respond because of the historical experiences and identity commitments in United States around issues of homosexuality and its role within the culture. The 'gay' frame encouraged a different sort of response from government policymakers.

The epistemic communities literature speaks of one epistemic community gaining influence and framing an issue when policymakers attempt to devise responses to transnational problems. This leads to an interesting quandary. If epistemic communities come together around a shared worldview and interpretation of a socially constructed reality, then why should we assume that there is only *one*? Arguing that only one epistemic community gains influence essentially says that most or all policymakers, though they may be scattered across the globe with radically different histories, identities, and worldviews, will interpret these new, complex transnational problems *in a nearly identical manner.* If that is the case, then the literature on epistemic communities contradicts its own epistemological heritage. Policymakers turn to epistemic communities because they need high-quality information in order to interpret and respond to new, emerging, complex transnational issues. It does not then follow that all these policymakers would turn to the same group or that only one group would emerge that could credibly discuss the issue. This simply does not make logical sense. It gives a technocratic gloss to an inherently political problem – a technocratic gloss that would be unthinkable in any other realm.

Different people are likely to have different interpretations and employ different frames to respond to emerging issues. The epistemic communities literature, though seems to assume that these communities are essentially engaged in zero-sum games to acquire influence. If Community A is recognized for its expertise on a particular issue, then Community A is *the* expert community for that issue. No other challengers need apply, for Community A has vanquished its competitors and all policymakers will turn to Community A for advice.

Why should this be the case? Does Community B stop having any role to play? Do Community B's supporters simply fold? In some cases, they do – but not always. After all, the problems being dealt with by epistemic communities are complex and transnational. Would it not be better to suppose that, in certain circumstances, Community A and Community B, both made up of scientists and experts recognized for their expertise and turned to for advice, could *both* find political champions and be regarded as valid sources of policy recommendations? The members of both communities may have similar impeccable, recognized credentials, but that does not necessarily mean that they share the same general worldview. They could interpret the realities of a particular problem in radically different ways, and those differing interpretations could lead to wildly divergent policy recommendations with different policymakers championing each. This does not mean that two competing epistemic communities will *always* exist, but rather acknowledges that different groups of scientific experts often come into play on the same issue.

The international arena is not always a realm of peaceful agreement. States vigorously disagree with one another. These disagreements could be rooted in epistemic communities opposed to one another. Though there may be a dominant epistemic community, that does not necessarily preclude the emergence of a counter-epistemic community that presents problem frames and policy suggestions in opposition to the dominant epistemic community. States interpret problems in different ways. In turn, they may well respond to different policy suggestions and privilege different epistemic communities.[1]

Building off Peter Haas' definition of epistemic community, I define a counter-epistemic community as a *network of professionals with recognized expertise and competence in a particular domain and an authoritative claim to policy-relevant knowledge within that domain or issue-area in opposition to the recognized expertise of the dominant epistemic community*. It serves as a counterweight to the dominant epistemic community by seeking to reframe the problem and offering alternative solutions to problems faced by the international community. It empowers a state or group of states to challenge the dominant position.

Of crucial importance, influential policymakers in some state must recognize the counter-epistemic community's expertise and empower that group to have a role in the policy process. The mere existence of a group of people with policy views on a particular issue means nothing unless policymakers within a state embrace and help promote those policy views. This embrace is crucial, as it makes the group relevant to other policymakers (not to mention scholars). The scientists who first discovered pollution's detrimental impact on the Mediterranean Sea shared information with each other and worked together prior to being recognized for their policy-relevant knowledge. The group existed without official recognition. With official recognition, though, those scientists became important players in faming the issue, setting the agenda, and crafting policy for the international community. That step moved them from being random academics to relevant political actors.

Counter-epistemic communities translate a state's history and identity into actual policy outcomes, just like epistemic communities do. They present a paradigm that resonates with a society's underlying values and normative patterns, which in turn

---

1 The notion of counter-epistemic communities shares a great deal with the burgeoning literature on the importance of discursive representations and re-representations of actors by other actors (see Hall 2003; Weldes and Saco 1996). They diverge largely because of the role of science. Epistemic and counter-epistemic communities are generally populated by natural scientists who can make a claim to scientific objectivity and political neutrality. Their authority comes from their supposed value-neutrality, whereas the experts who construct representations of the Castro regime or the Asian development model are largely politicians or political appointees.

greatly increases its chances of being accepted by policymakers (Radaelli 1995, 166–167). They do not shape a state's identity by themselves, nor are they created by states simply to provide scientific credibility for a particular policy. They transmit ideas to people who turn them into policy.

Epistemic and Counter-epistemic Communities

If we examine the debates over national AIDS policies in South Africa, we see two clearly defined epistemic communities influencing the debates – one that supports the mainstream consensus that HIV causes AIDS, and one that supports the dissident position that disputes a causal link between HIV and AIDS. Both communities consist of experts who share causal beliefs, causal mechanisms, truth tests, and policy options. More importantly, each community has the ear of at least some government officials and policymakers who can turn those ideas into policy. This gives the views of that community a certain level of currency and validity within the international debates on AIDS and how best to address the AIDS epidemic. The case of AIDS and its competing epistemic communities reinforces the idea that "scientific research and the uses to which it is put are as strongly shaped by existing social structures as vice versa" (Bernstein 2001, 124). Each epistemic community reflects and empowers a certain reality shaped by historical experiences and identity commitments.

Scientific opinion coalesced in the 1980s around the ideas that HIV was the sole cause of AIDS, that HIV was an infectious agent, and that AIDS is fatal in all cases. This epistemic community embraced a biomedical, behavioral discursive frame. The frame emphasized behavioral change as the most appropriate way to combat the spread of the disease. It also advocated the need to find a pharmaceutical remedy to treat those infected with the disease. Through organizations such as, but not limited to, the World Health Organization, the Global Program on AIDS, and UNAIDS, the mainstream AIDS epistemic community took center stage in creating, supporting, and funding national AIDS control programs. Their involvement enabled the transmission of the community's views and discursive frames. International conferences on AIDS, well-attended by government officials and extensively covered by international media sources, provided yet another platform from which community members could express their views to an international audience. Because they expressed these views through internationally sanctioned outlets such as international scientific conferences and leading scientific research journals, the mainstream AIDS epistemic community's discursive frame soon became equated with the only appropriate discursive frame on the disease.

As with any epistemic community, members did not agree with each other on every point. Bitter disagreements between leading researchers and intense competition over funding divided the AIDS research community into 'warring factions' for many years (Cohen 1996). Though this may have undermined efforts at collaborative research projects, it did not fundamentally alter the underlying shared causal beliefs. Members of the epistemic community did not differ over whether HIV causes AIDS or whether behavioral interventions are the most appropriate manner for combating the spread of AIDS. Instead, they bickered over ego (who received credit for what discoveries) and money (who received research grants from which prestigious sources). In addition, the AIDS epistemic community could not necessarily explain all the mysteries of the disease. Why, for example, did it infect so many people in sub-Saharan Africa, yet relatively few in Oceania? Why did HIV have such a long latency period, and what triggered the end of that period? Why did the disease emerge in the 1970s and 1980s and not earlier (or later)? These questions remained unanswered, but the research successes of the AIDS epistemic community encouraged an environment in which few worried that small questions about a complex new disease would hamper treatments.

Because of the influence of the AIDS epistemic community, few initially challenged it. By the mid-1980s, the mainstream AIDS epistemic community declared debates over the cause and origin of AIDS to largely be over. Questioning this emerging consensus meant scientists risked losing valuable research funds or access to prestigious publishing outlets. Further, the AIDS epistemic community had been so successful at transmitting its views and gaining access to policymakers, few stopped to question whether another frame even existed.

The counter-epistemic community, in many ways, emerged from the initial scientific debates over AIDS' cause. Prior to HIV's announced discovery in 1984, not all scientists agreed that AIDS was a viral disease. Some cast doubt on the methodologies and motivations of many scientists. They questioned why Margaret Heckler, the US Secretary of Health and Human Services, proclaimed Robert Gallo the discoverer of HIV as the cause of AIDS at a government-sponsored press conference in March before the findings underwent a traditional double-blind peer review process.[2] The early dissenters claimed that members of the mainstream epistemic community assumed a virus caused AIDS because they were virologists. If this new disease were viral, then these researchers could continue to use their established methodologies and ensure continued access to virological research funding. This emphasis, the dissenters claimed, blinded the scientists from considering other environmental or toxilogical causes. Dissenters also implied that the mainstream scientists had financial stakes in developing AIDS tests and drugs (Duesberg 1997). These seeds of doubt eventually bloomed into a full-fledged counter-epistemic community that actively challenged the basic tenets of the mainstream AIDS epistemic community at every turn.

Members of the counter-epistemic community, led most prominently by Berkeley virologist Peter Duesberg, share common beliefs about AIDS. Rather than being viral in origin, counter-epistemic community members argue that AIDS is essentially a

---

2   The story of HIV's discovery is one of intrigue and mystery. Robert Gallo of the US National Cancer Institute claimed to be the first person to discover and isolate HIV. Luc Montagnier of France's Pasteur Institute challenged this claim, arguing that he had actually discovered the virus first and that Gallo had improperly used samples from Montagnier's lab. Gallo denied this strenuously, and an international investigation commenced. In 1987, after high-level negotiations between US President Ronald Reagan and French Prime Minister Jacques Chircac, Gallo and Montagnier received credit as co-discoverers of HIV. Three years later, an investigation by the US National Institute of Health's Office of Scientific Integrity concluded that the samples in Gallo's lab were identical to Montagnier's. Gallo was investigated for scientific misconduct, but received no punishment.

political disease. AIDS serves as a convenient political moniker for a host of ailments that had afflicted various communities for years. What's more, they claim that the AIDS epidemics in Africa and the West are fundamentally different. For Africans, this means poverty, malnutrition, and underdevelopment. For intravenous drug users and gay men, this means repeated exposure to high amounts of illegal drugs, sexually transmitted diseases, and poor nutrition. In all cases, though, the counter-epistemic community asserts that governments seek to classify all of these afflictions under the rubric of AIDS to avoid potentially embarrassing discussions about sexual activity and global inequities. Calling AIDS a new disease allows governments to turn what members of the counter-epistemic community see as essentially a social issue into a medical issue, and this biomedical discourse saves the developed states from engaging in critical self-reflection.

The vitriolic research battles of the 1980s and early 1990s also convinced many AIDS dissidents that the HIV/AIDS connection is more about scientific ego and funding rather than actual science. They saw the battles over who first discovered HIV as diverting attention from the more important questions about *whether* HIV causes AIDS. The mainstream AIDS epistemic community was so fixated on finding a viral cause for AIDS that they blamed the disease on the first virus they could find, according to the counter-epistemic community. (Chapter 6 provides greater detail about the shared causal beliefs of the AIDS counter-epistemic community.)

Counter-epistemic community members also came together over their exclusion from the scientific debates about AIDS. As journals refused to publish articles that denied the connection between HIV and AIDS, many dissidents took this as a sign that they were on to something. The mainstream journals are afraid to publish dissident research, the dissidents asserted, because it would expose the scientific fraud being perpetrated by the mainstream. Each rejection reinforced and strengthened the counter-epistemic community. They saw every refusal to engage them, every denied research grant, and every article rejected by a prominent scientific journal as further proof that they were right – and that the mainstream AIDS epistemic community knew it. Mainstream AIDS researchers refused to debate them, they believed, because they did not want their fraud exposed. Instead of engaging in an honest debate, AIDS dissidents argued, members of the mainstream AIDS epistemic community protected each other and produced 'politically correct' science.

Since they found themselves excluded from the mainstream scientific debates, AIDS dissidents found other channels for disseminating their research and beliefs. They published in alternative and less-prestigious journals. They organized their own conferences. They self-published their books when the need arose. They turned to the Internet. (Indeed, Mbeki's association with AIDS dissidents allegedly began when he stumbled across one of their websites.)

Conditions Giving Rise to Counter-epistemic Communities

Historical experiences and identity commitments can contribute to a failure to arrive at shared intersubjective understandings. This failure can give rise to a counter-epistemic community that challenges the international regime that emerges for a particular issue. The question now becomes, why do counter-epistemic communities emerge on some issues, but not for all issues? Numerous regimes exist, but not all of them see competing epistemic communities. What's more, some South African policymakers may privilege an AIDS counter-epistemic community, but go with mainstream epistemic communities on other issues. What conditions make history and identity so salient that challengers to the dominant epistemic community emerge?

Two features appear particularly relevant for the emergence of a counter-epistemic community: the explicit assignation of blame, and the lack of channels that allow for broad participation. Carolan and Bell emphasize:

> Truth depends essentially on social relations ... thus, challenges to what constitutes the 'truth' are equally challenges to identities and the social networks of trust in which that truth is embedded (2003, 225).

Counter-epistemic communities emerge in those situations in which trust is lacking and groups feel they cannot participate in the creation or re-creation of identity commitments.

First, counter-epistemic communities are more likely to emerge when blame for a problem is explicitly laid at the feet of one state or a group of states. When AIDS first emerged, popular speculation blamed Africa for the disease's emergence. Accusations flew about bizarre religious and sexual rituals involving monkeys that allowed the virus to make the leap from animals to humans. Africans were subjected to a host of discriminatory visa requirements, special blood tests, and careful surveillance in many Western countries out of fear that they were infected with AIDS and would spread it to others (Fortin 1989). Many outsiders also imbued their accusations with a sense of morality. Since AIDS spread rapidly *and* is sexually transmitted, the argument often went, Africans must engage in immoral behavior.

Assigning blame for the problem that has led to the need for an international regime automatically puts the blamed party on the defensive. States are unlikely to react positively to others telling them that they have wreaked havoc on the international community. Dimitrov (2003) argues that recognition of an issue's transnational consequences is crucial for facilitating cooperation. When states do not share an understanding of these transnational impacts and instead blame the problem on one state (or a group of states), international cooperation is highly unlikely. A counter-epistemic community, then, essentially functions as a defense mechanism. For example, Algeria and Egypt both initially viewed the Mediterranean pollution control regime with skepticism because they felt that regime members blamed them for problems that, in their views, originated in other countries (Haas 1989, 392). Feeling that they were being chastised for a problem they did not cause, they contributed very little to the regime and backed up their arguments with their own scientists. This does not mean that a counter-epistemic community is simply a political tool, but it highlights how blame can foster the development of divergent viewpoints on a given issue.

The other factor contributing to the formation of a counter-epistemic community is a lack of channels that allow for broad participation in the regime. If states feel that a regime is being imposed upon them, or that their voices are not being heard, they are unlikely to participate in a constructive manner and may actively oppose the regime's scientific bases. An epistemic community's credibility often depends on sharing a common culture or common cultural understandings (Lidskog and Sundqvist 2004, 210). Closing the channels of participation precludes the creation of the mutually shared intersubjective understandings crucial for the acceptance of 'expert' advice. Channels are not the same as formal institutional mechanisms, though they can certainly play a role. Instead, channels refer to opportunities for a wide array of states to contribute to the formation and sharing of the shared intersubjective meanings that uphold and support the regime. States want to have a voice, or at least have the *option* of having a voice, within a regime. Alienation from the policymaking process is significantly related to questioning the scientific knowledge used by government officials or outright rejection of these new policies. Proximity to the process does not guarantee acceptance of the resultant policies, but it does allow for a greater appreciation of the promises and limitations of the proposed policies (Rüdig 1993).

To return to the Mediterranean pollution control regime example, both Algeria and Egypt eventually overcame their skepticism and became active participants in the regime. Why? Haas traces this to the active cultivation of relationships with scientists and policymakers in these two countries (Haas 1989, 394–396). Members of the regime sought out to include influential people from both of these countries, and to incorporate the perspectives and understandings these people brought with them into the regime itself. This allowed the regime to overcome initial opposition, and turned two states who could have posed a serious threat to regime's goals into active participants.

Despite good intentions, the international community initially offered few opportunities for non-Western states to play a major role in formulating strategies, agendas, and understandings of the AIDS epidemic. The regime's organizations, funding, and personnel largely came from Western states. Because of this, non-Western states had few inroads to contribute to the direction of the regime. They instead found the ideas of regime being handed down to them without their active input. African scientists and policymakers decried how the international AIDS control regime often failed to understand their perspective or ask for their input. They note how the calls for cultural sensitivity often strike them as hypocritical, as Western researchers sometimes treat Africa as one large laboratory for AIDS research (Fredland 1998). This has certainly improved in recent years, but African leaders still voice complaints about having outside programs imposed upon them by Western states without consultation (Sontag 2004).

The combination of these two factors – blame and a lack of channels to allow input – appears to favor the creation of a counter-epistemic community. In isolation, it is unlikely that a counter-epistemic community would emerge. A state may be blamed for a particular problem initially, but it is unlikely to actively challenge the regime if it has an opportunity to communicate its perspective to that regime.

Further, a state that simply lacks inroads with a regime is unlikely to cause a problem if it largely agrees with the regime's underlying principles.

The apparent importance of these two factors shows that the emergence of a counter-epistemic community is not simply a political ploy by one side to advance its own arguments. Counter-epistemic communities instead emerge organically out of sincere and profound disagreements about how to understand and interpret a particular phenomenon.

Possible Objections

Three objections may arise to the notion of counter-epistemic communities. First, some may argue that the emergence of a counter-epistemic community is unique to AIDS, and even then unique only to South Africa. Second, other may object that the counter-epistemic community is essentially an interest group. Third, some scholars might posit that the AIDS dissidents do not represent a distinct epistemic community; rather, they signal the epistemic community's immaturity. Let me examine and answer each of these objections in greater detail.

Objection #1: This Concept Applies Only to South Africa and/or AIDS

The first objection addresses the issue of generalizability. Two epistemic communities may have emerged on AIDS. If that is the only case in which that has occurred, though, then the research here tells an interesting story but does little to advance our understanding of international regimes or the flow of knowledge in the international community.

A cursory examination of the issues and problems facing the international community proves that AIDS is not the only issue in which opposing epistemic communities operate. Recent debates about Kyoto Accord and climate change present perhaps the clearest example. A mainstream climate change epistemic community argues that developed states need to implement aggressive measures to reduce their emissions of greenhouse gases like carbon dioxide, methane, and nitrous oxide. When these gases collect in the atmosphere, they hamper Earth's ability to radiate heat back into space. The result is increased temperatures, which disrupts agricultural production and can cause wild fluctuations in temperature. These gases also cause holes in the ozone layer, which means that people are exposed to higher levels of UV radiation from the sun – which, in turn, increases vulnerability to skin cancer. Since these changes are largely the result of human activity, the climate change epistemic community recommends that states undertake measures to dramatically reduce greenhouse gas emissions. These measures include minimum fuel standards for automobiles, pollution controls on industrial activities, and the development of alternative sources of energy.

Through the work of this epistemic community, climate change is an important and prominent issue on the international agenda. Many states have passed laws to put some of the epistemic community's suggestions into practice, but significant improvement requires coordinated international action. After talks in 1997, international negotiators presented the Kyoto Accord for ratification by national governments. The Accord mandates that industrialized nations cut their emissions of greenhouse gases by 5.2 percent by 2012. Developing countries, though included in the treaty, are exempted from the emission control quotas. Members of the climate change epistemic community hoped that the Accord would not only spur the development of alternative energy sources that emit less pollution, but also prevent placing too much of a burden on any particular state (Gough and Shackley 2001).

All was not smooth sailing for the Kyoto Accord. The treaty required 55 percent of the industrialized nations to ratify it before it entered into effect. Both the United States and Australia refused to ratify the treaty. Part of their objection was economic, arguing that it placed an undue burden on American and Australian industries while doing little to control emissions in rapidly-industrializing countries like China. More importantly, a counter-epistemic community emerged to question the science behind the treaty. These climate dissidents doubted that the global warming was even a problem, arguing instead that this was simply the natural climactic fluctuations that Earth underwent on a regular basis (Christy 2000). They shared the belief that global warming, if it existed at all, was due to natural fluctuations (Cohen 2004; Jacoby and Reiner 2001; Robinson and Robinson 1997). Therefore, signing the Kyoto Accord would depress economic growth and activity for no reason.

The vast majority of climate scientists support the mainstream climate change epistemic community (Oreskes 2004). What makes the climate dissidents so influential and important is that they have the ear of high-placed and influential policymakers. US President George W. Bush has called for further research into whether global climate change is due to human activity, while US Senator James Inhofe has held multiple hearings on the global warming 'conspiracy' in the media (Coile 2006). The dissidents in the climate change counter-epistemic community do not need to convince everyone that they and their science are correct; they just have to convince the right people.

It should come as no surprise that epistemic and counter-epistemic communities can emerge. No two states will necessarily interpret a newly-emergent problem in the same way, nor will they necessarily share beliefs about the best response to that problem. States have different historical experiences and identity commitments, which in turn color how states interpret newly emergent problems. States respond to international issues in different manners as befits their varying interpretations of the problem. The subsequent interpretations, especially when the problem is new and novel and epistemic communities are likely to play the largest role, are likely to reflect a state's identity, history, and other relevant interests. In the case of climate change, just as with AIDS control, one sees the emergence of two distinct communities of scientists and experts who share causal beliefs about a particular international issue and to whom government officials and policymakers defer when it comes to implementing and crafting appropriate policy responses.

A variant on this first objection asserts that, while an AIDS counter-epistemic community may exist, its influence is limited to South Africa. While it may be true that members of the South African government have offered the most support and credibility to the AIDS dissidents, it is a mistake to equate that prominence with being the *sole* platform. Government officials in other states have also given some credence to the views of the AIDS counter-epistemic community. Zimbabwe's Robert Mugabe has long rejected the public health interventions of Western states, arguing that the West was attempting to essentially recolonize Africa under the guise of preventing AIDS (Boone and Batsell 2001).[3] Daniel arap Moi, Kenya's former president, lashed out at the international community for rejecting the possibility that African scientists could possibly find a cure for AIDS when so few reporters showed up for the press conference announcing the discovery of Kemron. The drug turned out to be useless, but Moi interpreted the reaction as a wholesale rejection of the possibility of successful African AIDS science. Even Uganda, which is often extolled by the international community for its behavioral interventions that have reduced HIV infection in the span of 15 years, has cautioned the international AIDS control regime against reading too much into the behavioral side. While changes in behavior certainly account for some of the reduction, Ugandan officials also point out behavioral changes alone are insufficient (Ingham 2004).

Further, this counter-epistemic community has clearly had an effect on international AIDS policy responses. Its continued existence, in the fact of overwhelming pressures to the contrary, demonstrates this. If this counter-epistemic community were truly as epiphenomenal as its detractors suggest, it would have long ago disappeared. The counter-epistemic community of AIDS dissidents has proven its staying power and required the mainstream AIDS epistemic community to respond. Many were outraged that Mbeki placed so many AIDS dissidents on his Presidential AIDS Advisory Panel, but their presence required the mainstream AIDS epistemic community to engage the dissidents on some level.

Objection #2: Counter-epistemic Communities are Identical to Interest Groups

To some, the concept of competing epistemic communities may look like competing interest groups. In the domestic arena, different interest groups compete for influence over legislation, with the more successful groups gaining more influence. If competing epistemic communities are really just competing interest groups, then does that not undermine the whole concept of the epistemic community? Can we not simply employ the theoretical tools already in existence to study interest groups?

Interest groups and epistemic communities certainly share some commonalities. Both seek to influence policy outcomes, and both share basic beliefs about a particular issue (McFadden 1995, 14). Despite these similarities, interest groups and epistemic communities are two very distinct concepts that cannot simply be collapsed into the same idea. Haas distinguishes between the *causal* beliefs shared by epistemic community members and the *principled* beliefs shared by interest group members. Because an epistemic community shares certain causal beliefs about an issue, its members are less likely to pursue an explicitly political agenda. They invoke the

---

3   Interestingly, Zimbabwe is one of the only countries in Africa experiencing a decline in its HIV prevalence rates. Zimbabwean government officials see this as evidence that their programs are working. Critics claim this shows that HIV has saturated the country's adult population (UNICEF 2005).

language of scientific objectivity to cloak any political interests. Interest groups, on the other hand, do not necessarily withdraw from the debate when confronted with contradictory evidence (Haas 1992, 18). Peterson (1992) shows how epistemic communities and interest groups differ when confronted with negative information. While issue-oriented environmentalists continued to press for policy changes despite evidence that contradicted their position on whale management, whale scientists largely withdrew from the debate as new scientific information emerged. Further, epistemic community members come together over this shared knowledge and intense interest on a particular topic. This distinguishes them both from the larger scientific community, which exhibits consensual knowledge but not shared interests, and interest groups, whose members possess shared interests but not necessarily a consensual knowledge base (Haas 1992, 18–19). This does not mean that alliances cannot form between epistemic communities and interest groups, but it does mean that we should recognize the different vantage points from which these two groups approach a given issue.

The political distinction between interest groups and epistemic communities is perhaps the most crucial. Neither members of the mainstream AIDS epistemic community, nor the counter-epistemic community of AIDS dissidents, see their work as inherently political. Nearly all would explicitly deny this. They argue that they are simply responding to what the scientific evidence tells them (though both communities would likely argue that the other side's science is overly political). Interest groups, on the other hand, explicitly exist to advance particular political goals. They may portray themselves as non-partisan, but interest groups, by their very nature, have some sort of political agenda which they wish to further.

Interest groups and epistemic communities also target different groups. Interest groups lobby legislators and government officials about particular bills. Epistemic communities, on the other hand, attempt to influence how those government officials understand the issues contained within bills. Epistemic communities define a problem and frame the discussions and perceptions on that issue. This framing, in turn, can give rise to interest groups. Without scientists warning about the dangers of global warming and framing public perceptions of the problem, a group like Greenpeace would be less likely to exist – because the issue itself would not exist. Epistemic communities can bring a problem to the agenda; interest groups work on the fine points of implementing legislation on that problem. Interest groups are primarily local or national phenomena, whereas epistemic communities tend to be international. Though some evidence suggests the burgeoning of transnational interest groups or advocacy coalitions (Keck and Sikkink 1999; Klotz 2002), most interest groups appear to be rooted in one state. This makes sense, as interest groups are specifically targeting policy changes, and the international community has few substantive policymaking bodies that can implement legislation with any degree of force on a regular basis.

None of this should suggest that interest groups and epistemic communities are necessarily opposing concepts. Both can provide information to policymakers and attempt to influence how states respond to particular problems. Combining these two groups into the same analytical term ignores the different functions, memberships, and targets of interest groups and epistemic communities. Each plays a distinct and unique role.

Objection #3: Any Counter-epistemic Community will Eventually Disappear

Finally, some may counter that a counter-epistemic community will disappear once as scientists learn more about an issue. In the early response stages of any problem, we should expect a degree of dissension. Epistemic communities emerge precisely because a new issue emerges and policymakers are uncertain how to respond. If the issue is so new, then we should expect some early disagreements. Over time, though, that dissension and disunity will give way as one epistemic community 'beats' the other and is recognized as *the* epistemic community and an international regime emerges around the issue.

This argument, though intuitive, fails to fatally undermine the notion of counter-epistemic communities for a number of reasons. First, it may be right. A counter-epistemic community may indeed disappear as scientists learn more about a particular issue. Nothing about counter-epistemic communities posits that competing epistemic communities will *always* exist. Since knowledge is dynamic, as are actors' perceptions of their interests on a particular issue, then it is certainly possible for the number of epistemic communities to change. Certain causal beliefs may wither away in the face of scientific evidence or with the passing of a community's leaders. A completely new manner for approaching a particular issue may emerge and prove itself superior to previous modes of thought. The problem that spawned the epistemic communities in the first place may disappear. Any number of reasons may redraw the battle lines, so to speak, between competing epistemic communities – and one cannot predict when and where these changes will occur.

It is incorrect, though, to assume that this will automatically happen. A counter-epistemic community may disappear, but there is no reason to assume that it *must* disappear. Additional counter-epistemic communities could emerge. We would expect the epistemic communities to change as knowledge changes; that does not mean that we can predict the future and know how these epistemic communities will look in response to future knowledge.

Second, it assumes that consolidation is merely a function of age, but knowledge does not transfer to all parties in the same way. Some issues may invite more controversy than others. Take an epistemic community devoted to whaling and one devoted to space flight. The members will be different, the economic considerations will be different, and the simple importance of the issue to member-states will be different. With all these differences, it makes little sense to automatically assume that both epistemic communities would develop in the same manner.

Along these same lines, if we assume that authoritative knowledge is a function of age, then we should also be able to specify at what age a regime will be mature enough to have one epistemic community. AIDS emerged 25 years ago, and we still witness competing epistemic communities. SARS, on the other hand, quickly emerged onto the international agenda, but a scientific consensus quickly emerged, and no one speaks of dissident SARS scientists. Why would such a new issue be seemingly uncontested, while older issues still exhibit sharp disagreements between competing epistemic communities? If differences exist, then the issue must be about something other than age.

Third, this objection fails to understand the underlying reasons that competing epistemic communities exist in the first place. If the problem were as simple as needing more research or more time, then we simply have to wait a while for all disagreements to resolve themselves. Disagreements between epistemic communities, though, are not over tactics or peripheral issues; they are over fundamental root causes, about how competing communities understand and evaluate truth statements. They are at the heart of how a community sees and interprets the world around it. Such beliefs, so central to an identity, are unlikely to disappear quickly – even in the face of "overwhelming evidence." Most scientists now agree that overwhelming proof exists that HIV causes AIDS, but that has not silenced the counter-epistemic community of AIDS dissidents. They still believe that no connection exists between HIV and AIDS, and that the mainstream AIDS epistemic community does more harm than good. Evidence, then, is not enough. Beliefs that form the core of a group's identity are unlikely to disappear over night.

History offers another example. Scientists first recognized that cholera spread via contaminated drinking water by 1854, but sharp disagreements existed between competing epistemic communities. While the contagionists believed that a microbial agent was to blame, miasmists held to the belief that foul vapors caused cholera. This clash effectively prevented writing international sanitary guidelines until the late 1890s (Howard-Jones 1975). Why would two competing epistemic communities last for so long? Were the miasmists simply callous and unconcerned with the suffering of others? That is hardly likely. Instead, the miasma theory of cholera was deeply enmeshed within a larger set of beliefs about religion, society, social class, and politics. The theory about disease fit within a broader framework about society.[4] Denying theories about cholera's origin, then, threatened these other beliefs that were central to identity.

Conclusion

A counter-epistemic community is a group of experts who share common causal beliefs, yet whose causal beliefs fundamentally differ from the mainstream epistemic community. They are not simply a group of crackpots; they generally have the same advanced degrees from the same prestigious institutions as members of the mainstream epistemic community. This divergence in causal beliefs leads to highly different policy suggestions. It is at this point that counter-epistemic communities become important for scholars to examine. Once they have the ear of policymakers, they can influence a state's policy outcomes. Most research on epistemic communities

---

4   Interestingly, the miasmist theory of cholera contagion led to significant health improvements that contributed to cholera's decline. Edwin Chadwick, secretary of Britain's Poor Law Commission, wrote a report, heavily influenced by miasmist theories, on living conditions in London slums in 1842. In it, he argued for the construction of sewage systems and improved drinking water supplies (Tesh 1988, 28–29) – the same steps that ultimately proved successful for stopping cholera. Though the miasmists may have had the wrong theory, their policy recommendations were ultimately beneficial.

has either overlooked or dismissed the possibility that such a counter to a mainstream epistemic community could exist.

Government officials do not turn to members of a counter-epistemic community to hear what they want to hear. Instead, the counter-epistemic community is important because it embodies the history and identity commitments that resonate with that society. It bridges the gap between a society's norms and values, on the one hand, and its understanding of a problem, on the other. This competing group of experts is more likely to emerge when a state feels blamed for a transnational problem and when participatory channels are cut off.

Some may object that this concept is too unique to AIDS in South Africa to be important or that a counter-epistemic community will necessarily disappear with enough time. These objections demonstrate a failure to fully understand whence and why counter-epistemic communities emerge. They are not attempts by a particular state to be obstinate. Rather, they are reflections of the important, yet often overlooked, connection between *trust* and *truth*. They frame a problem in terms that make sense given a state's history and identity commitments.

How does this occur? The next two chapters will examine South Africa's history with public health interventions and its attempts to foster an African Renaissance-inspired identity commitment for the post-apartheid era. In-depth explorations of these two concepts will show how and why the AIDS counter-epistemic community resonates so much with an influential segment of the South African government.

Chapter 4

History and Public Health in South Africa

Health and disease are not apolitical. They can have profound social, political, and cultural consequences for a state. Diseases are not simply pathological in nature; they also reveal historical truths about the social body (Fassin 2003, 35). This includes the causes of disease. "Social factors including gender, ethnicity ('race'), and socioeconomic status may each play a role in rendering groups and individuals vulnerable to extreme human suffering ... *simultaneous* consideration of various social 'axes' is imperative" (Farmer 2005, 42–43). The marginalization of particular groups makes them more vulnerable to disease outbreaks in the first place.

The subsequent responses to these outbreaks are also very telling. They reflect how a state interprets the disease and its origins and how a state perceives those affected by the disease. Van der Vliet writes: "Epidemics are not merely medical phenomena. They have their roots in social conditions, and major epidemics can in turn profoundly affect how societies evolve" (1996, 11). Barnett and Whiteside concur, "Histories of infectious disease reflect the ways in which channels and paths of infection have been created as a part of the material and cultural lives of societies" (Barnett and Whiteside 2002, 65–66). We find a situation in which certain groups are more predisposed to infection, which in turn makes them less likely to receive adequate medical attention, which further marginalizes the group. A group's status within the political arena not affects its chances of getting ill, but also its chances of getting better.

States do not respond to all diseases in the same way, and their responses are often quite telling. As Altman notes, "How we conceptualize the epidemic will determine what sort of responses we apply" (1999, 560). Our conceptualizations of disease imply judgments about human rights, social cohesion, mobility, wealth, and, in the case of a disease like AIDS, patterns of sexual behavior. These judgments have profound implications for the manner in which states mobilize to combat a disease (Altman 1999, 566–568). Even the words used to describe a disease can shed a great deal of light on perceptions. The way we describe a disease privileges some aspects of society, while simultaneously obscuring others. "How AIDS has been theorized has had profound implications, not only for how we understand the disease, but for our responses to it" (Lee and Zwi 1996, 362).

This chapter places the South African government's response to the AIDS epidemic within the broader context of the country's history. In particular, I highlight how previous governments repeatedly used public health measures to justify racist, discriminatory, and segregationist policies. For many, this created an inextricable link between public health and control, which inspires a mistrust of groups claiming to solve public health issues. I begin by examining state public health responses in history, and in South African history in particular. I then delve into detailed investigations of inoculation campaigns and the controversies surrounding them. The next two sections look at how officials justified early moves toward apartheid on public health grounds and then how the apartheid government put public health programs into practice. Finally, I consider early governmental responses to AIDS in South Africa and the racial divide in government programs.

State Public Health Responses in an Historical Context

Disease outbreaks have long served as a catalyst for major political changes. Thucydides describes a plague that ravaged Athens during the Peloponnesian War. Crowded within the city walls to protect against a Spartan offensive, this new disease ravaged the population. Not only did it weaken Athens, but the unrelenting rate of death shattered morale, undermined public order, and weakened community ties (Thucydides 1982). Moore singles out bubonic plague for facilitating the end of feudalism (1966, 5). McNeill (1976) demonstrates how disease outbreaks played crucial roles in changing Asian and European political relations, establishing the Westphalian system of states, and colonizing new lands in the Americas and Africa. These outbreaks profoundly altered not just the trajectory of state development, but also the way in which peoples saw themselves. More recent work by Diamond (1999) has further reinforced the idea that disease can play key roles in understanding the historical evolution of the international system.

The colonization of the Americas depended upon infectious disease, albeit unwittingly. The spread of infectious diseases, especially smallpox, from Europe to the so-called "Neo-European" colonies wiped out indigenous populations and facilitated colonization just as much, if not more, than armies (Crosby 1986). The Incan Empire was one that fell to smallpox. The disease traveled to South America with Francisco Pizarro and his army in the 1520s and 1530s. Finding a virgin population lacking immunity, smallpox quickly spread among the Incas. The Incas' well-developed infrastructure greatly facilitated this process, allowing the disease to reach throughout the empire in a relatively short time (Mann 2005, 87–88).[1] In addition to its direct impact on the Incan Empire (killing large numbers of people), smallpox also precipitated a political crisis. The entire Incan royal court died of smallpox, introducing a political vacuum into the society while it was under attack from Pizarro's men. With no clear lines of succession, a civil war erupted among the Incan elite (Mann 2005, 88). When Pizarro finally made his final assault on the Incan capital, the army had been decimated by disease and divided by civil war, and Pizarro easily took control.

---

  1   Smallpox and other diseases often traveled ahead of colonizing forces, even to areas where Europeans had not yet stepped foot. The disease would move along major transportation routes, sickening populations years before European conquerors arrived. Mann writes of one Caribbean island, "When Europeans actually arrived, the battled, fragmented cultures could not unite to resist the incursion" (Mann 2005, 90–91). Europeans could then take advantage of the combination of disease and factionalization to take the land.

Disease also proved important for understanding the dynamic between Native Americans and European settlers. During battles in modern-day New England in 1616, the Native Americans captured a number of British settlers. A number of the settlers carried viral hepatitis, a disease to which they had been repeatedly exposed throughout their lives but one completely foreign to the Native Americans. Over the course of three years, viral hepatitis spread rapidly among Native Americans. Reports suggest that up to 90 percent of some towns succumbed to the disease (Mann 2005, 55). Interestingly, both the British settlers and Native Americans interpreted viral hepatitis' spread in religious terms. William Bradford, the Governor of the Plymouth Colony, attributed the disease to the "good hand of God" who "favored our beginnings" by "sweeping away great multitudes of the natives … that he might make room for us" (Mann 2005, 55–56). In other words, God sent the disease to prove that he wanted the British to take over North America. The settlers did not intentionally spread the disease, nor would they have understood the mechanisms of disease transmission, but they saw the disease's spread as a sign of God's favor. On the other side, Massasoit, the leader of the Wampanoag tribe, saw the devastation wreaked by viral hepatitis on his people and concluded that "their deities had allied against them" (Mann 2005, 56).

Disease outbreaks can also have profound consequences for how knowledge is understood and valued. During the outbreaks of bubonic plague in the 14th Century, physician-clerics led the charge to battle the disease. They derived their medical knowledge from the Bible, and believed that the plague was spread through vapors. As a result, they recommended treatments like burying the dead very deeply and ventilating crowded rooms (Tesh 1988, 27). It quickly became apparent that these methods failed to halt the disease's spread. The physician-clerics proved themselves unable to control the spread of a disease that was wiping out vast swaths of the European population. This large-scale failure called the physician-clerics' knowledge into question. People began to doubt the appropriateness of medical knowledge rooted solely in Christian doctrines. The failure of the physician-clerics encouraged the development of secular medicine. It also spurred the development and implementation of public health measures (Van der Vliet 1996, 15). The failure of one group of experts to combat the disease encouraged the development of a *new* group of experts who interpreted the disease in a different manner and who privileged different types of knowledge.

Glenn illustrates this reality using an example from early American history – inoculation against smallpox. In the early 1720s, a smallpox epidemic raged throughout the Northeast. In 1721 in Boston alone, smallpox killed 77 of every 1000 residents (Glenn 2004, 279). To combat the disease's spread, Lady Mary Wortley Montagu suggested that Bostonians begin an inoculation program. Montagu saw inoculation's successes firsthand while her husband served as British ambassador to the Persian Empire in the late 1710s (Glenn 2004, 280). Boston's medical establishment rejected this idea out of hand, claiming that it was scientifically unproven, dangerous, and even heretical.

In fact, a scientific paper explaining the benefits and processes associated with inoculation in Turkey had been published in the *Philosophical Transactions of the Royal Society*, a leading learned journal. It attracted little attention and held little credibility because its author, Emanual Timonius, was "a Turk – who would have been considered a heathen in Eighteenth Century Christendom (and worse, a non-

White one at that!)" (Glenn 2004, 280). The ethnic and racial status of the paper's author led to a rejection of its insights, even though those insights could have saved thousands of lives.

Interestingly, inoculation only started to receive acceptance in the American colonies once ministers took up Lady Montagu's campaign. They recast inoculation as a citizen's Christian obligation. Opponents of inoculation claimed that smallpox was a punishment from God for humanity's sins. Proponents conceded that God may be punishing humanity with smallpox. They added, though, that God was *also* showing humanity how to save itself through inoculation. By this argument, it would be an even greater sin to rebuff God's offer of compassion (Glenn 2004, 283). As this latter argument gained favor, the medical establishment and the citizenry at large came to accept, if not embrace, the usefulness of inoculation. It was only by casting inoculation within the cultural and religious context of the time that it gained acceptance. Reconceptualizing the disease fundamentally changed how officials responded to it.

Infectious Disease, Public Health, and Colonialism

The colonial mind invariably linked Africa and disease. During the 1800s, many described Africa as the "White man's grave" because of the high mortality rates among settlers and explorers. Whites died from a host of new diseases to which the indigenous populations had long been exposed and developed immunities, while Europeans brought with them new diseases and pathogens to which African immune systems were unaccustomed (Lund 2003, 90). A lack of biomedical immunity was not the only reason that European diseases proved so lethal to Africans. Colonialism largely served to destroy the cultural patterns and modes of production that allowed pre-colonial African societies to adapt to changing health circumstances and associated diseases (Doyal 1981, 104). By imposing new, alien belief systems on a society without considering that society's social and historical context, colonial health programs led to unsatisfactory outcomes. The result was a high degree of lethality for diseases that Europeans largely considered manageable. While the spread of these diseases was largely unintentional, it did serve to reinforce the political aims of European states by weakening resistance.

South Africa was a settler colony, and this greatly impacted its political, social, and health programs. Most European colonies in Africa had small White populations, but settler colonies, like Kenya, Rhodesia (now Zimbabwe), and South Africa, received significant White emigration. These colonists saw Africa as their permanent home. They wanted to develop the area politically and economically. Because settler colonies had a critical mass of Whites, they tended to have strong social, political, and cultural ties to Europe and North America (Barnett and Whiteside 2002, 147). European intellectual fashions were in vogue in many of these settler colonies. This helped frame how White settlers saw their appropriate roles in relation to the indigenous populations. "The settlers shared a vision of 'civilization' which distanced them from the rest of the population and by which they legitimized their dominance" (Barnett and Whiteside 2002, 147).

Whites wanted to develop the colonies in which they lived, but they did not see themselves as "Africans." Rather, they saw their mission as one of bringing the intellectual and political currents of Europe and North America to Africa to make it a civilized place. Given the close cultural and intellectual ties between Europe and Whites in South Africa, the emergence of eugenics and Social Darwinism in the former soon impacted the political and social realities of the latter. "Positive" eugenicists used the ideas to scientifically derive the means for bettering the African population, while "negative" eugenicists employed these doctrines to justify discriminatory measures that prevented the degradation of the White population (Dubow 1998, 71–72). Both positive and negative eugenicists used their theories to reinforce White dominance over Africans and reassert their privileged position. They also sought to use their superior status to help civilize and elevate the African population.

The "civilizing" mission of colonialism became invariably intertwined with a "healing" mission. Missionaries played a prominent role in the transmission of European norms to Africa and in encouraging Europeans to settle in Africa, and often combined their medical work with attempts to convert Africans to Christianity (Doyal 1981, 251). John Ross, the son of a Scottish missionary in South Africa, wrote a pamphlet in 1887 that advised, "People must be taught that attention to public health is a moral duty, that cleanliness, avoidance of excess, and health preservation go hand in hand with mental and moral training, and that morality consists as much in a hearty submissions to the precepts of health as to the observations of creed" (cited in Lund 2003, 91).

The following sections detail how South African government officials used public health in the colonial, post-colonial, and apartheid eras. In each period, Whites employed public health measures to control and reinforce dominance over Blacks. This, in turn, caused Blacks to resent the imposition of these measures and doubt their motivations. Table 4.1 provides a brief summary of some of the relevant disease outbreaks during the early period, as well as the government's response to those outbreaks.

Table 4.1   Important South African Disease Epidemics and Responses, 1895–1940

1895	Contagious Diseases Law No. 12 (Transvaal) – required all Blacks to report to District Surgeon for syphilis testing
1896–7	Rinderpest – decimated cattle herds; government inoculation campaigns largely failed and led to suspicion among Black herdsmen
1900	Bubonic plague reaches South Africa – government uses Public Health Act of 1883 to justify the creation of "Native locations" to separate Blacks and Whites
1909	Pass Act – required all Blacks to obtain certification that they were free of syphilis to receive a work permit
1918–9	Influenza – rumors spread among Blacks that flu inoculation campaign was a plot to wipe out Blacks
1920s–1930s	Deverminization campaigns in Durban – subjected Blacks to chemical dips

Inoculation Campaigns: Rinderpest and Influenza

Given the colonial South African government's general apathy toward their public health, Blacks often greeted these programs with suspicion and mistrust. The rinderpest epizootic in South Africa in the 1890s provides a clear illustration. Rinderpest is an acute viral disease that primarily affects the respiratory and gastrointestinal systems in cattle. Outbreaks of the disease, while rare, are devastating because nearly all animals infected with the disease die of severe diarrhea within a week of infection (Vogel and Heyne 1996, 164). Not indigenous to Africa, rinderpest arrived on the continent in 1889 when the Italian government inadvertently imported a number of infected herds to help sustain troops occupying present-day Somalia (Reader 1999, 589). The disease quickly spread throughout the continent, reaching South Africa a few years later.

Rinderpest's spread caused much consternation. Rumors suggested that the colonial government planned to use it as a pretext to take over Black-owned land for gold prospecting, and groups organized to repel any invasion (Van Onselen 1972, 475–478). Further, cattle were a symbol of wealth among both Whites and Blacks. "Cattle had long been accepted as a form of wealth that endowed their owners with power and authority. Almost instantaneously, rinderpest swept away the wealth of tropical Africa" (Reader 1999, 590). The colonial government erected a 1600-kilometer barbed-wire fence from Bechuanaland (now Botswana) to the Cape-Natal coast, replete with police patrols and disinfection stations, in a vain attempt to prevent the pest's entry into South Africa (Reader 1999, 589–590).

Blame for rinderpest in South Africa quickly fell to Black herdsmen. White farmers alleged that Black farmers failed to properly restrain their infected cattle that then infected White-owned cattle. One colonial official from Transvaal implied that Blacks were actively allowing rinderpest to spread, claiming, "In the south they [Blacks] have had all their cattle destroyed by the pest and now they wish to do likewise by the cattle of the Boer and so involve the whole country in ruin" (cited in Van Onselen 1972, 479–480). In response to the outbreak, colonial officials in late 1896 began a program to quarantine "promiscuous" Black-owned herds to prevent them from spreading the disease to White-owned herds. As a part of the quarantine program, Black-owned herds were doused with harsh chemical disinfectants in an attempt to eliminate rinderpest. These same chemicals were then applied to the Black cattle herders themselves (Carton 2003, 204). Though some of these measures also applied to White cattle owners, they were enforced less assiduously, and only Black cattle owners were required to undergo complete disinfectant dips themselves. This process entailed soaking the whole body in disinfectant, treating all clothing, and destroying any milk, meat, or cattle products (Van Onselen 1972, 480). The disinfectant had almost no effect on rinderpest, but it did lead to the destruction of large numbers of Black-owned cattle.

The government also sought to prevent the spread of rinderpest by severely restricting the free movement of Blacks. People could easily transport rinderpest on their clothing if they had recently visited an infected area or had leather goods from infected cattle. According to the government's logic, since people could transport rinderpest, and Black-owned cattle were the main source of rinderpest, it made sense to limit the movement of all Blacks. After establishing a fence, the government of the Cape Colony barred nearly all Blacks from entering the colony under any circumstances; Whites could enter after disinfection (Vogel and Heyne 1996, 165–166). For many Blacks, this was evidence that the disease was actually a plot by Whites targeted against them. The initial policy for containing rinderpest, killing all cattle in an affected area, wiped out the wealth and livelihood for many Black families. The timing of the epidemic also fanned many conspiracy theories. Rural residents, who were overwhelmingly Black, in the 1890s had already suffered through droughts and a (literal) plague of locusts (Vogel and Heyne 1996, 165). Both had taken their toll on rural families, and the rinderpest epidemic added insult to injury. Colonial officials throughout southern Africa reported on revolts "against the White man's rule, which in the natives' view had caused the disease" (Vogel and Heyne 1996, 167).

Colonial officials tried a new approach to treating rinderpest in 1897. Robert Koch, one of the fathers of serology and the recipient of the 1905 Nobel Prize for Medicine for his work on disease control and the development of vaccines, came to South Africa to address the rinderpest problem. He began a program that inoculated cattle against rinderpest with a serum taken from the gall bladders of infected cattle. Koch and his supporters hoped that this would immunize the cattle against rinderpest and quickly bring the epidemic under control.

Unfortunately, the serum was in short supply and only had a limited effectiveness. It often took 6 to 10 days for the serum to take hold, and immunity periods were as short as 20 days (Vogel and Heyne 1996, 169). More problematically, injecting healthy cattle with the serum temporarily induced symptoms of the disease. In essence, colonial officials told Black herd owners that they would protect their cattle against a dreaded disease, but herd owners witnessed their cattle apparently coming down with that very disease. This encouraged suspicion and resistance among Black cattle owners. Carton writes, "If the Europeans came to cure, they [Black herd owners] asked, why was he 'bringing the disease nearer'? This question was often posed by Black people in southern Africa, who suspected rinderpest was the 'White man's' weapon of death in 'the imperial apocalypse' wasting their land" (Carton 2003, 204). One traditional leader queried a colonial official, "They tell me you are a doctor, and that you are a great doctor, but you do nothing but kill?" (cited in Van Onselen 1972, 482).

This is not the only example of colonial inoculation programs fomenting mistrust. In the fall of 1918, a massive influenza epidemic spread worldwide. Between 20 and 40 million people worldwide died before the epidemic ended in 1919. South Africa was not spared from the devastating consequences of this outbreak. Called *umbathalala*, the Xhosa word for 'disaster,' influenza spread rampantly throughout the rural Eastern Cape region between September and October 1918.

Both Whites and Blacks blamed each other for causing and spreading the epidemic. Some segments of the White population blamed it on migrant Black laborers, while some Blacks thought influenza originated among "malevolent Whites wanting to exterminate Africans" (Phillips 2004, 33). Calls for restrictions of movement to prevent influenza's spread were nearly all couched in racial terms. A number of towns introduced measures that required Blacks to obtain a clean bill of health before being allowed within city limits, and others searched passenger trains for "sick natives." One newspaper editorial wrote at the time, "Statistics prove that Natives are more susceptible to the disease than Europeans, and this being so, it is the duty of the authorities to take special precautions in regard to them" (cited in Phillips 1990, 80).

Some Blacks blamed the epidemic on Whites. Rumors flew that the influenza epidemic was a plot by the government to kill Blacks. A Black correspondent for *Territorial News*, a Transkei newspaper, wrote that the flu epidemic "threatens the existence of the entire race" (cited in Phillips 1990, 82). A missionary in the Transvaal reported hearing an interesting twist on this logic. Instead of being a plot to wipe out Blacks, the missionary reported that some Blacks claimed that the epidemic was actually targeted against Whites as a divine punishment for their mistreatment of Blacks (Phillips 1990, 148). Regardless, the influenza outbreak quickly became imbued with racial connotations and accusations of blame. These connotations influenced responses to both the disease and potential treatments.

Soon after the outbreak began, colonial officials sent flu inoculations to rural areas, hoping to stop the spread of the disease before it hit urban centers. The response among Blacks to the inoculation program was largely negative, as vaccination temporarily induced symptoms of the flu. Blacks claimed that "the 'long needle' of the 'White man' came to inject more harm" (Carton 2003, 204). Others dissuaded their neighbors from receiving the inoculations by claiming that it was administered by sticking a long needle into the jugular vein or blaming the spread of influenza on smallpox vaccinations given a few years prior (Phillips 1990, 86–87). Native Commissioners reported that Blacks ran from any official that appeared to be administering medicine (Ranger 1988, 178). One newspaper report from 1918 noted that Xhosa-speaking messengers warned people of "a device of the Europeans to finish off the Native races of South Africa, and as it had not been quite successful, they were sending out men with poison to complete the work of extermination" (cited in Carton 2003, 204). In other parts of the country, the "drugs" used to treat influenza were little more than colored water and lacked any curative effects (Tomkins 1994). This merely served to reinforce fears of a government-sponsored plot against Blacks, because the supposed treatment did nothing to treat the disease.

By this time, germ theory had largely gained acceptance by the medical community. Rejecting previous ideas, doctors had largely come to believe Louis Pasteur's argument that microorganisms cause most disease.[2] This finding revolutionized medical science. It also contributed to the development of segregationist ideologies in South Africa, as it showed the need to separate the races. Bear in mind that much of the South African medical establishment at this time argued that Africans were inherently more prone to contract and spread diseases, and the medical establishment wanted to prevent Blacks from spreading disease to the White population. With germ theory, South African medical authorities saw that social intercourse could in fact

---

2   Pasteur was not the first to propose this idea; references to germ theory appear as early as the First Century BCE. Pasteur's 1878 book, *Germ Theory and Its Applications for Medicine and Surgery*, was one of the first scientific books that offered definitive proof of germ theory's validity.

be dangerous to the health of Whites. It was no longer a simple matter of Africans being more prone to disease; now, they could spread those diseases to the White population simply by being in close proximity to Whites. Black bodies in and of themselves constituted a direct threat to the health of Whites (Lund 2003, 96). With such a framework in place, it is small leap to argue that Blacks and Whites must be physically separated from one another.

Bubonic Plague, Tuberculosis, and Apartheid

Public health measures played a crucial role in implementing segregationist policies in South Africa. Fear of cholera and plague rationalized calls by Whites to segregate Blacks, Coloureds, and Indians. Officials believed that Blacks were reservoirs of disease and therefore a potential danger to the White population (Vaughan 1991, 39). Medical officials in South Africa during this time often saw infections and the spread of disease as a social metaphor that interacted powerfully with current racial attitudes in both Great Britain and South Africa (Swanson 1977, 387). "The metaphoric equation of 'coolies' with urban poverty and disease became a steady refrain of White opinion and a preoccupation of police and health officers in the South African colonies long before 1900" (Swanson 1977, 390). Public health and prevention of epidemics then largely justified movements toward racial segregation, as reflected in the provisions of the Public Health Act of 1883 (Fassin and Schneider 2003). The Act mandated vaccinations and public notification of infectious diseases, and gave local authorities extensive emergency powers, including the ability to establish quarantines and sanitary corridors.

The provisions of the Public Health Act of 1883 soon entered into effect. In the midst of a worldwide pandemic, plague reached South Africa in 1900. The plague pandemic had already contributed to the rise of nationalism in India, the Great Fire in Honolulu, the rise of anti-Asian prejudice in the United States and Australia, and the development of separate 'African' quarters in cities like Dakar and Salisbury (now Harare) by the time it arrived on South Africa's shores (Echenberg 2002, 434; Swanson 1977, 388–389). The discovery of bubonic plague in Cape Town in 1900 led to the forcible movement of the city's African population into "Native locations." Colonial officials argued that plague came to South Africa because of the Africans and their unsanitary conditions, even though there were fewer cases of plague among Africans than among Whites or Coloureds (Swanson 1977, 392–393). Government officials relied on the provisions of the Public Health Act of 1883 to justify the creation of these "Native locations." *This was the first time that separate locations for Blacks, a hallmark of apartheid, were created in South Africa, and it was justified on the grounds of public health.* Echenberg notes:

> Throughout the epidemic, fingers were pointed at the 'raw natives' and the 'dirty Jews'; little mention was made of the South African War, which turned Cape Town into an overcrowded military and refugee center (Echenberg 2002, 447).

Of course, by placing Africans into crowded "Native locations" which lacked appropriate sanitary or health care infrastructures, colonial officials actually created the conditions for plague to spread among Africans – which only served to reinforce their ideas about the need to segregate the city's African population away from Whites.

The outbreak of plague did not create the calls for segregation itself. Instead, it concentrated the anxieties and fears that already existed among the White population, and advanced the segregationist agendas (Swanson 1977, 392). During this time, Whites, especially in the urban areas, became increasingly vocal about the dangers posed to them by the poor health of the poor Black workers (Packard 1989, 15). These White urban voices were not necessarily promoting new ideas; rather, they had found a 'hook' for segregationist ideas that already existed among South Africa's Whites. Through the logic of the times, though, segregation was both a conservative and a liberal idea. Conservatives argued for segregating Blacks because they spread disease to Whites. Progressive reformers argued for the creation of "Native locations" because they believed the spread of disease among Blacks reflected their lack of experience and ability to cope with Western industrialized life (Lund 2003, 92; Packard 1989, 194–195). Both sides could advance segregationist agendas under the guise of protecting the Black population through public health measures.

Other infectious diseases also led to the passage of discriminatory laws that specifically targeted Blacks. Syphilis was of particular concern to many colonial officials, as they saw it as a sign of the moral laxity among Blacks (Jochelson 2001)[3] In 1895, the provincial legislature in Transvaal passed the Contagious Diseases Law No. 12. This act required that any and all cases of syphilis among Blacks be reported to the district surgeon. It also included a provision whereby the government could require any Black person to appear for testing, though no such provision existed for Whites (Jochelson 2001, 46–48). Fourteen years later, the government strengthened the law via the Urban Areas Native Pass Act No. 18 of 1909. This act required that any Black man wanting a pass to work either in the mines or in an urban area must prove that he is free of syphilis (Jochelson 2001, 48–51). Again, Whites were exempt from this law.

Tuberculosis also raged in South Africa during the early 1900s, and it reinforced calls for racial segregation. Vaughan writes:

> The shape which the medical constructions on the disease [tuberculosis] took in South Africa can only be interpreted by reference to the fact of sickness and debility amongst Black miners, and the problem that this posed for employers of Black labor (1991, 7).

Around 1900, tuberculosis began to spread among urban Blacks, who suffered from higher mortality rates than Whites. No public officials linked the crowded urban living conditions of most Blacks to the high rate of tuberculosis fatalities. Instead, medical officials relied on theories emphasizing inherent racial differences. Africans,

---

3   The nature of syphilis is quite controversial in South African history. Syphilis is a sexually transmitted disease. Yaws, a related disease that often displays symptoms very similar to syphilis, is a skin infection and not sexually transmitted. During the colonial era, though, many assumed that the diseases were the same. Evidence suggests that most of the supposed cases of syphilis in South Africa was actually cases of yaws. Jochelson (2001) provides an excellent, in-depth examination of both the distinction between syphilis and yaws, as well as their impact on South Africa.

they argued, were naturally susceptible to tuberculosis. Framing the medical debate in this racialized context framed subsequent research on diseases among Blacks (Packard and Epstein 1991, 771). One line of research examined the "dressed native" hypothesis. This theory argued that Blacks were unaccustomed to wearing Western-style clothes when they moved to urban areas, and therefore did not know to change their clothes frequently or to observe proper hygiene standards (Packard 1989, 48–51). This explanation blamed Blacks themselves for the spread of tuberculosis. It did not explore the underlying conditions that put Blacks in the conditions that spread disease in the first place (Packard and Epstein 1991, 771–772). Urban Blacks largely lived in squalid, cramped conditions and rarely had access to proper sanitation or potable water. These conditions fostered tuberculosis' spread. As a result, "Africans were chastised for living in overcrowded slums and eating non-nutritious foods as if they chose to do so out of perversity rather than economic necessity" (Packard 1989, 51), and increased calls for segregated Black locations went up among the White population. The government said this would protect the health of both Whites and Blacks, but it rarely provided the "Native locations" with the necessary health care resources (Packard 1989, 52–56). Instead of adopting proactive public health measures, the colonial government instituted programs that stigmatized the Black population. In one case, public health officials conducted "deverminization" campaigns in Durban in the 1920s and 1930s. During these campaigns, over 50,000 Black men were subjected to "dipping" in effort to rid them of diseases for which they were presumed to carry (Marks and Andersson 1984, 34).

The African population understood how White colonial officials used public health measures to justify segregation. Swanson notes, "Blacks were especially resentful at the discriminatory application of the plague quarantine regulations ... The horses of Blacks had been quarantined; those of neighboring Whites had not. The possessions of Blacks had been burned; the goods, the stores, and the warehouses where they worked and contracted the plague had not been touched because those belonged to Whites" (Swanson 1977, 402). As with the rinderpest epizootic, White colonial officials told the Black populations that measures were being taken to protect their health, but Africans saw that these measures actually made them worse off. Africans saw that these public health measures served to extend the reach of the colonial state over them (Lund 2003, 92). These actions inspired some of the earliest resistance campaigns to the colonial government. Durban's "deverminization" campaigns, for example, inspired strikes by the Industrial and Commercial Workers' Union, leading to a temporary cessation of the practice. Even after the strike, these campaigns "remained a constant source of serious discontent amongst Coloureds and the African elite, and a focus for political action" (Marks and Andersson 1984, 34).

Public Health during the Apartheid Era

Marks and Andersson describe the public health system for Blacks in South Africa during apartheid as "hidden violence" (Marks and Andersson 1987, 177). The apartheid era government's failure to implement an effective public health system not only turned easily treated diseases into epidemics, but it also undermined local family structures and humiliated the Black majority into seeing themselves as second class citizens.

Assessing the state of public health of Blacks under apartheid is difficult because the government kept few detailed records in these areas. Throughout the apartheid era, the government did not require any official recording of births or deaths among Blacks (Seedat 1984, 9). This fact alone reveals the lack of attention the apartheid government paid to the public health concerns of Blacks.

The few available statistics from this era amply demonstrated the lack of attention from the apartheid government to Black health needs. By the mid-1970s, life expectancy rates for White South Africans were comparable to those in the United States and Western Europe. By contrast, government estimates of Black life expectancy rates ran approximately 15 years lower than those for Whites – and evidence suggests that even these dismal figures overestimated actual life expectancy among Blacks (Thompson 1995, 203). Whites largely fell victim to chronic diseases like cancer and heart disease. Blacks predominantly died of infectious diseases like pneumonia and tuberculosis. In fact, tuberculosis rates among Blacks rose at the same time they were falling among Whites (Thompson 1995, 204). Whites had a better chance of being *diagnosed* with tuberculosis, but Blacks were 27 times more likely to actually fall ill with tuberculosis (Andersson and Marks 1988, 673). Even this statistic may underestimate the true rates of tuberculosis. Official government estimates at this time specifically excluded the supposedly independent Bantustans, whose health care resources were incredibly meager. Most strikingly, rates of cholera infection were 100 times higher for Blacks than Whites. As inadequate sanitation and lack of clean drinking water transmit cholera, this disparity is particularly illustrative of the disparities in health care during apartheid.

Infant mortality rates reinforce the picture of inequality. The official Black infant mortality rate estimate in the 1970s was 100 to 110 per 1000 live births – six to seven times higher than the White rate, and the third worst rate in all of Africa (behind only Burkina Faso and Sierra Leone) (Thompson 1995, 202–203). The top causes of death for non-White children were gastroenteritis, chest infection, and diarrhea (Andersson and Marks 1988, 671). Accidents, particularly drownings, were the top causes of death for White children (Brown 1987, 259).

At the most basic level, state resources for public health varied widely depending on which racial group the services served. Writing in 1984, an exiled South African doctor wrote, "Hospital attendance for Blacks is a test of endurance requiring endless patience and fortitude – and this when the person could be very ill" (Seedat 1984, 63). Hospitals and health clinics for non-White groups were often located far from population centers, and they were severely overcrowded with few resources. Health care facilities for Blacks often lacked reliable electricity, telephone service or potable water (Seedat 1984, 70). The distribution of government health care resources reinforced the lack of equality. Government spending on hospital stays was 2 to 5 times higher for Whites than Blacks and Coloureds during apartheid (Andersson and Marks 1988, 678). The entire annual health budget of KwaZulu during the 1970s and 1980s was less than the annual expenditure for the main (White) hospital in Johannesburg (Brown 1987, 259). A 1980 survey showed that spending on hospitals in the Cape Province, most of which went to large White hospitals, was

12 times higher than the total national expenditure to control tuberculosis, a disease that primarily afflicted Blacks (World Health Organization 1983, 219). Based on these differences, the World Health Organization declared that, by its definition of health, it could not consider South Africa's Black population "healthy" (World Health Organization 1983, 28).

The government used its health care resources as a means of control over various groups. It established a myriad of health care-related bureaucracies, using them to reward or punish Black communities for their actions (Andersson and Marks 1988, 670). They also found ways to exacerbate tensions among different groups through the public health system. After discovering the wide disparity in cholera rates between Whites and Blacks in one area of KwaZulu, the government required landlords to either install proper sanitation or remove the renters from the property. Because of the incredible cost of installing proper sanitation, few landlords could afford to do it, and would therefore be required to remove the renters from the land. In this area, most landlords were Asian and most renters, Black. The government essentially attempted to deflect Black anger from itself to the region's Asian population (Andersson and Marks 1988, 677). It put Asians in the unenviable position of either bankrupting themselves to install sewer lines or kicking Blacks off their land. If the former occurred, it could cripple the economy. If the latter occurred, the government could claim to Blacks that the root of their problem truly rested with the Asians. South Africa's apartheid government imperiled the health of Blacks in an attempt to maintain their dominant societal position.

When the government did spend significant resources on health care for Blacks, it often came with ideological baggage. Starting in the mid-1970s, the government undertook a major national family planning campaign throughout the country, encouraging contraception and smaller families. The campaign itself was curious. White fertility rates had been in decline for a number of years, and the government heavily subsidized White emigration from abroad. This campaign almost exclusively targeted Blacks. The government considered the higher fertility rate for Blacks a major problem, fearing that the Black population would overwhelm Whites. This would make it impossible for them to maintain their dominant position within South African society. While Blacks always outnumbered Whites, the apartheid government feared that a growing Black population would place too great a strain on the system. A larger Black population could also lead to increased calls for majority rule.

With this program came a substantial increase in spending. In just 10 years, the government's outlays for family planning increased 13 times over (Brown 1987, 264), most of which was targeted toward Blacks. The government largely sold this program to the public in terms of poverty and underdevelopment; limiting the number of children would allow resources to be used more efficiently and reduce the surplus labor supply (Brown 1987, 261). For many Whites, the real objective behind the program was to provide a cover for the inequities of apartheid, quash rising Black militancy for equality, and fend off the feared *swart gevaar* (Afrikaans for "Black peril") (Brown 1987, 261–263). Politicians realized that they could not be so overt with their desires if they wanted the Black population to respond to the program. "[W]hen the government's birth control program got under way, White leaders became increasingly circumspect in stating publicly the linkage between the size of the population and a Black revolt. They are fully aware that the program would be killed by Black suspicion of any political motivation" (Brown 1987, 264). Many Blacks did apparently believe just that, especially when some employers threatened to fire women who did not receive injections of Depo-Provera and politicians spoke of the possibility of forced sterilization (Brown 1987, 268–269).

The apartheid-era government generally responded to outbreaks of infectious diseases in one of two ways. These reactions drew upon the public health legacy of the colonial era, which served to reinforce the negative perceptions of public health interventions among the African population. The first was "authoritarian intervention in the case of disease which it was feared 'would know no color bar'" (Marks and Andersson 1984, 33). When the government feared that a disease could spread to Whites, it took draconian actions like quarantining Black populations and the forced removal of Blacks from urban areas. Because Whites and Blacks initially lived in close proximity to each other in urban areas in the late 1800s and early 1900s, many advocated for urban residential segregation. Doctors were among the foremost advocates of such a policy. "The 'metaphoric equation' of Blacks with infectious disease and the perception of urban social relations in terms of 'the imagery of infection and epidemic disease' provided a compelling rationale for major forms of social control, and the removal of segregated African housing to the edges of the town" (Marks and Andersson 1984, 33).

The second theme was "the non-recognition of the full impact of those diseases which would remain confined to Blacks in rural areas" (Marks and Andersson 1984, 33). The government showed little concern for diseases that remained in the hinterlands, away from the urban areas in which the vast majority of the White population lived. Outbreaks of disease among Blacks rarely received much attention from colonial officials until the disease threatened Whites. The large numbers of Black men who moved to work in urban factories or in the diamond and gold mines received limited health services, and most of their ailments went untreated (Barnett and Whiteside 2002, 151). Government neglect of health services for Blacks caused a critical shortage of basic services and hospital beds (De Beer 1984; American Association for the Advancement of Science 1990). Polio, cholera, and typhoid epidemics swept through the South African Bantustans throughout the 1980s. The South African government instead focused on covering up epidemics to prevent "moments of hysteria when it was feared they would cross the lines into 'White' Durban, or even Johannesburg and Pretoria" (Marks and Andersson 1984, 32). Marks and Andersson, commenting on apartheid-era public health programs among Blacks, remark, "For Blacks, typhoid is now an everyday occurrence, but it is only when it encroaches on the 'White preserve' that it causes a stir. In general, the state has been able to take its *laissez faire* attitude because the epidemics have remained amongst South Africa's 'surplus population' within the Bantustan borders" (Marks and Andersson 1984, 32).

Early Responses to AIDS in South Africa

With the advent of AIDS, the negative image of public health and outside health interventions became even more pronounced. "The fact that it [AIDS] is sexually transmitted and that HIV is believed to have its origins in Africa have, on the one hand, fueled racist stereotypes, discrimination, and Afro-pessimism, and, on the other, prompted anger, denial, and genocidal conspiracy theories" (Van der Vliet 2001, 153). AIDS was almost immediately imbued with particular judgments about those infected with the disease, just as earlier epidemics were. Many of these value judgments originated with the theories about the origins of AIDS. To this day, questions over the origins of AIDS remain controversial and hotly contested.

When AIDS first emerged, many people blamed Africa for the disease. They claimed that it moved from monkeys to humans through the eating of chimpanzees or elaborate tribal rituals involving monkey blood (Sabatier 1988, 88). These accusations immediately led to suspicion among African researchers about *any* hypothesis that placed AIDS' origins within the African continent. Sabatier notes that these early theories often included racist, ill-informed speculations and offensive assumptions about African sexualities, and that little, if any, of this research was conducted by Africans or even in Africa (Sabatier 1988, 88–90). Many in Africa saw these accusations as symptomatic of continued Western racism (Chirimuuta and Chirimuuta 1989). African leaders claimed that Western states engaged in "imperialist scapegoating" by blaming Africa for AIDS (Packard and Epstein 1991, 773). They were also suspicious of Western interest in the disease, as many stories circulated in the press that AIDS was created in and deliberately spread by American labs (Fassin 2002, 64).

Linking AIDS to hostile American actions is a common theme in many developing countries. Treichler writes, "The notion that AIDS is an American invention is, like so-called conspiracy theories, a recurrent element of the international AIDS story. It is one not easily incorporated within a Western positivist frame – in part, perhaps, because it often reveals an unwelcome narrative about colonialism in a post-colonial world" (Treichler 1999, 103). *Sechaba*, an official publication of the African National Congress during the apartheid era, described a direct connection between biological weapons research programs in the United States and its allies and the spread of AIDS (Mzala 1988). This helped lay the foundation for suspicion and hostility about public health and outside intervention when it came to AIDS.

Apartheid did little to assuage fears and doubts about AIDS among Black South Africans. Early government efforts to prevent an AIDS epidemic focused on testing and repatriating migrant Malawian workers, not preventing the spread of disease among local populations (Larson 1990, 11). Anti-apartheid groups decried early government anti-AIDS programs as "typical racist propaganda" for focusing on stereotypical images of African sexuality (Van der Vliet 1994, 110). In one early campaign:

[T]he campaign was largely aimed at the heterosexual population, and it was both ill-conceived and racist. Different images were selected for White and Black audiences. That for Whites was a fairly clichéd representation of graffiti on a wall: 'Kevin loves,' the poster proclaimed, followed by many girls' names, the list of conquests crossed out and added to. Implicitly it linked AIDS to promiscuity and emphasized the benefits of a single partner relationship. The 'Black' poster showed mourners gathered round a graveside burying an 'AIDS victim,' with the caption 'AIDS kills' – linking AIDS to death. It was an extremely unpopular campaign. It dealt insensitively with the issue and took little heed of international experience, which taught that messages based on fear, judgment, doom, and gloom do not work (Crewe 1992, 61).

Such messages exploited existing racial stereotypes and undermined prevention efforts. They reinforced the notion that AIDS was qualitatively different for Whites and Blacks, and offered little useful information.[4]

Apartheid provided almost ideal social conditions for fostering the AIDS epidemic, with its migrant labor systems and disruption of traditional norms and cultural systems. Given that the disease's spread among the Black population, politicians quickly found an ideological basis for talking about the disease in strictly racial terms (Fassin 2002, 64). In a debate in Parliament in 1990, Dr. F.H. Pauw, a Conservative Party member, alleged that members of the ruling National Party was telling White South Africans that they need not worry about majority rule because "AIDS will be responsible for the large-scale elimination of the Black population, to such an extent that Blacks will in reality become a minority in South Africa within five years" (Republic of South Africa 1990, 9761). Dr. E.H. Venter, the Minister of National Health and Population Development, denied these accusations. She responded that it was actually the Conservative Party that was at fault. She quoted Conservative Party Member of Parliament Clive Derby-Lewis, who stated, "If AIDS stops Black population growth, it would be like Father Christmas" (Republic of South Africa 1990, 9797).[5] Crewe notes that the Conservative Party during the 1980s spread the view that AIDS could be spread through "coughing and sneezing, by water, milk, food and fruit; by personal contact and by biting insects" (Crewe 1992, 73). Right-wing newspapers in the day regularly published so-called evidence that HIV could be spread through casual contact to "low-risk groups," i.e. Whites (Van der Vliet 2001, 157). Apartheid's supporters used this rhetoric to argue against scrapping apartheid, *employing nearly identical rhetorical tools as used in the early 1900s to justify segregation along the lines of public health.*

In response to these historical experiences, Fassin and Schneider identify two common themes in the South African government's response to AIDS. The first is racialization. Discussions of AIDS or AIDS policies often take on racial overtones, with the government's critics labeled racist. For example, in the midst of one controversy over the provision of AZT in 1999, Dr. Nkosazana Dlamini-

---

4   The first AIDS cases in South Africa were among gay White men, a group hardly held in favor by the apartheid government. This may have had an impact on the government's initial programs. By the mid-1980s, though, government programs squarely targeted White and Black heterosexual populations, though in very different ways.

5   Derby-Lewis is currently serving a life sentence in prison for his role in the 1993 assassination of Chris Hani, leader of the South African Communist Party and head of the African National Congress' military wing. Derby-Lewis supplied Janusz Walus with the gun that Walus then used to kill Hani. He applied for amnesty from the Truth and Reconciliation Commission in 1997, but was denied. He has defended his actions in the Hani assassination on religious grounds, saying that it was his highest duty as a Christian (and member of the pro-apartheid Afrikaanse Protestante Kerk) to fight communism (*National Catholic Reporter* 1997).

Zuma, then the Minister of Health, lashed out at opposition parties and AIDS service organizations for being racist (Van der Vliet 2001, 168). On another occasion, she charged, "If they [opponents of the government's AIDS policies] had their way, we would all die of AIDS" (Power 2003, 59). Second, it claims that Western responses to AIDS are a conspiracy against Africans. AIDS, and its treatment, is a plot to wipe out the African population by this thinking (Fassin 2003, 55–56; Fassin and Schneider 2003). One joke claimed that AIDS stood for *A*frikaner (or *A*merican) *I*nvention to *D*eny *S*ex, and others said that condoms promoted impotence.

Such images would be patently absurd if they were not hints of reality associated with them. After the first multi-racial elections in South Africa in 1994, the government established the Truth and Reconciliation Commission (TRC) to uncover the horrors of the apartheid era and explain some of the atrocities that took place by all sides. During the commission's hearings, one man testified about his work for Roodeplat Research Laboratories (RRL). RRL was a front for the government's secret biological weapons program. One of RRL's projects focused on developing an infectious agent that would induce sterility among African women. High levels of sterility would lead to declining African birth rates, with the hopes that this would reduce the domestic resistance to apartheid. This man reported that RRL spent a great deal of time and money on utilizing HIV as this agent, though the effort ultimately failed (Fassin and Schneider 2003). This resonated with rumors that spread among Zulu-speaking communities in the 1980s and early 1990s. These rumors talked about a White "doctor of death" who unleashed a poison, widely assumed to be AIDS, on Blacks. Shockingly, many of these rumors specifically mentioned one man by name – Wouter Basson. Basson was the head of RRL and directed the program on inducing sterility (Carton 2003, 206–207).

In another TRC hearing, two former security officers claimed that they took HIV-positive *askaris*[6] and deployed them in two hotels in Hillbrow, a Johannesburg township. The security officers explicitly instructed the *askaris* to infect the hotels' sex workers with HIV. By infecting sex workers, the security officers hoped that the disease would spread more widely throughout the population. Men would then infect their wives and any future children. The hope was to slowly infect large swaths of the country's African population with HIV, again with the ultimate aim of weakening domestic opposition to apartheid (Whiteside and Sunter 2001, 64–65). Thus, accusations suggest that the apartheid-era government in South Africa may have attempted to deliberately spread AIDS among the Black population with the goal of wiping it out and enabling the continued functioning of apartheid.

Conclusion

South African history contains numerous examples of public health programs being used to further segregation, discrimination, and apartheid. Blacks were blamed for the spread of rinderpest, bubonic plague, influenza, and tuberculosis, among other

---

6   *Askaris* were former ANC operatives who went to work for the apartheid government's security forces.

disease. In response, the government established programs that segregated Blacks from Whites, placed severe restrictions on the mobility of Blacks, and subjected the Black population to degrading and ineffective "treatments." These actions relied upon stereotypical representations of African sexuality and hygiene. They made crude assumptions about the health behaviors of Blacks, while simultaneously claiming to "rescue" Blacks from their misery. Most Africans instead witnessed a government implementing programs that detrimentally impacted them.

Similar events occurred during the early days of South Africa's AIDS epidemic. Many discriminatory public health tropes from earlier epidemics re-emerged. Hypersexualized and promiscuous Blacks were blamed for spreading the new disease, and early government actions sought to isolate Blacks to "protect" the White population. At the same time, this history of racist public health interventions conditioned how Blacks responded to government claims. In many ways, AIDS concentrated the fears and anxieties among the Black population about public health programs. Many segments of the Black population blamed the apartheid government for perpetrating a plague to advance genocidal aims. This fear, in turn, generated suspicion and mistrust of anti-AIDS programs. The racist, naïve early anti-AIDS campaigns led some segments of the Black population to reject *all* anti-AIDS messages, or to at least greet them with suspicion.

Chapter 5

Identity, AIDS, and Public Health in South Africa

Disease epidemics do not just make us question what we know; they also force us to examine who we are. Epidemics can also lead a society to question its obligations to others. We question why members of certain groups seem particularly prone to contracting a certain illness. Is it because of where they live? Their behaviors? Their genetic backgrounds? Who they are? The social construction of target populations influences how we think about those groups and how we implement policies that impact them above and beyond simple calculations of political power and influence (Schneider and Ingram 1993). For example, in the United States, tuberculosis primarily afflicts the poor. What does this reality tell us about the structure of American society and how these groups are (or are not) incorporated into the greater community? Diseases are uniquely able to raise such questions.

AIDS raises many of these same concerns, as it has often had a negative impact on a state's identity and perception within the international community. When AIDS was first discovered, US government officials identified Haitians as one of the "Four Hs" – the groups most at risk for contracting the disease.[1] Haitians were unique to this risk grouping, as their only common bond was their national identity rather than any discernible behavior. Later, a number of physicians and activists with an understanding of Haitian culture came forward to challenge this claim. They noted that Haitian men were largely unwilling to acknowledge intravenous drug use or having sex with other men. They argued that Haitians *did* share the behavioral risk factors already noted for spreading the disease, but that a lack of cultural understanding prevented doctors from discovering this. The issue was not one of nationality, but rather behavior (Sabatier 1988, 44–47). Farmer (2003) calls attention to Haiti's political and economic plight over the past 20 years, showing that it is impossible to understand the country's AIDS epidemic without understanding this context. By the time this was understood, though, the damage was already done, and Haitian immigrants in the United States faced widespread discrimination, unemployment, and business difficulties.

Similar negative images plague the South African AIDS epidemic. These images directly contradict South Africa's attempts to promote a new post-apartheid identity inspired by the ideals of the African Renaissance. The South African government wants to use AIDS to mold the image of a positive, self-sufficient country with the scientific capabilities to propel it into the pantheon of the world's best scientific research. Members of the government have appropriated images of liberation and

---

1   The other three "Hs" were homosexuals, heroin users, and hemophiliacs.

resistance to justify their AIDS policies and President Mbeki's controversial responses to the disease. Critics of these policies are dismissed as racist (Mbali 2004, 104).

This chapter examines the idea of the African Renaissance, how it fits into the South African government's broader goals of remaking the country's identity within the international community, and why the government uses its AIDS policies to present a new identity to the rest of the world. The country's AIDS policies, according to policymakers, demonstrate the government's ability to foster African solutions for African problems and to question whether the received wisdom from outside experts resonates with the country's experiences and understandings. AIDS provides an opportunity for the government to assert itself, and Africa as a whole, as independent and self-reliant. Themes of liberation continually emerge, and these themes are often explicitly linked with the anti-apartheid struggle. The case of Virodene and the government's promotion of alternative therapies receive special attention, as they embody many of these goals. President Mbeki's discourse with other world leaders about AIDS and its impact in South Africa is also quite telling, and I discuss this in detail toward the end of the chapter.

The African Renaissance

Much of Mbeki's efforts to forge this new identity centers on the African Renaissance. The African Renaissance is not a new idea, though. Mbeki's current embrace of an African Renaissance embraces ideas and themes promoted by some of Africa's most prominent statesmen and scholars. One of the earliest proponents was Pixley kaIsaka Seme, a South African student at Columbia University. He won the school's most prestigious award for oratory in 1906 for his speech calling for "the regeneration of Africa" (Dunton 2003). Seme later went on to help found the South African Native National Congress in 1912 and served as president of its successor organization, the African National Congress, during the 1930s.

Calls for Africa's rebirth and self-reliance were at the heart of the Negritude movement of the 1930s in French-speaking Africa. Delegates to the sixth Pan-African Congress in 1945 passed a resolution asserting, "We are determined to be free [from colonialism] ... we demand for Black Africa autonomy and independence" (cited in Reader 1999, 643). Among the delegates to this conference were Kwame Nkrumah and Jomo Kenyatta, who would go on to lead Ghana and Kenya, respectively, to independence. Julius Nyerere (1964) saw his philosophy of *ujamaa*, or African socialism, as providing the means for self-reliant development on the continent. Various political leaders called for some sort of rebirth or resurgence of Africa during the era of decolonization and throughout the 1970s and 1980s.

Mbeki himself first publicly used the term in 1997 during a speech to the Corporate Council on Africa in Virginia, encouraging potential investors to share in the emergence of Africa as a significant player on the world stage (Mbeki 1997). Since then, Mbeki has repeatedly promoted the African Renaissance in his speeches and political activities both domestically and internationally. The ideas themselves may not necessarily be new, but he has given a new, prominent voice to previous calls for the continent's rebirth.

What does "African Renaissance" mean? The term is actually a bit vague. Various commentators have suggested different, yet complementary, definitions. Okumu (2002) offers a holistic view of the concept. His definition stresses the rebirth of Africa in all areas – cultural, economic, and political. Vale and Maseko provide more specifics, casting the African Renaissance largely in cultural and social terms. They say that the African Renaissance encompasses five key areas: encouraging cultural exchange, emancipating women from the patriarchy, mobilizing youth, broadening and deepening democracy, and promoting sustainable economic development (Vale and Maseko 1998, 274). Stremlau also focuses five core attributes of the African Renaissance, but his have a greater emphasis on political and economic factors. His definition emphasizes economic recovery, establishment of democracy, end of neocolonial relations, mobilization of Africans to control their destinies, and economic systems that focus on meeting the basic needs of the population (Stremlau 1999, 102–103). Stremlau's definition is of particular importance, as he presented it at a 1999 conference on the African Renaissance at which Mbeki was a featured speaker. Linking these definitions is a common emphasis on self-reliance, responsibility, and belief in Africa's ability to control its own destiny.

Mbeki clearly sees promoting the African Renaissance as central to his role as president. Gumede succinctly summarizes Mbeki's version of the African Renaissance, "Both intellectually and emotionally, Mbeki is intent on proving Afro-pessimists wrong" (2005, 203). Speaking to an audience in Cuba, Mbeki (2001a) stressed that the African Renaissance presented an opportunity for Africans to determine who they are and to challenge the West's conventional wisdom about Africa. Later that year, addressing a meeting of African central bank governors, Mbeki stressed, "When we speak of an African Renaissance, we speak of ending poverty and underdevelopment on our continent and, therefore, the building of a better life for the ordinary people of Africa, especially the poor, and the assertion of our pride as human beings, with a culture and identity that define our personality" (2001c, 127).

Mbeki's vision of the African Renaissance includes both economic autonomy for Africa and the creation of new African identity to challenge the negative stereotypes that prevail throughout the developed world. This does not mean that Mbeki is anti-West or that his views on HIV and AIDS are knee-jerk rejections of everything coming from the West. "Much like India's Nehru, Mbeki is strongly attracted to the political and economic examples of the modern West, but balks at imperialism and is little influenced by Western cultural models" (Gumede 2005, 242). This may make Mbeki appear "politically schizophrenic" (Gumede 2005, 54) at times, but it reflects his political education. Mbeki never embraced the socialist or Communist elements within the ANC, and he largely positioned himself as a centrist (if not conservative). His academic studies and work for the ANC while exiled gave him first-hand opportunities to see the positives and negatives of both the West and the East.

This African Renaissance-inspired identity extends to science policy and AIDS. One analysis of Mbeki's attitude characterizes as:

> defiance towards official scientific knowledge, a deliberate act to challenge established truths of AIDS, whether biological or social, and an identification with those on

the margins, whether of science or society. Such heterodoxy takes place within the framework of the ideological model of the African Renaissance, emphasizing the necessity for the black continent to find its own solution to its own problems (Schneider and Fassin 2002, 549).

Employing the framework of the African Renaissance allows Mbeki to alter the discursive terrain surrounding AIDS in Africa. Africa, according to Mbeki, needs to find solutions to its own problems, and these solutions must reflect the continent's unique needs.

We must be careful when describing Mbeki's views on AIDS. It is easy to picture Mbeki as an extremist who denies the suffering of his own people. The reality, though, is far more subtle and complicated. Mbeki's supporters and critics call him "a restless intellectual," "no stranger to challenging the establishment," and "a chief executive who challenges convention" (Swarns 2000). Others say that he "is very keen on doing things in an African way" (Daley 2000). In keeping with his widely-noted sphinx-like nature (Corrigan 1999; Schoofs 2000), he has never definitively stated that HIV does not cause AIDS. He did, though, convene a panel of scientists and experts, both mainstream and dissident, to look into "everything about AIDS" – including whether HIV causes AIDS (Schoofs 2000). AIDS dissidents consider Mbeki their champion, but he asked them to stop using his name in connection with their work in 2002 – though without renouncing his beliefs in their views (Power 2003, 65). Members of his Cabinet, most prominently Health Minister Dr. Manto Tshabalala-Msimang, have continued to publicly challenge the relationship between HIV and AIDS. To date, though, Mbeki has not challenged his Health Minister's assertions or given any indication that he disagrees with her. Even as Mbeki called the link between HIV and AIDS intro question, he never ordered his Ministry of Health to stop purchasing and distributing condoms. In recent years, Mbeki appears to have softened his rhetoric about AIDS somewhat, but many have expressed doubts about whether such temperance represents a genuine change of heart or a simple matter of political expediency (Copson 2003, 4). Late in 2003, his government announced a comprehensive plan to provide antiretroviral drugs to those who need them, but details of the plans are sketchy and many question whether the government has the resources or political will necessary to undertake such an ambitious goal. Some argue the government made the announcement for political expediency's sake, but that it will later scale back or cancel its commitments (Innocenti and Reed 2004, 17). By March 2005, the government had established at least one ARV access point in each of 53 districts around the country. In late 2006, Deputy President Phumzile Mlambo-Ngcuka reported that 213,000 South Africans received ARVs through government-sponsored programs, with 11,000 people being added to the program every month (*Mail and Guardian* 2006d). This means that approximately 20 percent of those who need ARVs at the end of 2006 receive them.

Mbeki's views, and those of members of his government, about AIDS go beyond a simple rejection of the disease's existence or ignorance. His policies are intended to craft a new and unique response to South Africa's ADS epidemic that is in line with his belief that African is best suited to solve Africa's problems.

Virodene, Alternative Therapies, and International Pharmaceutical Companies

In 1997, three scientists at the University of Pretoria – Olga Visser, Dirk du Plessis, and Kallie Landaure – held a press conference to unveil a startling discovery. They announced that dimethylformamide, an industrial solvent used in cryopreservation and commonly known as Virodene, proved to be a cheap, effective cure for AIDS. In an unorthodox move, the scientists announced their findings prior to submitting them for independent peer review and conducted their research on human subjects without receiving formal clearance to do so. This seriously breached scientific ethics, but the celebratory atmosphere surrounding the discovery initially overshadowed those concerns. Newspapers rejoiced that it was a proud day for South African science, and politicians celebrated the low cost of the drug. Shortly after their announcement, the trio approached the government's Medicines Control Council (MCC) for permission to conduct additional human tests and sell the drug.

The MCC refused. It chastised the University of Pretoria researchers for conducting human tests without any oversight and announcing their findings before submitting their data for peer review, a standard protocol in scientific research. Independent research by the South African Medical Research Council highlighted that dimethylformamide causes severe liver damage (Gumede 2005, 154). Some research also suggested that the drug may actually trigger HIV (Van der Vliet 2001, 163).

After the MCC's rejection, the researchers approached the Cabinet directly, asking for permission to test the drug. They alleged that the MCC refused to license their drug because it was beholden to the Western pharmaceutical companies. The researchers justified their direct appeal to the Cabinet because the MCC and the "AIDS research establishment" blocked their work. Virodene threatened the economic livelihood and intellectual hegemony of the Western pharmaceutical companies, they charged, and their rejection by the MCC proved this (Van der Vliet 2001, 164). Mbeki, then South Africa's deputy president and head of the National AIDS Council, came out strongly against the MCC's decision (Power 2003, 58). He claimed that the MCC was simply doing the bidding of the international pharmaceutical industry, which wanted to deny Africans access to an inexpensive AIDS drug.[2] Mbeki championed Virodene, and he urged Health Minister Dlamini-Zuma to fast-track its production (Gumede 2005, 154). He also sharply criticized the MCC for its refusal to certify a product of African science, which he claimed had been suppressed and denigrated for far too long. Mbeki then sacked the head of the MCC, Professor Peter Folb (Daley 2000).[3] Tony Leon, leader of the opposition Democratic Alliance, chastised Mbeki for being so obsessed with "finding African

---

2   Later investigations suggested that the African National Congress stood to profit from Virodene. Allegations surfaced that the ANC received stock in the company that produced Virodene. Party officials strenuously denied the allegation (Daley 2000).

3   Though Virodene did not receive a license for public use, reports suggest that the drug is still available through various Internet sources. Virodene Pharmaceuticals still maintains an active website, extolling the drug's virtues and encouraging people to "secur[e] the Exclusive Product Distribution" in their countries (South African Press Association 2005).

solutions to every problem" that he supports "snake-oil cures and quackery" like Virodene (Gumede 2005, 154).[4]

After assuming the presidency in 1999, Mbeki continued to face criticism at home and abroad for his policies on AIDS drugs. The Bill of Rights in the South African Constitution guarantees its citizens the right to health care. On this basis, the Treatment Action Campaign (TAC), one of the South Africa's leading AIDS activist groups, brought suit against the government for failing to provide AIDS drugs to HIV-positive pregnant women. Drugs like nevirapine and AZT, the TAC noted, had been shown remarkably effective at reducing the risk of HIV-positive mothers passing the disease on to their children, while also improving the quality of life for the mothers. At the same time, Glaxo Wellcome offered to provide the South African government with AZT at a heavily discounted rate (Epstein 2001, 190). Mbeki rejected Glaxo Wellcome's offer and refused to provide anti-AIDS drugs to HIV-positive pregnant women. He specifically cited concerns about safety and possible toxic side effects (Epstein 2001, 190).

AIDS drugs can have potentially serious side effects; this is true for nearly all pharmaceuticals. Mbeki's criticisms went beyond just challenging the safety of AIDS drugs, though. He followed a line of argumentation first put forward by Anthony Brink in his online book, *Debating AZT*. Brink asserts that AIDS drugs like AZT are toxic and actually *cause* the disease that they are supposed to combat. Looking at the side effects associated with these drugs, he posits that these side effects are actually symptomatic of infection with a new disease. Brink goes so far as to call AZT "a medicine from Hell" (Brink 1999).

Mbeki employed these same ideas as he argued against providing AIDS drugs. He claimed that Glaxo Wellcome's offer was a thinly-veiled attempt to use Africa as a testing ground for drugs. Because so few people in South Africa can afford these drugs, he argued, international pharmaceutical companies wanted to use South Africa as a dumping ground for untested and potentially dangerous drugs (Epstein 2001, 191) – just as drug companies had used developing countries as testing grounds for contraceptives deemed too dangerous for use in developed states (Brown 1987; Doyal 1981, 283–284; Zwi and Bachmayer 1990, 319). In a March 1999 interview, presidential spokesperson Parks Mankhlana asserted,

---

4   The Virodene incident bears a striking similarity to the discovery of another AIDS "cure" discovered in Africa. In 1990, the Kenyan Medical Research Institute announced its discovery of Kemron, a drug combination that reversed the symptoms of AIDS in several patients. At a time when the world was scrambling to find any effective AIDS treatment, the Kenyan researchers anticipated that their announcement would be greeted with international praise and demonstrate the robustness of African science. Instead, only two journalists from the international press corps attended the press conference. The scientists, and the Kenyan government, pointed to this as evidence that the West was fundamentally unwilling to take African science seriously (Hyden and Lanegran 1993). When Western governments and scientists raised doubts about the effectiveness of Kemron and refused to license it as a treatment, the hostility and suspicion only increased (Fredland 1998, 564). Daniel arap Moi, then Kenya's president, decried those who doubted the effectiveness of Kemron as unpatriotic (Schneider 2002, 151). Subsequent studies found that Kemron had no therapeutic efficacy (Garrett 1992).

Like the marauders of the military-industrial complex who propagated fear to increase their profits, the profit-takers who are benefiting from the scourge of HIV/AIDS will disappear to the affluent beaches because of the world to enjoy wealth accumulated from a humankind ravaged by a dreaded disease … Sure, the shareholders of Glaxo Wellcome will rejoice to hear that the South African government has decided to supply AZT to pregnant women who are HIV-positive. The sources of their joy will not be concern for those people's health, but about profits and shareholders value (cited in Epstein 2001, 190).

This attitude led to an international outcry, with many people dumbfounded that a government leader would make such pronouncements that flew in the face of established science and could lead to as many as 60,000 infants born with HIV each year (Schoofs 2000).

Mbeki and other South African government officials continue to claim that international pharmaceutical companies only want to use Africans as guinea pigs for research. One study in particular raised their ire. The United States government sponsored research in Uganda on nevirapine's effectiveness between 1997 and 2004. Known as HIVNET012, the study sough to "identify a safe, effective means of preventing mother-to-infant HIV transmission that would be applicable and affordable in resource-limited settings" through two short-course antiretroviral drug treatments. Results indicated that a regimen of nevirapine given to the mother at the onset of labor and to the infant within 72 hours significantly reduced MTCT among breastfeeding mothers (HIV Prevention Trials Network 2005). On this basis, President Bush promoted a $500 million initiative in 2002 to provide AIDS drugs like nevirapine to Africa. News reports in December 2004 cast doubts on HIVNET012's findings. Journalists discovered that U.S. officials told the Ugandan government in 2002 that the research violated international patient safety standards. Researchers failed to receive participants' consent for changes in the study after it started, administered improper dosages, and under-reported fatal and life-threatening complications (Kaiser Network 2004). These same reporters alleged that U.S. government officials knew about the problems with the Uganda research as early as January 2002, but neglected to tell President Bush until after he made his announcement (Solomon 2004). A subsequent investigation into HIVNET012's research protocols and findings by the US Institute of Medicine and National Academies acknowledged some shortcomings, but reaffirmed the study's overall conclusions (Institute of Medicine 2005).

South African government officials quickly seized on HIVNET012's flaws. Some claimed that it justified their reluctance to provide the drug to HIV-positive pregnant women (Wilson 2005). Others announced that they "welcomed further questioning of the safety of nevirapine" (cited in UNIRIN 2004) and withdrew their already-lukewarm support of the drug's use. An anonymous editorial in *ANC Today*, the ruling party's official weekly newspaper, boldly asserted:

Clearly, what was important for Dr. [Edmund] Tramont [head of the US National Institutes of Health's AIDS Division and overseer of HIVNET012] was not the health of the African people, but the success of President Bush's visit to our continent, during which he would market nevirapine to convince all of us that he is concerned about our health, not knowing that the US state medical research authorities had kept him ignorant about the serious concerns relating to the use of nevirapine. In other words, Dr. Tramont was happy that the peoples of Africa should be used as guinea pigs, given a drug he knew very well should not be prescribed ... But obviously the TAC does not agree. It is determined to continue to pursue its mission to promote the widest possible use of anti-retroviral drugs in our country, at all costs. In this regard, despite the fact that it is a mere NGO, and not a body of suitably qualified scientists, it is quite ready even to deny the reality of established scientific truths (*ANC Today* 2004).

Meanwhile, the Treatment Action Campaign encouraged use of the drug, since it proved so effective at reducing MTCT. The group lambasted the government for inciting hysteria and misinterpreting the concerns associated with the study (Muleme 2004). The government responded by questioning in whose interests TAC worked and asking whether it was a front for Western pharmaceutical companies (African National Congress 2004).

Supporters of AIDS dissidents suggested more sinister motivations on the part of the government, pharmaceutical companies, and research scientists. Farber (2006), a prominent AIDS dissident journalist, lambasted the study's authors for shoddy science, ethical lapses, and fudging data. The study, she claims, violated the basic precepts of scientific testing for the benefit of the pharmaceutical companies that would benefit from their drug's approval.

Why would scientists, who presumably want to protect health, engage in such practices? Dissidents like Farber claim that the regulatory agencies, the scientists overseeing the study, and international pharmaceutical companies have interdependent financial interests that encourage them to overlook problems. Farber charges, "Today's scientists are almost entirely dependent upon the goodwill of government researchers and powerful peer-review boards, who control a financial network binding together the National Institutes of Health, academia, and the biotech and pharmaceutical industries. Many scientists live in fear of losing their funding" (Farber 2006, 51). The financial interests of Western pharmaceutical companies, and the reliance of many scientists upon the largesse of those companies for research funds, perverts the scientific process and encourages the intentional prolonging of the AIDS epidemic simply to bolster profits.

The South African government has responded to the HIVNET012 study's flaws and other questions about antiretroviral drugs by promoting alternative therapies. Health Minister Dr. Manto Tshabalala-Msimang has been particularly vocal on this front. She advised in 2004 that "a diet of garlic, olive oil, and lemon juice helps fend off the effects of AIDS" (Wines 2004). This diet, she claimed, was more appropriate for Africans and would better protect their health than taking antiretrovirals. Most members of the international AIDS control regime greeted her recommendations with derision and disbelief.

Despite such condemnation, Tshabalala-Msimang has continued her nutrition-as-cure crusade. As part of its 3×5 Initiative to provide antiretroviral drugs to 3 million people in developing countries by 2005, the World Health Organization pushed countries to establish treatment targets. Tshabalala-Msimang resisted because she claimed the drugs had severe side effects. Instead, she counseled, "Raw garlic and a skin of a lemon – not only do they give you a beautiful face and skin, but they also protect you from disease" (Boseley 2005, 16). The following year, at the 2006 International AIDS Conference in Toronto, Tshabalala-Msimang and other health officials placed lemons, garlic, and beetroot on their official stand, seemingly presented them as alternatives to ARV treatment (though condoms and ARVs were also part of the display). US Senator Barack Obama chastised the minister for sending mixed messages, and UN envoy Stephen Lewis called her part of the "lunatic fringe" (*Economist* 2006, 39). In these instances, she based her claims on the idea that this nutrition-based treatment for HIV was more appropriate for Africa than taking antiretroviral drugs manufactured by Western pharmaceutical companies.

More recently, Tshabalala-Msimang has become an advocate for Dr. Matthias Rath. Rath, a German physician and scientist, heads an eponymous organization dedicated to the establishment of a "New Global Healthcare System." His approach emphasizes the use of vitamins and micronutrients to address medical maladies like high blood pressure, heart disease, cancer, and AIDS. He also claims that medical research conducted at top universities like Harvard corroborates his claims (Dr. Rath Foundation n.d.).[5] Rath promotes and sells vitamins in South Africa (and other countries) to cure AIDS, cancer, and a host of other diseases. He calls his vitamins a cheap, easily accessible cure, and charges international pharmaceutical companies with conspiring with powerful governments worldwide to suppress this information. He charges that the pharmaceutical industry is:

> the largest investment industry on earth, maintaining and promoting one of the largest deception and fraud schemes in the history of mankind. While the advertisements promise 'health' the very market place of this investment industry is the existence and expansion of diseases. Prevention, root cause treatment and eradication of diseases threaten the pharmaceutical 'investment business with disease' and are therefore fought by the so-called pharmaceutical cartel (Dr. Rath Foundation 2003).

Significantly, Rath ties his struggles against the international pharmaceutical industry to international peace and development. By promoting costly drugs instead of natural alternative therapies, Rath argues that the international pharmaceutical companies manage to stifle international development, retard economic growth in developing countries, and promote war. In the early 1990s, Rath studied with Dr. Linus Pauling, a two-time Nobel laureate (chemistry in 1954, peace in 1963) who saw a direct link between his scientific work on cancer and his social activism against nuclear weapons. Rath sees his work in this same vein. He takes out full-page ads in newspapers like the *New York Times*, *Sowetan*, and *International Herald Tribune* rather than going through the traditional double-blind peer review process to gain more direct access to the people. He lauds pronouncements by South African government officials like Tshabalala-Msimang as the first step in the "global health

---

5   Rath claims that research conducted in Tanzania by Wafaie Fawzi and David Hunter, both of the Harvard School of Public Health, proves that multivitamin treatments are far more effective than ARVs at preventing opportunistic infections in HIV-positive women. Fawzi and Hunter claim that Rath is taking their research out of context, While they agree that proper nutrition is important for ensuring the health of HIV-positive persons, they say that their findings in no way imply that nutritional support can replace ARV therapies (*Independent Online* 2005).

liberation from the drug cartel" (Dr. Rath Foundation 2005). He acknowledges that the pharmaceutical industry criticizes him, but he claims this is because he is uncovering the truth. In essence, Rath sees his work and himself as a liberating force which vested interests desperately want to stop.

Rath has no love for TAC. He alleges that it is merely a front for international pharmaceutical companies. Rath's website includes reports from a "TAC mole" who "entered the evil heartland" by attending TAC's 2004 national conference. It cloaks its message in grassroots support and promoting good health, according to Rath, but it operates as a shill for the big drug companies. In response, the TAC sued Rath for libel and violating national advertising standards. On 3 March 2006, the High Court in Cape Town found for TAC and enjoined the Dr. Rath Health Foundation from making any claims that TAC received funding from pharmaceutical companies (Reuters 2006). This ruling has not stopped Rath; if anything, it has emboldened him. After the High Court's decision, Rath released a press release arguing that the case actually exposed TAC's true motivations. He states that the High Court found that TAC "encourages people to take medicine which is harmful to them and will kill them," "forces the government to spend millions of Rand on toxic drugs," "force[s] the government of South Africa to deliberately spread diseases and death to its own people," and "destabilizes democracy" (Dr. Rath Foundation 2006). Rath and his foundation employ rhetoric emphasizing liberation, freedom, and challenging received wisdom similar to those invoked by members of the South African government itself to justify its actions.

Rath's efforts have apparently received at least tacit approval from members of the South African government. Tshabalala-Msimang held a private meeting with Rath in April 2005 to discuss "his concern for people infected with HIV and suffering from the impact of AIDS" (South African Press Agency 2005). When asked if she would distance herself from Rath's assertions about the toxicity of antiretrovirals, she replied, "I will only distance myself from Dr. Rath if it can be demonstrated that the vitamin supplements that he is prescribing are poisonous for people infected with HIV" (South African Press Agency 2005).[6] Though she claims not to recall "endorsing" Rath's work, the Health Minister noted that "the Foundation's focus on good nutrition in fighting disease is complementary to the government's program to fight AIDS" (Pressly 2005). Tshabalala-Msimang earlier claimed that she had treated her two HIV-positive nieces solely by adjusting their diets and without ARVs.[7] "I can tell you, I have sustained them on good nutrition and food supplements, because they don't take anti-retrovirals. One of them has gone back to work," she reported (Terreblance and Battersby 2003).

Other units of the South African Department of Health also have ties with Rath and his Foundation. Dr. Anthony MBewu, the head of the Medical Research Council (MRC), has reportedly met with Rath on numerous occasions, leading to charges

6   Dianne Kohler-Bernard, a member of the opposition Democratic Alliance who first questioned Tshabalala-Msimang about her meetings with Rath, later claimed that the Health Minister had formally aligned herself with Rath (South African Press Agency 2005).
7   Later during this same press conference, Tshabalala-Msimang acknowledged the ARVs may have a role in treating HIV, but she strongly downplayed their importance.

that the MRC is providing moral and academic support for Rath's operations to counter the TAC (Keeton 2006). Newspaper articles show that the MRC received R200,000 from Rath in 2004 to run a series of workshops. These same reports included a note, apparently written by MBewu, that states, "NAPWA (National Association of People with AIDS) – good group. TAC is paid by pharma cartel. NAPWA has an open mind and will be a great advocacy tool as a counter-balance attack" (cited in Shlensky 2006). NAPWA has received financial support in recent years from Rath, and TAC alleges that the organization is now merely a front for the Dr. Rath Foundation's activities in South Africa (Thom 2005). MRC officials claim that the meetings and workshops were merely a common courtesy afforded to any group that wants them (Shlensky 2006), though notes from a meeting between Rath and Sam Mhlongo, chair of the Presidential Advisory Panel, suggest that government officials, including Mbeki, were actively looking to Rath to find a grassroots organization to counter TAC's message and influence (TAC n.d.).

Mbeki's relationship with Rath appears more complicated. News reports indicate that Mbeki denied claims that he had explicitly encouraged Rath to set up shop in South Africa, but they note that he has taken no steps to shut down Rath's operations in the country (*Mail and Guardian* 2005). Other evidence suggests at least an ideological affinity between the two. Anthony Brink, the Dr. Rath Health Foundation's spokesperson in South Africa and a long-time campaigner against AIDS drugs, notes, "As a journalist, you're either hip to colossal, murderous fraud or you're not. Mbeki is; Tshabalala-Msimang is; and the highest level of [the South African government] is" (Cairns 2005).

In all of these cases – support for Virodene, promotion of alternative therapies, and support for Dr. Matthias Rath – the South African government has justified its actions through reference to the ideals of the African Renaissance. Virodene demonstrated the robustness of African science and its ability to indigenously find solutions to its medical problems. Alternative therapies were better than pharmaceuticals because they took account of the African context and responded to the unique nature of the AIDS epidemic in Africa. Suspicion of international pharmaceutical companies fits with questioning received outside wisdom and a desire for liberation. Advocating on behalf of Rath is yet another step toward liberation from oppression by outsiders. These stances all point toward an emphasis on self-reliance and independence, and therefore fall in line with Mbeki's broader promotion of the African Renaissance's ideals.

Explaining South Africa's Position to the World

The South African government's unorthodox AIDS policies – questioning the links between HIV and AIDS, discounting the efficacy of ARVs in favor of untested alternative treatments, promoting the views of AIDS dissidents despite widespread condemnation from the international community (even while other parts of the government continued to promote condom usage) – garnered negative international attention throughout the late 1990s. As the country's HIV infection rate continued to increase, journalists, academics, and activists increasingly questioned whether the government could effectively address the epidemic. Mbeki sought to correct any misrepresentations of his ideas or his government's policies. This was especially important, as South Africa was hosting the 13th International AIDS Conference in Durban during the summer of 2000 – the first time a developing country hosted the conference.

Prior to the conference, Mbeki sought to allay confusion over his AIDS beliefs. As part of his effort, he wrote letters to a number of world leaders, including Bill Clinton, Tony Blair, and Kofi Annan, in April 2000. In explaining South Africa's strategy to combat AIDS, Mbeki lays out his thinking about the epidemic. He cites UNAIDS figures adult HIV infection rates in southern Africa, and implies that these figures might be so high because of the struggle against apartheid. He goes on to examine the characteristics of the AIDS epidemics in the West and in Africa. He writes:

> Accordingly, as Africans, we have to deal with this uniquely African catastrophe that
> * contrary to the West, HIV/AIDS in Africa is heterosexually transmitted;
> * contrary to the Wets, where relatively few people have died from AIDS, itself a matter of serious concern, millions are said to have died in Africa; and,
> * contrary to the West, where AIDS deaths are declining, even greater numbers of Africans are destined to die (Mbeki 2000c).

Note the emphasis that Mbeki places on treating the "African catastrophe" by Africans. This is one of his most explicit attempts to connect the struggle against AIDS with the spirit of the African Renaissance.

Mbeki goes on to write, "It is obvious that whatever lessons we have to and may draw from the West about the grave issue of HIV-AIDS, *a simple imposition of Western experience on African reality would be absurd and illogical*" (Mbeki 2000c; emphasis added). He added: "We will not eschew this obligation [to treat AIDS in a manner appropriate to Africa] in favor of the comfort of the recitation of a catechism that may very well be a correct response to the specific manifestations of AIDS in the West" (Mbeki 2000c). In both of these sentences, Mbeki emphasizes the need to utilize a distinctly "African" approach to combating AIDS, while simultaneously questioning the scientific assumptions underlying AIDS in the West – including the connection between HIV and AIDS.[8]

Of particular interest are Mbeki's comments about his discussions with AIDS dissidents. He notes that he has received condemnation from a number of sources

---

8   These criticisms resonate with other critiques of international AIDS programs. Campbell and Williams state, "The language of HIV prevention has become the language of western science and western policy approaches, unmediated by an appreciation of the extent to which these are inappropriate for local conditions" (2001, 136). They find that many of the policies that international donors have attempted to implement in South Africa are actually imported from the Tanzanian experience, even though the scope and scale of Tanzania's AIDS crisis is not entirely comparable to South Africa. The lack of 'fit' with the realities of local conditions undermines the programs' effectiveness (Campbell and Williams 2001, 136). Both Mbeki and Campbell and Williams emphasize how international responses to AIDS in South Africa fail to appreciate the epidemic's distinctive nature in South Africa.

for questioning Western orthodoxy on AIDS by consulting them. Mbeki rises to their defense, objecting, "In an earlier period in human history, they [the AIDS dissidents] would be heretics that would be burnt at the stake!" (Mbeki 2000c).

He then proceeds to explicitly tie the work of the AIDS dissidents in with the struggle against apartheid. He writes:

> Not long ago, in our own country, people were killed, tortured, imprisoned, and prohibited from being quoted in private, and in public, because the established authority believed that their views were dangerous and discredited.
>
> We are now being asked to do *precisely the same thing that the racist apartheid tyranny we opposed did*, because, it is said, there exists a scientific view that is supported by the majority, *against which dissent is prohibited* (Mbeki 2000c; emphasis added).

Mbeki not only connects his questioning of the connections between HIV and AIDS with the African Renaissance, but he explicitly identifies it with the struggle against apartheid. Mbeki equates the fight against white minority rule in South Africa with the fight against the international AIDS control regime. He casts himself and the AIDS dissidents as freedom fighters resisting the imposition of an inappropriate worldview. One of Mbeki's aides remarked: "Western scientists once said to us the earth was flat. Now we know it's round. I bet one day we will look at AIDS the same way .... The world will have President Mbeki to thank" (cited in Power 2003, 56).

Mbeki's letter generally stunned and confused its recipients. Fears arose that Mbeki's sentiments would spread to other governments in Africa, undermining international efforts to control the AIDS epidemic. Some likened Mbeki's stance to that of Holocaust deniers. Concerned by its tone and message, two of President Clinton's staffers investigated whether the letter was a hoax (Daley 2000).

The international outcry over President Mbeki's views on AIDS swelled at the 13th International AIDS Conference in Durban. During his welcoming address on 9 July 2000, Mbeki welcomed the participants with a note of optimism. He encouraged the participants to ask tough questions, as he felt silenced when he questioned AIDS orthodoxy. Continuing, he stated:

> As I listened to this tale of human woe, I heard the name recur with frightening frequency, Africa, Africa, Africa! As I listened and heard the whole story told about out country, it seemed to me that we could not blame everything on a single virus. *The world's biggest killer and greatest cause of ill health across the globe, including South Africa, is extreme poverty* (cited in Fassin 2003, 54; emphasis added).

With this speech, Mbeki publicly challenged the scientific orthodoxy that HIV is the sole cause of AIDS – and did so in front of an audience of the very people who crafted that orthodoxy. He raised the questions asked by AIDS dissidents in a prominent international venue. In the process, he declared to the world that Africa's experience with AIDS differs fundamentally from the West's.

Reaction to Mbeki's address was swift and angry. Within days, over 5000 scientists signed the Durban Declaration and published it in the scientific journal *Nature* (Sidley 2000, 67). The document states in no uncertain terms that HIV is *the* cause of AIDS and lays out the supporting scientific evidence. The signatories affirmed, "HIV causes AIDS. It is unfortunate that a few vocal people continue to deny the evidence. Their position will cost countless lives." It concluded:

There is no end in sight to the AIDS pandemic. By working together, we have the power to reverse the tide of this epidemic. Science will one day triumph over AIDS, just as it did over smallpox. Curbing the spread of HIV will be the first step. Until then, reason, solidarity, political will and courage must be our partners (Durban Declaration 2000).

The declaration's signatories intended it as an affirmation of the scientific community's consensus on HIV and AIDS. Instead, it generated greater controversy and disagreement. Presidential spokesperson Parks Mankhlana pithily responded, "If the drafters of this declaration expect to give it to the president, or the government, it will find its comfortable place among the dustbins in the office" (Agence France-Presse 2000). A group of AIDS dissidents published a point-by-point refutation of the Durban Declaration on their website (Johnston et al. 2001), and lambasted the signatories for turning science into a battle of public opinion.

In a 2001 speech at Fort Hare University, Mbeki further developed these themes that linked AIDS with racism within the international scientific and policy communities. He asserted:

Thus does it happen that others who consider themselves to be our leaders take to the streets carrying their placards to demand that because we [Black people] are germ carriers and human beings of a lower order that cannot subject its [*sic*] passion to reason, we must perforce adopt strange opinions, to save a depraved and diseased people from perishing from self-inflicted disease ... convinced that we are but natural-born promiscuous carriers of germs ... they proclaim that our continent is doomed to an inevitable mortal end because of our devotion to the sin of lust (cited in Mbali 2004, 111).

Here, Mbeki explicitly ties his AIDS policies to a challenge to the international community's image of Africa as inherently disease-prone and hypersexualized. He contrasts his position with those of AIDS activists who march in the street to protest his government's actions. In essence, he calls AIDS activists un-African. By marching in the streets against the government, according to Mbeki's logic, activists are buying into racist caricatures of Africa. Mbeki's critics called this speech "bizarre" and "evidence that he is a closet AIDS denialist" (Forrest and Streek 2001).

Mbeki is not the only government official who explicitly links the government's AIDS policies with attempts to forge an African Renaissance-inspired, independent identity. In January 2005, Minister of Health Tshabalala-Msimang addressed the delegates to the First International Conference on Natural Products and Molecular Therapy, held in Cape Town. The meeting brought together scientists from around the world who advocate greater research on herbal extracts, plant therapies, and dietary supplements to treat a wide variety of illnesses, including AIDS. The delegates also seek to understand how traditional or folk remedies work and why international pharmaceutical companies do not invest in them. In her remarks, Tshabalala-Msimang commented:

> It [the study of indigenous knowledge] provides an opportunity to reclaim our scientific and socio-cultural heritage, which was stigmatized and discredited as primitive rituals and witchcraft during many years of colonialism and apartheid ... This forum should expose the false dichotomy that has arisen between natural medicine and allopathic medicine, a division fostered by the need to make money from patented drugs through discrediting the use of natural products (cited in *Mail and Guardian* 2006a).

Again, we see here an explicit attempt to link the promotion of alternative therapies and etiologies to the promotion of an independent identity. Tshabalala-Msimang sees alternative therapies as a way for South Africans (though not just South Africans, in this instance) to redefine their relationship with the rest of the world. It is a means by which local knowledge and understandings can be promoted against the hegemonic medical discourse promoted by the pharmaceutical companies, who, as she claims, place a premium on maximizing profit rather than finding the most appropriate form of treatment.[9]

AIDS in a Broader Identity Context

It is tempting to see Mbeki's views on AIDS as misguided and crackpot ideology. Fassin argues, though, that Mbeki's statements on AIDS fit within a collective South African experience with epidemics. Mbeki employs a narrative discourse of political resistance to white domination and its global order, and relies on the tropes of the African Renaissance and rejecting domination by outsiders (Fassin 2002, 66). He builds on the arguments advanced by Chirimuuta and Chirimuuta in the late 1980s. They argued that the West dramatically exaggerated the extent of AIDS in Africa to discredit African culture and sexuality (Chirimuuta and Chirimuuta 1989, 80–81). More importantly, Mbeki's views fit within the larger epidemiological debates about how one frames disease.

Instead of relying on the standard Western biomedical discourse about disease, which emphasizes behavior and risk, Mbeki relies on a socioeconomic discourse. He emphasizes that AIDS is a disease of poverty, and that poverty is the world's greatest killer. He chastises international pharmaceutical companies for wanting to profit from the suffering of South Africans. Mankhlana has highlighted the

---

9   One of the organizers of the conference at which Tshabalala-Msimang presented her remarks, Professor Girish Kotwal of the University of Cape Town, later ran into trouble due to activities related to the conference itself. After Kotwal published an article in the *Annals of the New York Academy of Science* (Kotwal et al. 2006) touting Secomet-V, an herbal tonic sold under the name "Ithemba Lesizwe" (Hope of the Nation) as a long-term treatment for AIDS, University of Cape Town officials suspended Kotwal for possible professional misconduct (*Mail and Guardian* 2006a). Kotwal claimed that Secomet-V was "effective against poxviruses, HIV, herpes, SARS corona, and flu viruses, including the H5N2 bird-flu strain, rendering them all inactive" (Pope 2006). He also allegedly had a financial stake in the company.

importance of this discourse about disease to the government. Speaking on 24 March 2000, he stated, "He [Mbeki] has broken the tradition that seeks to make the disease just a health problem. HIV/AIDS is a socioeconomic problem. It is a political problem that has reached the proportion of an international crisis" (cited in Altman 2003, 420).

This frame focuses on the social conditions which make disease possible. While it is certainly true that certain behaviors will place individuals at a higher risk of contracting HIV, it is also true that certain economic and social conditions make it more likely that a person will be placed in the sort of situation where they are forced to make that choice. People do not rationally choose to expose themselves to fatal, incurable diseases. They make choices, though they may increase exposure to HIV, because they lack the funds or social status to choose otherwise. Mbeki picks up on this socioeconomic discourse, and sees himself as a freedom fighter trying to expand the debate beyond the narrow biomedical and behavioral frame. Limiting the arguments about the AIDS epidemic strictly to the biomedical discourse has consequences. "Had a social epidemiology of HIV been more prominent in the scientific arena, rather than the dominant biomedical and behavioral approach, Mbeki might have found interesting alternatives to the explanation of the epidemic given on the dissidents' websites" (Fassin and Schneider 2003). By circumscribing the realm of debate, large amounts of energy and resources have been diverted away from treating the epidemic and toward recriminations and name-calling.

Promoting a new South African identity is central to many aspects of the country's interactions with the international community. South African foreign policy under Mbeki has been guided by a desire to forge stronger "South-South" links to strengthen the role of non-Western states in the post-Cold War era. The ideals of the African Renaissance reinforce this move by enabling South Africa to make a "conscious move away from a 'Western' profile to an 'African' and 'independent' international role" (Broderick 2001, 232–233). He wants to counter the popular notion that Africa is a place of starvation and failure, and that it has moved beyond the "Heart of Darkness" imagery that continues to color international perceptions of the continent (Dunn 2003). Mbeki sees this Afro-pessimism as a genuine pattern in international relations, and wants to counter that by demonstrating that African countries can and will take responsibility for their own problems (Corrigan 1999, 93–94). He writes,

> There will be a time when a highly respected columnist for one of America's best newspapers will not casually dismiss South Africa's achievements of the past decade as the result of luck, but will point instead to the character of our continent's people and the substance of the policies of the governments they elect...It is up to Africans to create the conditions for that to occur. No one can do it for us (Mbeki 2004a, A19).

We must bear in mind that Mbeki's attempts to forge a new identity based on the ideas of the African Renaissance do not automatically translate into an acceptance of this identity among South Africans. The South African public still sees its primary identity as "South African" as opposed to "African" (Nel 1999). AIDS activists in South Africa have not embraced the African Renaissance as the solution to the country's AIDS epidemic. They instead agitate for government programs that would provide antiretroviral drugs and encourage the government to challenge international intellectual property regulations that prevent the importation of generic AIDS drugs (Power 2003). Even among government officials, unity does not exist regarding an African Renaissance identity. Members of the ANC are divided on the issue, as some see Mbeki's use of the African Renaissance as precluding effective intervention in Zimbabwe (Mallaby 2005). The opposition Democratic Alliance claims that the African Renaissance has become an excuse to avoid dealing with issues like human rights (Klotz 2004, 11). The fact that the African Renaissance ideals do not appear to be resonating yet with the South African public may provide clues about how successful Mbeki will be in the long run. Recent surveys demonstrate that an African identity resonates with few South Africans. Instead, South Africans are far more likely to identify with their racial, ethnic, or religious groups (Mattes 2004).[10]

That does not mean that one should dismiss the importance of the African Renaissance. It remains true that Mbeki and other high government officials, people who have power over the country's AIDS policies, *do* embrace the African Renaissance and see it as central to the state's identity. The existence of divisions on the issue instead provides insights into why divisions may exist, even within the government, on AIDS policies.

The divisions within the ANC, the government, and the country itself over an African Renaissance-inspired identity suggest that Mbeki's drive has met with limited success. Moreover, it highlights the limits of an interest-based explanation for Mbeki's actions. From an interest-based perspective, Mbeki's embrace of this African Renaissance-inspired identity would represent political calculations. He wants to adopt this identity in order to solidify his own political base or to ensure that voters overlook his inattention to AIDS policies when casting ballots. If this identity is not resonating with his domestic constituencies, though, it is difficult to see what sort of political advantage Mbeki receives by hanging onto it. Even within his own government, there appears to be some disagreement among Cabinet members over the importance of Mbeki's African Renaissance project. Thus, one cannot make the argument that Mbeki had embraced the African Renaissance simply to maintain his political position among his government ministers or the ANC. These all suggest that interest-based explanations do not go far enough to explain Mbeki's position.

Why would Mbeki feel the need to create a new African identity? With the demise of the Cold War, Africa largely disappeared from the foreign policy agendas of developed states, and from the study of international relations in general (Behrman 2004, 65; Benatar 2002, 168; Murphy 2001, ix). Since the Cold War, and particularly after its demise, African leaders often found themselves co-opted into accepting neoliberal agendas that both bankrupted their states and left them with little popular legitimacy. By accepting the neoliberal orthodoxy, leaders found themselves opposed to the wants and needs of their populace. Promoting a

10 As will be discussed in the next chapter, nearly all of the AIDS dissidents come from Western states. This may also contribute to the South African public's failure to relate to the African Renaissance-inspired identity.

new identity allows leaders like Mbeki to both enhance their own legitimacy and bring Africa back to the international table. Mbeki highlighted this in a speech to the annual meeting of the Non-Aligned Movement in Durban in 1998. He said:

> In as much as the slave cannot ask the slavemaster to provide the strategy and tactics for a successful uprising of the slaves, so must we who are hungry and treated as minors in a world of adults also take upon ourselves the task of defining the new world order of prosperity and development for all and equality among the nations of the world. For the weak to challenge the strong has never been easy. Neither will it be easy to challenge the powerful vested interests on the current and entrenched orthodoxies about the modern world economy (cited in Corrigan 1999, 42–43).

These comments reiterated the points he made during a 1997 interview with *The Citizen*, when he stated, "We in the developing world who have borne the brunt of human injustice over decades and centuries issuing from other nations' desire to accumulate and aggrandize, should play a central role in defining what should constitute the new world order" (cited in Corrigan 1999, 42). Mbeki ties his efforts to establish a new African Renaissance-inspired identity with challenging the current international order that has largely excluded Africa.

This still begs the question of why Mbeki would situate the fight against AIDS as a central part of his attempt to fashion a new identity for South Africa. Bosia (2005) argues that the embrace of neoliberalism in the political and economic spheres has a detrimental impact on a nation's AIDS policies by constraining the government's actions. At the same time, Elbe (2005) notes that the 'securitization' of AIDS increasingly brings a country's AIDS policies under international surveillance. Outside actors play a progressively larger role in setting and evaluating the appropriateness of a given state's response to the epidemic. Johnson situates the South African government's response within the broader challenges posed by globalization. As globalization limits the policy space available for non-Western states, the South African government has repeatedly sought to assert its autonomy where possible. "At a time when the AIDS pandemic has finally drawn the attention of the international community and was increasingly being defined by the international community, the South African government sought to develop a uniquely African response to the pandemic" (Johnson 2005, 320).

Evidence of this can be seen in the South African government's refusal to declare a medical state of emergency, which would then trigger certain constitutional measures that ease access to antiretroviral drugs. By not declaring a medical state of emergency, Mbeki is essentially reasserting South Africa's sovereignty within the international community (Sitze 2004, 787). Resisting the dictates of the international community allows Mbeki and his government to reassert South Africa as an actor with agency – not simply a state that is acted *upon*. It is an attempt to wrest control away from international actors who have little concern for or understanding the contours of the AIDS epidemic within South Africa.

This is not necessarily unique to AIDS or Africa. Disease prevention measures often serve as markers of community borders. Fidler writes, "Infectious disease measures historically have served as demarcations by which 'we' protect ourselves from the diseases of 'others'" (Fidler 1998, 9). Public health measures have long been deeply intertwined with national identities. Mbeki attempts to turn this relationship on its head. Instead of using public health to protect South Africa from others, he wants to use public health to challenge others.

Are Mbeki and members of his government wrong? Answering this question is difficult, but the short answer is – not necessarily. Links certainly do exist between South Africa's international identity and its AIDS epidemic. Early responses to AIDS in Africa *were* largely racist. Africans in and of themselves were considered a "high-risk group" and faced discriminatory policies worldwide. Early theories about the disease's origins posited that Africans regularly engaged in sexual relations with monkeys, could not control their unbridled sexual desires, or injected monkey blood into their genitals during sex. Pro-apartheid politicians in South Africa saw AIDS as evidence of the need to keep Blacks away from Whites and publicly (and approvingly) argued that the disease would wipe out the anti-apartheid movement. These responses are an accurate reflection of the historical record of the world's response to AIDS, and members of the South African government employ these instances to justify their policies.

Doing so may reflect the history of AIDS responses, but it does not necessarily reflect *contemporary* responses to and interpretations of the epidemic. Mbali (2004) argues that South African government officials have largely overlooked policy and discourse changes within the international community's response to AIDS. She argues that the international community's AIDS discourse now emphasizes human rights and respect. This shift to a rights-based AIDS discourse allows for more rational policymaking that can address both the biomedical and social conditions that give rise to the epidemic's spread (Mbali 2004, 117). Instead of recognizing this shift, though, the government's AIDS denialism reflects an "obsess[ion] with colonial and late apartheid discourses of race, sexuality, and disease in Africa" (Mbali 2004, 104). Mbeki's policies seek to challenge an anachronistic identity beyond which the international community has largely moved. The *contemporary* response is appropriate for a *previous* conceptualization of the disease.

Conclusion

The South African government sees AIDS as having a negative impact on its identity within the international community, and it has used AIDS to remake its post-apartheid identity. Its AIDS policies highlight and reinforce the notion of finding African solutions for African problems, questioning received outside wisdom, and charting a course that it considers appropriate for the South African experience. Instead of being acted upon, the South African government uses its AIDS policies to demonstrate its agency within the international community. President Mbeki's enthusiastic support of Virodene, even in the face of contrary scientific evidence, reflected his desire to show the world that African science was not an oxymoron. Health Minister Tshabalala-Msimang's embrace of alternative, natural AIDS treatments, despite international ridicule and a lack of scientific evidence, demonstrate her commitment to challenging the 'objective knowledge' of outsiders that do not necessarily understand the context in which South Africa finds itself. When President Mbeki wrote his letter to world leaders and addressed the International AIDS Conference delegates, he saw his actions as a continuation of the spirit of independence and liberation that motivated the anti-apartheid movement – the same movement where he got his political start and whose political party he now leads.

The South African government's response to the AIDS epidemic and its clashes with the international AIDS control regime must be understood within the government's broader ideological and identity-based struggles. Mbeki and his allies approach the disease from a fundamentally different perspective than many members of the international AIDS control regime. The two sides lack shared intersubjective understandings of the AIDS epidemic. In and of itself, this may not be a problem. Tensions arise, though, when a counter-epistemic community can translate South Africa's history and identity commitments as they relate to AIDS into actual policies. It allows the South African government to counter the demands of the international community on a more equal footing. The next chapter examines the development and operation of the AIDS counter-epistemic community.

Chapter 6

South African AIDS Policies and the Counter-epistemic Community

History and identity commitments are important for understanding South Africa's unorthodox AIDS policies, but there must be a mechanism for translating history and identity commitments into policy outcomes. It is not enough to say that history and identity simply matter; the key is to show *how* and *why* they matter. How do such abstract concepts become real-world government policy?

This is where the counter-epistemic community comes into play. It embodies and reflects the outlook generated from the historical and ideational legacies. It frames the issue within these contexts and provides policy solutions that it believes to be appropriate given this frame. Its policy suggestions resonate with South Africa's historical experiences and identity commitments. Members of the counter-epistemic community couch these suggestions in terms of democracy and struggles against oppression. It offers South African policymakers the opportunity to challenge the mainstream consensus on HIV and AIDS on its own terms, matching the experts of the counter-epistemic community against the experts of the mainstream epistemic community.

In this chapter, I focus on the details about the AIDS counter-epistemic community. I start by examining what members of the counter-epistemic community believe and their origins. I then profile key members of the AIDS counter-epistemic community and show how their scientific credentials offer a certain level of credibility in these debates. These members have either advised Mbeki on AIDS policy or are prominent in the debates about appropriate AIDS treatments in South Africa. The following section examines how members of the AIDS counter-epistemic community came to work with Mbeki in the first place. It also explores how the AIDS dissidents have translated their ideas into policy outcomes. In particular, I show how the common accusation of 'AIDS denialism' on the part of the South African government is an outcome of the influence of the AIDS dissidents. Finally, I discuss how the AIDS counter-epistemic community employs a rhetoric of democracy and liberation that resonate with the country's historical experiences and identity commitments.

Roots and Beliefs of the AIDS Counter-epistemic Community

Signs of the development of an AIDS counter-epistemic community and its role in AIDS policies in Africa go back to the earliest days of the epidemic. In 1985, the first international conference addressing AIDS in Africa took place in Brussels. Its organizers hoped that the conference would bring together experts from the West and Africa to create a plan of action for combating the disease. Instead, most African scientists refused to attend the conference. They accused the Western scientific community of unfairly stigmatizing the continent with subtly racist theories about AIDS' African origins and for not appreciating the experience and wisdom of the African scientists (McFadden 1995, 176). This early conflict heightened the competition for scarce resources for treating the disease, and bred distrust between Western and African scientists.

Other African scientists reported similar experiences. One Nigerian scientist, commenting on Western interventions and the work of Western AIDS scientists in Africa, observed, "Experts come and say we must be culturally sensitive and then ignore my knowledge" (Fredland 1998, 566). A 1992 article on AIDS in Africa noted that many African elites saw foreigners as the real source of AIDS on the continent, and that Western interventions were attempts to make "Africans conform to Western norms" (Caldwell et al. 1992, 1171). Thus, from the earliest recognition of the AIDS epidemic, conflicts existed among scientists about the best methods for approaching and treating the disease. This fissure finds its contemporary expression in the counter-epistemic community.

The scientific orthodoxy about HIV and AIDS is well-established. The human immunodeficiency virus (HIV) infects individuals through the exchange of bodily fluids, generally transmitted through sharing needles for intravenous drug use, sexual intercourse, or breastfeeding. Once infected, the virus gradually weakens the person's immune system by attacking the T-cells that fight infection. With HIV attacking the T-cells, those cells cannot then fend off other opportunistic infections. Once a person loses enough T-cells, they are clinically diagnosed with AIDS. Most scientists believe that HIV causes AIDS, that AIDS is incurable, and that the disease is ultimately fatal in all instances.

AIDS dissidents share their own causal beliefs, challenging the established orthodoxy at almost every turn. These shared causal beliefs unite the counter-epistemic community of AIDS dissidents. Members of the counter-epistemic community generally deny that HIV causes AIDS. The dissidents charge mainstream scientists with failing to adhere to Koch's necessary and sufficient postulates of disease etiology. In the late 1800s, the German bacteriologist devised four criteria for judging whether a given organism causes a particular disease. An organism causes a disease if:

1. The organism is found in all animals suffering from a particular disease, but not in healthy animals,
2. The organism can be isolated from a diseased animal and grown in a pure culture,
3. When introduced into a healthy susceptible animal, the organism causes the disease, and
4. The organism can then be reisolated and recoverable from the newly-infected animal.

Dissidents allege that the scientific community has failed all four of these tests with HIV; therefore, we cannot assert that HIV is the cause of AIDS (Kistner 2002).

They argue that not all who have AIDS are HIV-positive, and that some who are HIV-positive never develop AIDS. They claim that HIV has still never been isolated and grown in a pure culture. They dispute evidence that HIV causes disease when introduced into uninfected persons and that scientists have not re-isolated the virus in these instances (Johnston et al. n.d.). In essence, they disagree with all of the arguments made by mainstream AIDS epistemic community (NIAID/NIH 2003). Mainstream virologists, they assert, are subverting the scientific process in their quest to blame HIV for AIDS.

The mainstream AIDS epistemic community responds to this critique in two primary ways. First, and most simply, they argue that they have in fact met Koch's four criteria. The AIDS dissidents may not like their methods or findings, but mainstream AIDS scientists assert that repeated studies over the past 20 years have satisfied Koch's postulates. Second, they argue that the dissidents ignore the evolution of Koch's thinking. Koch did establish strict postulates between 1878 and 1884, but he later revised his definitions in light of the challenges posed by viruses. Not all bacteria can be grown in a pure culture, and some human diseases have no counterpart in the animal kingdom. Those exceptions do not invalidate Koch's postulates, but they do require scientists to approach these tests with caution. Thus, the AIDS dissidents rely on a model of etiology that Koch himself later revised (Kistner 2002, 56–57).

If AIDS is not a new viral disease, then what is it? In the words of one article by leading dissidents, AIDS is "a collection of chemical epidemics, caused by recreational drugs, anti-HIV drugs, and malnutrition" (Duesberg et al. 2003, 383). Dissidents argue that the manifestations of AIDS in North America and Western Europe and in Africa are so incredibly dissimilar as to be different diseases. They also claim that, despite claims to the contrary, the disease in the West remains almost exclusively contained within several risk groups identified in the 1980s – namely, intravenous drug users and gay men – but that AIDS in Africa is far more randomly distributed throughout the population (Duesberg 1992; Duesberg et al. 2003). These findings lead the dissidents to deny that AIDS is a unique disease. What the world calls AIDS does not conform to the characteristics associated with all other viral and microbial epidemics. Instead, the 30-odd opportunistic infections associated with AIDS are more indicative of exposure to toxins (Duesberg 1992, 1997). Duesberg and Rasnick (1998) argue that people with AIDS are suffering from the debilitating side effects of exposing their bodies to large quantities of hard recreational drugs.

Instead of being a fatal agent, HIV is a simple passenger virus that has inhabited humans with no ill effects for millennia and continues to do so (Duesberg 2000). HIV, they assert, takes the blame for the maladies affecting heavy drug users. AIDS, according to the dissidents, is a convenient political moniker for a host of unrelated illnesses that allows policymakers to absolve themselves of dealing with the issues of drug use and abuse.

The "heavy drug use" hypothesis could conceivably hold some plausibility in the West, but supporters of the mainstream belief note that is not the case in Africa. Intravenous drug use is extremely rare in Africa, and the spread of the disease does not conform to those populations. The AIDS dissidents are quick to respond. They say that the relatively equal prevalence of AIDS in men and women in Africa proves that the disease is not sexually transmitted. Since men and women are not equally susceptible to contracting sexually transmitted diseases, the fairly-even gender split for African AIDS cases actually proves that the disease could *not* be sexually transmitted (Papadopulos-Eleopulos et al. 1995). They further note that AIDS in Africa is not a specific clinical disease, but rather a battery of previously known diseases like chronic diarrhea, shingles, candidiasis, and fevers lasting for more than a month. "Since these diseases include the most common diseases in Africa and in much of the rest of the world, it is impossible to distinguish clinically African AIDS disease from previously known, and concurrently diagnosed, conventional African disease" (Duesberg 2000, 4). Like in the West, the dissidents argue, AIDS in Africa is not a specific disease, but rather a convenient label for a host of problems that have plagued the continent for years. Duesberg (2000) argues that what the world calls AIDS is simply the result of malnutrition, parasitic infections, and poor sanitation – none of which are new to Africa. Geshetker (1997) says that "African AIDS" is a manifestation of international racism and underdevelopment. Because the international community still views Africa as dirty and diseased, it just assumes that the continent's problems are the result of illness, ignoring the West's role in actively hindering African development. Papadopulos-Eleopulos et al. (1995) posit that Western prejudice blinds researchers from appreciating that AIDS is just a new name for diseases that have long caused death in Africa.

AIDS dissidents heap vitriol on the full range of anti-AIDS drugs like AZT and antiretroviral therapies. Many assert that these drugs themselves *cause* the very disease which they supposedly treat (Duesberg 1997; Duesberg and Rasnick 1998). These drugs poison the body, causing toxic reactions that imperil the health of those who take them. Duesberg equates AZT with chemotherapy, arguing, "You lose your hair, you lose weight, you get pneumonia, you get immune deficient, you literally get AIDS, you have nausea, all the AIDS symptoms because it's severe cellular intoxication" (Guccione 1993). They applauded Mbeki's decisions in the late 1990s not to provide AZT to HIV-positive persons in South Africa. In fact, Mbeki cites the work of AIDS dissidents about anti-AIDS drugs, largely published on the Internet, for stimulating his decision not to provide AZT (Cohen 2000, 590).

Why, though, would all of the credentialed, intelligent, respected scientists in the mainstream AIDS epistemic community ignore evidence that could definitely answer what causes AIDS, and thus save millions of lives? The AIDS dissidents blame money. Discovering an infectious microbe means that pharmaceutical companies can develop antibiotics and antiviral vaccines – an incredibly lucrative business proposition (Duesberg 1997, 10). David Rasnick, a former pharmaceutical company researcher who worked on protease inhibitors, claims that these drugs work but are irrelevant because AIDS patients are not suffering from any effects as the result of HIV (Rasnick 1996). Instead, the drugs sicken patients – and fatten the bank accounts of the pharmaceutical companies. The drugs 'work' by convincing people they have a viral disease and that they need this drug. In one interview, Rasnick stated that Abbott Laboratories, the maker of the protease inhibitor Norvir, made US$10 million from the drug in the first three weeks it was available on the market (Conlan 1998).

Even more importantly, the federal government largely controls funds for scientific research in the United States. With the advent of the Cold War, the government poured billions of dollars into scientific research to prevent losing ground to the Soviet Union. Concomitantly, politicians bemoaned the lack of scientists in the United States and developed programs to encourage the training of more. As a result, the number of PhDs and MDs rapidly grew. Duesberg sees these two factors as undermining genuine research on AIDS. He argues that having so many scientists competing for funds from one central agency leads to "regression to the mean" and discourages the development of hypotheses that challenge established dogmas (Duesberg 1997, 64–66). Instead of encouraging innovation, the system demands conformity. "The successful researcher – the one who receives the biggest grants, the best career positions, the most prestigious prizes, the greatest number of published papers – is the one who generates the most data and the least controversy" (Duesberg 1997, 66–67).

The system also shuns challengers to its orthodoxy. "As AIDS grew in the 1980s into a global, multibillion-dollar juggernaut of diagnostics, drugs, and activist organizations, whose sole target in the fight against AIDS was HIV, condemning Duesberg became part of that crusade" (Farber 2006, 48). Thus, the system for allocating research monies, combined with the financial interests in pharmaceutical therapies, conspire to create an AIDS epistemic community that is unwilling and unable to generate truly relevant hypotheses about AIDS and see the disease for what it is.

Duesberg, widely considered the leader of the AIDS dissident movement, argues that much of the world's obsession with an African AIDS epidemic can be traced back to a single report written in the 1980s by Philippe and Evelyne Krynen, two French charity workers. The Krynens wrote of entire villages abandoned and "a sexually transmitted AIDS epidemic that threatened to depopulate" an entire region of Tanzania (Duesberg 1997, 291). The couple left their jobs to train as tropical medicine nurses, and returned to Tanzania in 1993 to found the Partage Tanzanie, "the first and largest AIDS organizations for children in Tanzania" (Hodgkinson 1993). The media latched onto this report and its dramatic imagery, thus giving birth to the African AIDS epidemic.

What the media failed to notice, Duesberg writes, is that the Krynens later changed their mind.

> The abandoned homes were empty because the occupants had moved to urban areas. Children were called AIDS orphans because it was fashionable. African doctors picked up on this invented epidemic because AIDS came with far more money than other diseases" (Duesberg 1997, 291–292).

A front-page article in the *Sunday Times of London* by Neville Hodgkinson[1] focused on the Krynens and their growing doubts. Entitled "The Plague that Never Was,"

---

1   Many AIDS dissidents consider Hodgkinson a leading and authoritative voice in questioning the mainstream scientific consensus on AIDS. He left the *Sunday Times* in 1994, but has continued to write dissident articles for publications like *Continuum*, *New African*, *Mothering*, and *The Business Online*.

Hodgkinson's article said that the Krynens no longer believed AIDS was sexually transmitted. They did not deny that people had died from a strange wasting disease, but they offered other explanations. Evelyne proclaimed:

> Was it a special booze? Was it an amphetamine or aphrodisiac? It is difficult to give more than hints, but when you listen to the people's descriptions of those first affected, you find they were saying they had been poisoned. If the local people said that, for two or three years before the word AIDS came to the region, why don't we believe them a bit, and look at what could have poisoned them? There is not a trace of evidence for it being sexually transmitted. I will spent a night with an HIV-positive person, if he's handsome enough I'll do it to prove it (Hodgkinson 1993).

Philippe was even more blunt: "There is no AIDS. It is something that has been invented" (Hodgkinson 1993). For AIDS dissidents, this article clearly demonstrated the failings of AIDS-as-infectious-disease model from a first-hand perspective, while also offering some confirmation that bodily toxins may cause AIDS. Instead of relying on science, they claim, the West's racist assumptions about Africa led it to uncritically adopt a biomedical framework to explain this phenomenon without actually conducting any real research.

AIDS dissidents accuse members the mainstream AIDS epistemic community of trying to fit square pegs in round holes. They note that many members of the community are "virus hunters" who made their names in discovering, combating, and, in some cases, eradicating, viral diseases like smallpox. Because of their training in virology and microbiology, Duesberg argues, community members consider those methodologies the only useful ones. This, he asserts, is their greatest flaw. Instead of trying to find the best solution to the problem, the virus hunters try to make the problem fit the techniques with which they are already comfortable. They bring their existing mental frameworks about disease with them, trying to make these frameworks fit a fundamentally different disease. Duesberg chastises the AIDS epistemic community, alleging:

> The transition from small to big to megascience has created an establishment of skilled technicians but mediocre scientists, who have abandoned real scientific interpretation and who even equate their experiments with science itself. They pride themselves on molding data to fit popular scientific belief, or perhaps in adding nonthreatening discoveries. But when someone strays outside accepted boundaries to ask questions of a more fundamental nature, the majority of researchers close ranks to protect their consensus beliefs" (Duesberg 1997, 67).

This counter-epistemic community believes itself to be the last bastion of scientific integrity. To illustrate his point, Duesberg tells the story of SMON, an illness that spread rapidly throughout Japan in the 1950s and 1960s (Duesberg 1997, 11–27). Most research on the disease initially centered on trying to find a bacterial or viral agent, "ignoring strong evidence to the contrary" (Duesberg 1997, 11), because the lead researchers came from that background. After 15 years of fruitless searches, ineffective public health measures to combat its spread, and a mounting number of lawsuits, researchers came to the conclusion that SMON was not a new disease; it was merely a series of side effects to two then-popular drugs prescribed to treat diarrhea. Duesberg uses the SMON experience to demonstrate how scientific consensus within a research community can inhibit exploring all possible causes of a disease. He sees the same situation occurring today in AIDS research.

Mainstream science initially avoided engaging the AIDS dissidents, hoping they would disappear. Instead, the dissidents took this as proof that mainstream AIDS scientists could not refute their claims (Epstein 1996, 109). As Duesberg's theories continued to spread throughout alternative and mainstream media sources, mainstream science's efforts to ignore the dissidents largely proved futile. *Science* decided to critically examine the arguments of both the proponents and opponents of the HIV/AIDS hypothesis, concluding:

> Although the Berkeley virologist [Duesberg] raises some provocative questions, few researchers find his basic contention that HIV is not the cause of AIDS persuasive. Mainstream AIDS researchers argue that Duesberg's arguments are constructed by selective reading of the scientific literature, dismissing evidence that contradicts his theses, requiring impossibly definitive proof, and dismissing outright studies marked by inconsequential weaknesses (Cohen 1994, 1642).

The article in *Science* failed to persuade the dissidents. Instead, they took it as further proof that the mainstream AIDS epistemic community was running scared and trying to stifle honest scientific debate.

Members of the AIDS Counter-epistemic Community

Epistemic communities have no formal membership procedures; one does not "join" an epistemic community per se. Membership in, or rather allegiance to, an epistemic community depends upon shared causal beliefs. Even without a formal membership process, though, leaders emerge in any epistemic community. These leaders may serve as public spokespeople or be prolific authors. They help manage and advance the debate. For the AIDS counter-epistemic community, these leaders include Peter Duesberg, David Rasnick, Harvey Bialy, the Perth Group, Sam Mhlongo, and Matthias Rath.

Peter Duesberg

Peter Duesberg, perhaps the most prominent AIDS dissident, first generated international attention for his work on the role of retroviruses in cancer. A native of Germany, he received his Ph.D. in chemistry from the University of Frankfurt in 1963. The following year, he joined the University of California at Berkeley's Department of Molecular and Cell Biology in 1964 as a postdoctoral fellow and has been a member of its faculty ever since. Duesberg made a scientific splash by mapping the genetic structure of retroviruses believed to be associated with cancer. He published academic articles on cancer, retroviruses, and oncogenes prolifically, and other researchers cited his work with great frequency. "Between 1975 and 1979, for example, 76 of his publications were cited more than one thousand times" (Epstein 1996, 106). In recognition of his pioneering work on cancer research, he was named California Scientist of the Year for 1971 and received the first annual American Medical Center Oncology Award in 1981, among other honors. In 1986, Duesberg was elected to the National Academy of Sciences (NAS). Members of this most prestigious group of scientists are chosen based on recognition of previous path-breaking discoveries. Election to NAS demonstrates not just the importance and validity of a scientist's work, but also the recognition by science's elite of that work. It is a tremendous vote of confidence. That same year, Duesberg received an Outstanding Investigator Award (OIA) from the National Institutes of Health. The OIA is a special award that recognizes the importance of a scientist's work and its ability to contribute to the national health. Though many considered Duesberg a maverick by the mid-1980s for his dissension from the dominant cancer theories, his fellow scientists held his work in high regard (Epstein 1996, 106).

Duesberg entered the HIV/AIDS debate in March 1987 with an article in *Cancer Research* about retroviruses and cancer. The article attacked the growing consensus that retroviruses were causal agents for various types of cancer because many of these retroviruses could be found in healthy subjects. Toward the end of the article, Duesberg turned his attention to HIV, the most prominent retrovirus in biomedical research. He expressed doubts about the links between HIV and AIDS, noting many of the same objections he had earlier raised about the retrovirus-cancer link (Bialy 2004, 58–61; Epstein 1996, 108). Duesberg essentially argued that HIV was a harmless passenger virus unfairly blamed for causing AIDS by overzealous, virus-obsessed researchers desperate to increase their finding and demonstrate the applicability and relevance of their lab techniques. Duesberg had not actually conducted any research on HIV or AIDS; he simply extrapolated his earlier arguments about retroviruses and cancer and applied them to this case. This article made prominent the ideas of the AIDS dissidents and offered the first salvo in the battle between mainstream AIDS researchers and the dissidents.

With the publication of his 1987 article and his subsequent publications challenging the links between HIV and AIDS, Duesberg found himself at the center of a scientific storm. He battled journal editors to get his work published, and alleged that editors turned his articles down because they were too beholden to the National Institutes of Health (NIH) and National Institutes of Allergy and Infectious Diseases (NIAID), which support the HIV-causes-AIDS hypothesis. He blamed the loss of his Outstanding Investigator Award in 1992 on political forces that wanted to stifle him. He writes on his website, "Prof[essor] Duesberg's findings have been a thorn in the side of the medical establishment and drug companies since 1987. Instead of engaging in scientific debate, however, the only response has been to cut-off funding to further test Professor Duesberg's hypothesis."

Nevertheless, Duesberg has managed to remain prominent within the AIDS counter-epistemic community. Regnery published his tome, *Inventing the AIDS Virus*, in 1997, which laid out his arguments in one volume. Since then, he has published numerous articles that aim to offer scientific proof of the lack of a connection between HIV and AIDS. In 2000, Mbeki named Duesberg to his Presidential AIDS Advisory Panel.

As of December 2006, Duesberg remains a professor in the Department of Molecular and Cell Biology at Berkeley.

David Rasnick

Like Duesberg, David Rasnick has a scientific background and uses that training to critique the HIV/AIDS hypothesis. Rasnick received a Ph.D in chemistry in 1978 from Georgia Tech. After receiving his degree, he worked for pharmaceutical companies for nearly 20 years developing drugs to treat cancer, emphysema, arthritis, and parasitic infections. In 1996, Rasnick joined Duesberg's lab in the Department of Molecular and Cell Biology at the University of California at Berkeley as a visiting researcher.[2] During Rasnick's decade-long tenure at Berkeley, the pair collaborated on numerous articles challenging the dominant paradigms on both AIDS and cancer.

Rasnick draws on his experience in the pharmaceutical industry as the basis of his criticism of the HIV/AIDS hypothesis. His work for drug companies included designing protease inhibitors, a group of drugs which blocks a virus from making copies of itself and therefore unable to infect new cells. Protease inhibitors are the foundation of contemporary AIDS treatment. Rasnick does not doubt that protease inhibitors block HIV from replicating itself, but he claims that it is irrelevant because HIV has no connection to AIDS (Rasnick 1996). Instead, these drugs have toxic side effects that poison the body and cause the very symptoms they purportedly cure.

Rasnick blames the influence of money for corrupting the research process. The drug companies have an interest in selling their products and expanding their markets, and ARVs are an especially lucrative market because of their high cost. Scientists, he claims, are largely unwilling to challenge the status quo because they are too dependent upon the government for their research grants (Mahoney n.d.).

Rasnick himself has achieved a great deal of prominence and visibility within the AIDS counter-epistemic community. Bialy cites Rasnick for helping resuscitate Duesberg's research and ensuring that his ideas remained in the scientific debate about AIDS (Bialy 2004, 180–181). He served as the president of the International Coalition for Medical Justice, an organization that campaigns for "the right to make medical decisions without government interference" (Regush 1999). He is also past president of the Group for the Scientific Reappraisal of the HIV/AIDS Hypothesis, commonly known as Rethinking AIDS, and continues to serve on its board of directors. When Mbeki first contacted someone about his concerns and doubts about the efficacy of AZT, he turned to Rasnick. Rasnick served on South Africa's Presidential AIDS Advisory Panel.

As of December 2006, Rasnick is a senior researcher for the Dr. Rath Foundation in Cape Town, South Africa.

---

2   Questions exist over the exact nature of Rasnick's affiliation with Berekely. TAC's newsletter reprinted a letter Richard Harland, Professor and Chair of the Department of Cell and Molecular Biology, sent to Rasnick, informing him that he could not claim a University of California at Berkeley affiliation. The undated letter does not directly address whether Rasnick ever had such an appointment in any capacity, but it does indicate that Harland warned Rasnick of this impropriety as early as February 2003 (Treatment Action Campaign 2006a).

Harvey Bialy

Harvey Bialy received a Ph.D. in molecular biology in 1970 from the University of California at Berkeley. After teaching at institutions throughout the United States and Africa, Bialy served as the research editor of *Nature/Biotechnology* from 1984 to 1996. He subsequently assumed the role of editor-at-large from 1996 to 2000. In the late 1980s, Bialy invited Duesberg to publish a summary of his arguments about HIV and AIDS in his *Cancer Research* article in *Bio/Technology* (as *Nature/ Biotechnology* was then known). Epstein cites Duesberg's article in Bialy's journal as one of the two important publications that brought Duesberg and AIDS dissidence to the mainstream media's attention (Epstein 1996, 112). Though the *Cancer Research* article provoked a controversy after its publication, Duesberg's article in Bialy's journal reached a far wider audience and brought the controversy to widespread media attention. Bialy remains a prolific author on behalf of the AIDS counter-epistemic community to this day.

Bialy claims that HIV could not cause AIDS. In one interview, he stated: "HIV is an ordinary retrovirus. There is nothing about this virus that is unique ... There's no way it can do all these elaborate things they say it does" (Farber 1992).

He also doubts that Africa is in the midst of an AIDS epidemic. He argues, along with members of the Perth Group, that positive HIV tests in Africa are simply the result of parasitic infections endemic to the continent. These false positives, according to Bialy demonstrate not only the flaws within the tests themselves, but also the entire scientific enterprise underlying their use.

Bialy is a scholar in residence at the Institute of Biotechnology at the National Autonomous University of Mexico in Curenavaca and was one of the original founders of Rethinking AIDS. He served on Mbeki's Presidential AIDS Advisory Panel.

The Perth Group

The Perth Group is a cohort of scholars and researchers based at the University of Western Australia's Royal Perth Hospital that first formed in 1981. While the composition of the Perth Group has changed over the years, three people have remained at its core: biophysicist Eleni Papadopulos-Eleopulos, emergency physician Valendar F. Turner, and pathologist John Papadimitriou.[3] Members of the Perth Group assert that the mainstream AIDS epistemic community has failed to prove HIV causes AIDS or even that a unique retrovirus called HIV exists. They see

---

3   The nature of the Perth Group's relationship with the University of Western Australia and the scientific credentials of its members is disputed. Turner received his M.D. from the University of Sydney in 1969, but the nature of Papadopulos-Eleopulos and Papadimitrou's degrees is more ambiguous. An Australian newspaper reports that Papadopulos-Eleopulos holds only a Bachelor of Science degree and works as a medical technician, not as a faculty member, at Royal Perth Hospital. Hospital officials stress that she does not work with AIDS patients or conduct HIV research, and that the hospital does not share the Perth Group's beliefs (Roberts 2006).

no evidence for viral transmission of AIDS, believing instead that the disease will remain confined to the originally identified risk groups. They blame exposure to oxidants for causing AIDS.

The members of the Perth Group are prolific writers for both the academic and popular presses. They also maintain a website where they make their research publicly available, provide links to their various media and public appearances, and respond to criticisms from other scientists.

Two members of the Perth Group, Eleni Papadopulos-Eleopulos and Valendar Turner, served on Mbeki's Presidential AIDS Advisory Panel.

Sam Mhlongo

Sam Mhlongo received his medical training at the University of London and practiced cardiology in the United Kingdom for 30 years. In 1998, he returned to South Africa and is now chief specialist and chief family practitioner in the Department of Family Medicine and Primary Health Care at the Medical University of South Africa (MEDUNSA), part of the University of Limpopo near Pretoria. Mhlongo's role within the AIDS counter-epistemic community and its functioning in South Africa is unique, as he is one of its few prominent South African members.

According to Mhlongo, the illnesses associated with AIDS – fever, weight loss, diahhrea, tuberculosis – have long plagued Africa. Their presence in South Africa today is not indicative of a new viral disease. Such common illnesses are lumped together because the pharmaceutical companies can sell their expensive drugs to treat a non-existent disease and rob Africa of its already meager resources.

Mhlongo does not dispute the high rates of tuberculosis, fever, weight loss, and other AIDS-defining illnesses, but he disputes the notion that they can be traced to HIV. Instead, these illnesses are spread through poor sanitation, malnutrition, poverty, and substandard living conditions. If the government would focus on poverty alleviation, he argues, then they would disappear. What we call AIDS is better thought of as the manifestation of 50 years of apartheid, chronic underdevelopment, and societal breakdown.

Mhlongo served on the Presidential AIDS Advisory Panel, claims to be its chair, and argues that the panel's work is still ongoing.

Matthias Rath

One of the newest prominent AIDS dissidents is Matthias Rath, a German physician and head of the Dr. Rath Foundation.[4] Rath calls himself the founder of cellular medicine, "the systematic introduction into clinical medicine of the biochemical knowledge of the role of micronutrients as biocatalysts in a multitude of metabolic reactions at the cellular level" (Dr. Rath Foundation n.d.). He links a deficiency of micronutrients to health maladies like cancer, high blood pressure, heart failure, and

---

4   Rath's website notes that he studied medicine in Germany, but it does not list which medical school he attended. After graduation, though, he worked at the University Clinic in Hamburg and at the German Heart Institute in Berlin.

AIDS. In line with other AIDS dissidents, he argues that ARVs are toxic. Instead, he promotes vitamins as the way to cure all sorts of illnesses – including AIDS.

In 1987, Rath claimed to discover a link between vitamin C deficiency and a new risk factor for heart disease. This research brought him to the attention of Linus Pauling, the two-time Nobel laureate who studied the links between vitamin C deficiency and cancer and heart disease. Pauling had developed a reputation for being a scientific maverick by this time, and he explicitly connected his scientific research with his political activism. He invited Rath to join him at his Linus Pauling Institute in Palo Alto, CA. Rath accepted, and became the Institute's Director of Cardiovascular Research in 1990. He sees his work as a continuation of Pauling's work linking science and social justice. It "follow[s] in the spirit of Nobel Peace prizewinners like Linus Pauling, Albert Schweitzer, Martin Luther King Jr. and Nelson Mandela" (Dr. Rath Foundation n.d.).

Before he started working on AIDS issues in South Africa, Rath became known around the world for his full-page advertisements in major international papers like the *New York Times* and *International Herald Tribune*. In these ads, he advocated for natural treatments for many common afflictions and promoted the role of micronutrients in curing disease. He also called for international peace and a stop to the war in Iraq with these ads. He continues to use full-page ads in major international and South African newspapers to promote his theories about AIDS and vitamins and to challenge the motivations of international pharmaceutical companies.

Rath had no role on Mbeki's Presidential AIDS Advisory Panel, but he has become quite prominent in South Africa since his arrival in 2004. He has conducted many studies, without government permission, on the role of nutrition and vitamins in treating AIDS. He has also entered into public feuds with the Treatment Action Campaign, charging the group with being a front for international pharmaceutical companies.

Credentials and Expertise

Members of an epistemic community are recognized for their technical and scientific expertise. This is also true for members of a counter-epistemic community. Their credibility is established through their credentials. These leaders cannot easily be dismissed as crackpots. They often have advanced degrees from prominent research universities. They hold appointments in academic institutions and have, in many cases, published important articles on non-AIDS-related scientific topics. Duesberg and Rasnick have both held research posts at one of the Unites States' premier research universities. Bialy edited a scientific journal, putting himself in the thick of the preferred means for communicating scientific discoveries. The Perth Group works at a major teaching hospital. Mhlongo holds an important position at South Africa's major medical university and was an exile for many years. Rath worked with a Nobel laureate. These achievements and prominent positions are important because they can engage members of the mainstream AIDS epistemic community in the same language and on the same level.

Because members of the AIDS counter-epistemic community have many of the "right" scientific credentials, they cannot be dismissed as easily. They do not fall in the same category as the AIDS conspiracy theorists who blame the disease on biological warfare programs led by Henry Kissinger and Nelson Rockefeller, tainted polio vaccinations given in Third World countries in the late 1960s and early 1970s, or population control efforts targeted at "undesirable" groups. The conspiracy theorists receive little attention because they rarely have any scientific or academic credentials, publish in academic journals, or engage in professional scientific meetings. In short, they are dismissed because they do not follow the rules for establishing credibility and expertise, and this makes them easy to dismiss as uninformed.

Members of the AIDS counter-epistemic community, on the other hand, have followed the rules. They have demonstrated their knowledge, credibility, and expertise in a variety of scientific areas, and they go through and understand the scientific socialization process. They have established their scientific credibility and knowledge in a number of realms. They can speak the same language as the mainstream AIDS epistemic community, even though they do not agree with that community. They can come to the scientific table and argue with the scientific mainstream on its own terms, and that gives them far more credibility and influence.

Curiously, almost none of the members of the counter-epistemic community of AIDS dissidents are African. Since Mbeki justifies much of his questioning through reference to the African Renaissance and finding African solutions to African problems, this seems quite strange. What's important here, though, has less to do with ethnicity and more to do with policy. It is true that most of the AIDS dissidents come from Western countries. Despite that, their suggested policy responses largely echo many of Mbeki's ideas. They want to encourage locally-produced and locally-developed responses. They see the distinctness of Africa's AIDS epidemic and believe in responding to the unique conditions that gave rise to it. They challenge the major (Western) pharmaceutical companies' intentions and argue that African states must break free. These dissidents may not be Africans themselves, but their policy ideas, as discussed below, strongly resonate with finding locally-appropriate solutions to the local manifestations of the problem.

AIDS Dissidents in Action

The story about Mbeki's embrace of AIDS dissidents usually goes like this. Mbeki reputedly enjoys spending his time browsing the Internet for information. In the late 1990s, as his government was being pressed to provide AZT to HIV-pregnant women, he went online to find more information about the drug and its usefulness. During these online ventures, he came across websites devoted to the work of prominent AIDS dissidents like Duesberg and Rasnick. These websites strenuously argued that AZT and other anti-AIDS drugs do more harm than good, and that they actually cause the maladies that they are supposed to treat. They also claimed that Glaxo Wellcome, the maker of AZT, was party to a number of lawsuits in the United States, the United Kingdom, and South Africa for producing a harmful drug. Glaxo Wellcome denied that anyone was suing them over AZT, and argued that their drug had been proven safe and effective by national monitoring bodies. Nevertheless, Mbeki highlighted the dissidents' arguments against AZT when announcing in Parliament in 1999 that "it would be irresponsible not to heed the dire warnings which medical researchers have been making" (cited in Cherry 1999, 3; *Economist* 1999, 46).

Around the same time, an unknown Health Ministry official gave Mbeki a copy of *Debating AZT*, a book by AIDS dissident Anthony Brink[5] which calls AZT poisonous. Soon thereafter, Mbeki contacted Rasnick, and the two began an intense email correspondence about AIDS and the proper responses to the disease (Power 2003, 61–62). Mbeki then encouraged members of Parliament to read "the huge volume of literature on this matter available on the Internet so that all of us can approach this issue from the same base of information" (cited in Van der Vliet 2001, 169). These early investigations led to Mbeki reaching out to the dissidents and asking them to serve on his Presidential AIDS Advisory Panel.

Shock and outrage greeted Mbeki's pronouncements. Political leaders are generally seen as lacking technical scientific knowledge, which leads to their reliance on experts and an epistemic community. "When it comes to science, it seems, politicians are in much the same boat as the rest of us: disqualified from comment by virtue of a lack of relevant expertise" (Epstein 2000, B05). Instead, though, Mbeki positioned himself firmly in the middle of a vigorous debate. Epstein notes that Mbeki's apparent willingness to align himself with AIDS dissidents "was not a comment on an obscure technical debate. This was an intervention into a domain of science where truth matters with a vengeance – where getting it right has consequences that can be measured in billions of dollars and millions of human lives" (Epstein 2000, B05).

As part of his plan to investigate "everything about AIDS," Mbeki appointed a panel, with Cabinet's blessing, of scientists and experts to review the evidence on HIV, AIDS, and treatments in April 2000. The Presidential AIDS Advisory Panel's mission was to answer questions about the accuracy of HIV tests, the impact of poverty and malnutrition on AIDS, the relationship between AIDS and other illnesses like tuberculosis and malaria, and the relationship between HIV and AIDS itself (Presidential AIDS Advisory Panel 2001, 9). The group's final report would then "be used to inform and advise the government as to the most appropriate course of action to follow in dealing with AIDS" (Presidential AIDS Advisory Panel 2001, 9). Mbeki quickly sent out invitations. Twenty-five scientists from around the world attended both Panel meetings. An additional seven experts attended only the first meeting, and twenty (five invited by Mbeki, fifteen by the Secretariat organizing the meetings) attended only the second meeting. Eleven scientists who were invited attended neither meeting but participated in the deliberations online (Presidential AIDS Advisory Panel 2001, 10–11).

What made the panel so unique was its composition. Mbeki explicitly included members of the international AIDS control regime's epistemic community and the developing counter-epistemic community. Of the 34 Panel members invited by

---

5   Brink currently serves as a spokesperson for the Dr. Rath Health Foundation in South Africa and is convener and national chairperson of the Treatment Information Group (TIG). TIG is affiliated with the Dr. Rath Health Foundation and tries to counter the influence of the Treatment Action Campaign (TAC).

Mbeki and who attended at least one meeting, between one-third and one-half are considered "AIDS dissidents."[6]

The Presidential AIDS Advisory Panel met in person twice – in Pretoria on 6–7 May 2000, and in Johannesburg on 3–4 July 2000. In addition to the in-person meetings, panelists engaged in vigorous online debates through a secure Internet facility between 17 May and 28 June 2000. Distinct camps quickly emerged, and they vigorously disagreed with each other. The report produced by the Panel testifies to the level of acrimony among participants. For instance, the Panel debated whether HIV causes AIDS. The Panel's final report described these discussions in part:

> The opponents of the HIV/AIDS hypothesis described the assertion of AIDS as an infectious, viral, and transmittable syndrome as based on a set of beliefs and myths and not on scientific facts. They argued strenuously to refute the HIV/AIDS hypothesis and posted numerous references on the Internet site to support their stance ... Despite over 700,000 patients in the USA being treated, there is no example of doctors and researchers having contracted AIDS from exposure to HIV-positive patients, claimed Dr. [Peter] Duesberg. Dr. [Helene] Gayle, who stated that that she would be happy to provide information on the fact that there has been transmission to healthcare workers in both the US as well as in other continents, refuted this contention (Presidential AIDS Advisory Panel 2001, 21, 23).

This level and tone of debate dominated many of the discussions on nearly every issue. On most issues, panelists could not agree on a single set of policy recommendations. Panelists did agree on the need to collect more and better data on AIDS and the usefulness of a standardized definition of AIDS to be used across the country. Beyond that, though, panelists found little common ground. Proponents of the mainstream HIV/AIDS science would offer one set of policies, and AIDS dissidents would offer another (Presidential AIDS Advisory Panel 2001, Ch. 8). In addition to their policy proposals, the AIDS dissidents also suggested a number of research projects. These proposals addressed whether HIV tests are accurate in South Africa, whether HIV attacks CD4 cells, whether HIV and AIDS statistics in Africa are reliable and robust, and whether ARVs cause more harm than good (Presidential AIDS Advisory Panel 2001, Ch. 9). The research recommendations suggest that there may be differences in how HIV operates and the efficacy of HIV tests between the South African and American contexts. They assume that the scientific knowledge about AIDS from other contexts cannot necessarily be applied to South Africa, and that local tests must occur to test for this. Interestingly, research on the efficacy and accuracy of HIV tests is the one project conducted so far – and the results found no basis for assuming that HIV tests are any less reliable in South Africa than anywhere else (Cherry 2005).

---

6   This number reflects those scientists and experts listed on the Virus Myth (www. virusmyth.net) and Health Education AIDS Liaison-Toronto (www.healtoronto.com) websites as challengers of the international AIDS orthodoxy. Therefore, the number should be used not as an authoritative figure, but rather as illustrative of the deep divide on the panel. Interestingly, seven of the nine board members of the Group for the Scientific Reappraisal of the HIV/AIDS Hypothesis list the South Africa's Presidential AIDS Advisory Panel as one of their professional affiliations.

The results of the other experiments are largely unknown, since it is unclear who is in charge of the advisory panel or whether it even still exists. In 2004, the dissident members of the panel claimed that the committee would be reconvened sometime during 2004 or 2005, but many other members – the mainstream members – believed the group had been disbanded. The government itself appears unable to solve the question itself. When a reporter asked to whom the panel reported, Mhlongo, the self-described chair of the panel, reported that he was uncertain because their liaison in the Ministry of Health had moved to the Ministry of Foreign Affairs after the 2004 elections. President Mbeki's office referred the matter of the panel's existence to then-Deputy President Jacob Zuma, who chaired the National AIDS Council. Zuma referred the matter to Ministry of Government Communication and Information Systems, who referred the matter back to the Ministry of Health (Maclennan 2004).

Despite this uncertainty, the AIDS dissidents clearly still consider themselves an epistemic community. They see themselves as having a significant impact on the South African government's AIDS policies – even after Mbeki has somewhat distanced himself from them by asking dissidents to stop using his name in reference to their views (Makhanya 2002). Shortly after this announcement, though, Mbeki sent a rambling, 114–page email, largely written by former head of the ANC Youth League Peter Mokaba, to members of his government which "attacked drug companies, antiretrovirals, and the mainstream 'thesis' on HIV" and included a sarcastic monologue about racist stereotypes about African sexualities and AIDS in Africa (Power 2003, 65).

Mbeki's moves to institutionalize a counter-epistemic community on AIDS reflect his critique of the certainty of Western scientific knowledge. Mbeki has rejected accepting the Western scientific discourse on AIDS without subjecting it to stringent tests. His support for Virodene over the objections of the MCC was inspired by his championing of the African Renaissance and his support for African-directed scientific knowledge (Schneider 2002, 151–152). He dismissed the scientific consensus about the safety of AZT by noting, in a letter to HIV-positive Constitutional Court justice Edwin Cameron, that a similar consensus once existed on thalidomide (Power 2003, 62).[7] Mbeki, along with Zimbabwean President Robert Mugabe, has charged that the West's focus on AIDS diverts attention away from far more pressing issues in Africa like the impact of neoliberalism on their states or global inequality (Boone and Batsell 2001, 22). The West's efforts are not seen as attempts to help, but rather as "malevolent attempts to weaken countries already struggling with huge economic and social problems" (Boone and Batsell 2001, 21).

These same themes continue today, with Dr. Matthias Rath being their most prominent advocate. Rejecting antiretrovirals and using vitamins to treat AIDS is tantamount to "breaking the chains of pharmaceutical colonialism" (Dr. Rath Foundation n.d.). The international pharmaceutical companies and their allies,

---

7   Thalidomide was used in the 1950s and 1960s to combat morning sickness and insomnia in pregnant women. However, the drug caused severe birth defects in some 10,000 children in the United States alone and was withdrawn from the market in 1962. In May 2006, the US Food and Drug Administration approved the use of thalidomide, in conjunction with other drugs, to treat skin cancer under very tightly controlled circumstances.

among whom Rath includes the Treatment Action Campaign, is "the worst form of corporate colonialism built on the suffering of millions of people" and perpetrates a "fraud scheme" that has taken "more than the economies of the 40 poorest countries in Africa combined" (Dr. Rath Foundation n.d.). They do this in order to ruin South Africa's economy and destabilize the country's democratic government (Dr. Rath Foundation n.d.). In this way, Rath explicitly links resistance to AZT and challenging the mainstream AIDS science to protecting and saving South African democracy.

Rath set up a South African branch of his foundation in January 2004 and immediately began selling his vitamin treatments. Entering the debate about AIDS policies in South Africa, he also claimed in large newspaper advertisements that international pharmaceutical companies funded the activities of the Treatment Action Campaign. TAC sued for libel, and the courts ordered Rath to stop making this claim (Treatment Action Campaign 2006b). Rath also claims to have scientific proof that his vitamins are better than ARVs for treating AIDS. At a May 2005 press conference, he announced that his study (which had not received official government permission) proved that vitamins kept people healthier. When asked about his unorthodox manner of presenting the results of a scientific study, he claimed that the results were "so encouraging" that he chose not to submit them to peer review (Kapp 2005b, 1910–1911).[8] Rath did not make mention of the two HIV-positive women in Khayelitsha, where he conducted his study, who died within weeks of giving up their ARVs to take Rath's vitamins. Nor did he mention allegations of taking blood from patients without consent or forcing patients to strip to their underwear and have their photos taken (Kapp 2005a, 1837).

Denialism as Policy?

Critics allege that the South African government has responded to the AIDS epidemic by *not* responding to it. Instead of proactively taking steps to address a disease that has infected over 20 percent of its adult population, the government has essentially denied that any such epidemic exists. In response, many have labeled the government's approach toward AIDS callous, if not outright murderous. According to Cameron (2003):

> For South Africa, the significance of AIDS denialism is momentous. It has to be, since our president, President Thabo Mbeki, has publicly countenanced and officially encouraged it. The president's stand has caused predictable confusion and dismay among ordinary South Africans ... But more important still, it has bedeviled and unfortunately continues to bedevil our national response to the disease.

Why would the government take such a step, especially given its ambitious agenda on so many other issues? Many analysts link denialism and racism. "From its origins, the HIV/AIDS epidemic has been bound-up with far more than merely a battle of organisms and biology. Rather, the epidemic has also been associated with

---

8 Ironically, many AIDS dissidents criticize Robert Gallo, the co-discover of HIV, for announcing his discovery at a US government-sponsored press conference before submitting his findings for peer review.

prior cultural understandings of what induces vulnerability to the disease, including a prescribed pathology of certain groups" (Jones 2005, 425). The discourses surrounding AIDS throughout the world have often blamed certain groups for spreading the disease due to their "immoral" or "dirty" practices.

During apartheid's waning days, its defenders often explicitly linked desegregation with the spread of AIDS. They worried that racial mixing would lead to an explosion of AIDS cases among "low risk" (read: White) groups. They also blamed AIDS' emergence in South Africa on the return of ANC members who had been in exile. Unbanning the ANC and other liberation groups, by this logic, would only cause more AIDS cases (Van der Vliet 2004, 50–51). Mbali explicitly correlates government denialism and its reliance on dissident scientists with racist past public health policies and caricatured notions of African sexuality. Government leaders, according to Mbali, developed an obsession with the colonial and late apartheid era discourses on race, sex, and disease in Africa, and this obsession encouraged the new ANC government to deny the extent of the country's AIDS epidemic (2004, 104–105). The arguments of the dissident scientists fit within these discourses on race, and allowed the government to challenge the policy prescriptions of the mainstream international AIDS control regime from a "scientific" standpoint.

Defenders of a denialist stance have often positioned their views as a response to the perceived (and, in some cases, overt) racism they see within the orthodox position on HIV and AIDS. Denialists have often criticized the motivations of international pharmaceutical corporations, arguing that they support the mainstream views on AIDS simply as a way to sell more of their expensive drugs. One ANC official (who was later rumored to have died from AIDS himself) publicly argued that the promotion of antiretroviral drugs was simply an extension of the dehumanization of Africans. Drug companies used lies to sell these drugs, which AIDS dissidents believe actually bring on the symptoms that they supposedly alleviate, because they do not value the lives of Africans. They want to use Africa as a dumping ground for their toxic substances. Further, given the high cost of these drugs, selling them to Africans is simply another way of extracting resources from the continent and keeping it in a subservient, underdeveloped position (Jones 2005, 426). The implication in this position is that drug companies would not subject White populations to similar treatment, but that they feel justified in doing it to Black populations. Left unmentioned in this dissident argument, though, is how to explain the vast number of White AIDS patients who are taking antiretroviral drugs.

Though early AIDS discourses did prominently feature racist explanations, the South African government may be responding to outdated arguments. During the 1990s, the international AIDS control regime increasingly adopted and promoted policies that emphasized respect for human rights as key to combating the epidemic. Policies that placed too much emphasis on risk groups actually worked against encouraging people to seek treatment. Instead, by emphasizing respect, non-discrimination, and the freedom of information, the international community sought to diminish stigma. AIDS was not the problem of particular groups; it was a common problem for humanity. Mbali argues that Mbeki and his allies in the South African government largely missed this discursive shift (2004, 113). They raise valid points about the racism inherent in AIDS discourse and treatment, she posits, but they are essentially fighting a battle that the international community has already moved beyond. Instead of tapping into this new discourse emphasizing human rights and a holistic understanding of the epidemic, which could help them realize their visions of an African Renaissance and spur needed socioeconomic changes, the South African government finds itself trapped in the past.

Calling a policy denialist also comes with its own baggage that may not be fair or accurate. Johnson (2005, 310) notes: "The language of denialism connotes that the political leadership has failed to grasp 'the truth' or 'reality,' and must be educated so as to see this reality ... Is it possible that President Mbeki is responding to a different reality?"

That is, perhaps the issue is one of interpretation rather than implementation. If Mbeki is approaching AIDS from a socioeconomic perspective rather than a biomedical one, then some of his positions make more sense. Addressing AIDS is less about providing ARVs and more about fundamentally restructuring the international economic order. It is a problem of poverty and underdevelopment, not just sick bodies, and needs to be holistically addressed from that perspective. While Mbeki may have this different interpretation, there is no reason to assume that it is an either/or issue. A restructuring of the international economic order may indeed provide greater equity and justice, but that does not mean that those sick bodies here today should be sacrificed for a goal that is perhaps even *more* overwhelming than the AIDS epidemic.

Finally, Sitze argues that the West charges Mbeki and the South African government with denialism as a projection of its own failures to adequately respond to the AIDS pandemic. The international community could take steps to make ARVs more readily available to developing countries. It could provide greater resources to sub-Saharan Africa to combat the epidemic. It could change international institutions to offer countries like South Africa a greater voice. It could do these things, but it does not (Sitze 2004, 780–782). To absolve itself of its guilt and failure to do this, it projects these failures onto South Africa.

These cautionary arguments provide a welcome pause, forcing the rest of the world to examine its own actions and responses. However, that does not fundamentally change the response that the South African government has undertaken. A government cannot simply ignore the transmission of a deadly virus and the loss of a generation because it wants to see greater international justice. Calling for a fair shake in the international community does not mean that a government must actively question the scientific bases of a disease. Problems of affordability and access do not mean that a drug is toxic, that people are not dying of a fatal and incurable disease, or that there is a racist plot to wipe out the black population.

The AIDS counter-epistemic community's arguments fit into these denialist arguments. It allows the South African government to challenge allegations of denying the scope of the problem by arguing that the epidemic itself has been misunderstood. It is not denying anything; instead, it is responding to a different and more appropriate problem – and using more appropriate tools to do so.

Democracy, Liberation, and Racism

The twin forces of history and identity have made the South African government reluctant to embrace public health interventions for AIDS. This fact alone, though, is not necessarily unique to South Africa. The colonial experience is rife with examples of justifying repression in the name of protecting the public's health, and most states have attempted to carve out an independent identity for themselves in the post-colonial era. Why, then, do most states accede to the international AIDS control regime? Why would the South African government use this history and identity to challenge the international AIDS control regime? What makes South Africa unique is its ability to foster a counter-epistemic community to provide policymakers with the necessary tools to challenge the international AIDS control regime. Members of the South African government did not create the counter-epistemic community, but they have given them access to policymakers and influence in the policy process. This counter-epistemic community translates South Africa's historical experience with public health interventions and its attempts to create a new identity into actual policy outcomes. The members of the counter-epistemic community bring these experiences and feelings with them to the table, and they color the recommendations they offer the government. Science and medicine can be politicized. The counter-epistemic community interjects a different set of values and discourses into the debates about how to confront and treat South Africa's AIDS epidemic.

Scientific debate, the dissidents argue, is not only good for science, but is also a sign of a healthy democratic system. AIDS dissidents thus style themselves as the protectors of the democratic system for challenging the authorities and sticking up for the oppressed, using many of the same tropes as anti-apartheid protesters of an earlier era. They draw on the ideas of speaking truth to power, even if that truth may be unpleasant, and emphasizing liberation from hegemonic thought. Duesberg asserts:

> The charge of a scientist if to find the truth, to find the scientific basis of a problem. So you go for it irrespective of the political and moral and ethical consequences …. A scientist is not a politically correct crowd pleaser; he is supposed to find the cause of disease (Guccione 1993).

Rasnick writes:

> Ultimately, the AIDS blunder is not really about AIDS, nor even about health and disease, nor even about science and medicine. The AIDS blunder is about the health of our democracies. A healthy democracy demands that its citizens keep a skeptical, even suspicious, eye on its institutions in order to prevent them from becoming the autonomous, authoritarian regimes they are now" (Rasnick 2001).

The AIDS dissidents and Mbeki frame their discussions in terms of the democratic right to criticize and question official policies. Their activities reflect the highest expression of the freedom of thought that is part and parcel of a democratic system (Robins 2004, 661–662). They democratize science by criticizing the "official" scientific findings and arguing for including alternative viewpoints. Tshabalala-Msimang replied to the Durban Declaration by calling it elitist and arguing, "You can't have a certain exclusive group of people saying this is what we believe about HIV and AIDS" (cited in Van der Vliet 2004, 60). Hoosen Coovadia, the chairperson of the International AIDS Conference in Durban in 2000, pithily replied, "Science is elitist" (cited in Van der Vliet 2004, 60).

Many have wondered why dissident theories retain a certain level of currency among members of the South African government in light of scientific evidence to the contrary. Mainstream AIDS scientists allege that Duesberg and his allies exploit uncertainties about the details regarding how HIV causes AIDS to discredit the HIV/AIDS hypothesis in the press. Cohen noted in 1994: "It isn't difficult to understand why people at high risk of AIDS might be sympathetic to his revisionist views. Not only are there uncertainties about the pathogenesis – the precise way HIV causes disease and death – but also there isn't yet a cure or a vaccine" (Cohen 1994, 1643). The mere existence of uncertainty lends itself to alternative readings of the disease and its etiology.

The AIDS dissidents resonate with both South Africa's history with public health interventions and Mbeki's attempts to forge a new identity for the country. A recurring theme among the dissidents is fighting against the establishment. One popular website devoted to debunking the HIV/AIDS connection invites readers to "find out what the AIDS establishment and media do not want you to know" (VirusMyth). Another urges its readers to question "the validity of the most common assumption about HIV and AIDS" (Alive and Well AIDS Alternatives). A third sees its mission as "challeng[ing] the medical and scientific establishment to explain the many paradoxes within HIV/AIDS theory" (HEAL Toronto). Duesberg often casts himself as a heroic, anti-establishment figure whose genius and expertise, now considered heretical, will later be understood as revolutionary. One journalist asks, "Is he [Duesberg] the heretic the medical establishment claims, or a 20th Century Galileo?" (Guccione 1993). Note how this question introduces an oppositional, confrontational stance. One is either with the "medical establishment," or one sides with a modern Galileo – someone unjustly scorned during his own time but later validated as a paragon of scientific innovation. Epstein writes: "Darwin, Copernicus, Galileo – such names are often invoked to enhance the credibility of anti-establishment figures in science. These comparisons put a premium on challenge and innovation while equating 'normal' science with dogma, superstition, and intellectual stagnation" (Epstein 1996, 152).

In an interview, Rasnick commented:

> Peter Duesberg, I, and the other dissidents … we are very dangerous people. The question is, dangerous to whom? We're certainly not dangerous to HIV-positive people. We're not dangerous to hemophiliacs. We're not dangerous to Africans. But we are lethally dangerous to the HIV establishment. To the people who are on that $8 billion taxpayer gravy train in the USA every year that goes to AIDS. The $1.8 billion that goes to the National Institute of Allergy and Infectious Diseases only for HIV research. We're very dangerous to those folks" (Mahoney n.d.).

This leaves little room for compromise and debate, but it further reinforces the notion of the counter-epistemic community fighting against a stifling, hegemonic epistemic community. Further, the dissident scientists charge that the mainstream scientists, with their emphasis on anti-AIDS drugs, are simply playing into the hands of the very international pharmaceutical companies that want to bleed Africa dry. The pro-drug scientists, the dissidents claim, are really elitists and anti-poor, because they care more about the profits of pharmaceutical companies (Schneider 2002, 152). These themes ring true with Mbeki's views. Mbeki often conjures up images of the revolutionary fighting against the entrenched orthodoxies that denigrate Africa's position in the international community. He also frequently refers to the desires of international pharmaceutical companies to extract profits from South Africa, and Africa as a whole, without providing any real benefit to Africans. The dissidents provide support for Mbeki and celebrate his challenge to the international pharmaceutical companies. In one article, Farber wrote: "Because of his concerns about the toxicity of this [nevirapine] and other antiretroviral drugs, President Thabo Mbeki was pilloried in the international press as pharmaceutical companies and their well-funded 'activist' ambassadors repeated their mantra about 'life-saving drugs'" (Farber 2006, 50).

While challenging the scientific bases of mainstream thinking on HIV and AIDS, Mbeki's AIDS dissident advisors invoke the rhetoric and imagery of participatory democracy – emphasizing the need to involve stakeholders, the local knowledge that gets overlooked by mainstream scientific techniques, and the linkages between scientific participation and democracy. David Rasnick, one of the first scientists with whom Mbeki corresponded, has been the most explicit on these points. In a 2001 address, he focused on the democratic possibilities of science, stating, "By its nature, science is one of the most democratic of human activities … scientific discourse is not limited to privileged individuals, nations, races, or world-views … thus, science is democratic in its freedom of thought and activities" (Rasnick 2001). He explicitly links his work to democratic practices, noting that "the AIDS blunder goes to the very core of our democracies. If we continue to be hoodwinked by techno-babble and institutional blather, and allow ourselves to be manipulated by cheap sentimentality and red ribbons, then freedom and democracy will slip through our fingers" (Rasnick 2001). He sees connections between South Africa's liberation from apartheid and its attempt to liberate itself from mainstream AIDS science. "No sooner had South Africans freed themselves from the tyranny of a minority from within (apartheid) than they were subjected to the tyranny of the majority from without (mainstream AIDS establishment)," he wrote as a part of his contributions to the Presidential AIDS Advisory Panel (Rasnick 2000).

These concerns about the role of scientific knowledge are not necessarily unique to Africa. This is not a simple case of Africa-versus-the West. Most governments are wary of "foreign science" because it raises fundamental issues of state identity (Litfin 1994, 36). Science and state power are inherently related to each other because scientists are also citizens. States want to demonstrate to the world the superiority of their scientists and their abilities to solve problems. They believe that domestic scientists will better safeguard the interests of their fellow citizens, whereas foreigners may have ulterior motives. Litfin writes about the science over the ozone layer in the 1980s and 1990s, but the same lines of thought are present when one considers research on AIDS.

In its efforts to promote its African Renaissance-inspired identity, some have noted a curious irony. While promoting African solutions to African problems, the South African government has turned to Western dissident scientists while ignoring the local scientific community which largely supports the orthodox position.

> Moreover, determined to prove that Africans can run a sophisticated society as Africans and not merely as partners of self-serving whites, liberation movement leaders have been unwilling to defer to claims from others to know better. Ironically, in seeking an 'African solution,' many of them turned to 'dissident' scientific opinion in the United States (Butler 2005, 606).

As mentioned earlier, while most of the AIDS dissidents are not themselves African, their ideas reinforce the idea that there is something unique about AIDS in Africa. They believe that Africa requires its own distinct response to AIDS, and fervently argue for locally-appropriate remedies. The dissidents share Mbeki's belief in finding African solutions to a uniquely African problem.

Influence Waning?

On World AIDS Day 2006, the South African government announced yet-another new program to combat the country's AIDS epidemic. This new program aims to reduce the number of people being infected with HIV by 50 percent over the next five years and provide care to 80 percent of those who need it (*Mail and Guardian* 2006d). This policy proceeds unambiguously from the notions that there is an AIDS epidemic in the country, that HIV causes AIDS, and that ARVs help prolong the lives of HIV-positive persons (McGreal 2006). Commentators within and outside of South Africa have praised the new plan as reinvigorating a stalled response to the AIDS epidemic and demonstrating that the government now appreciates the epidemic's extent.

Much of the praise for the new plan focuses on the two people responsible for its implementation: Deputy President Phumzile Mlambo-Ngcuka and Deputy Health Minister Nozizwe Madlala-Routledge. Mbeki has largely turned AIDS policy to his deputy, as Mandela did with Mbeki himself, and Tshabalala-Msimang has played a less prominent role in policymaking due to her own health problems. As both the leading champions of the AIDS dissidents and the main directors of national AIDS policies, Mbeki and Tshabalala-Msimang held tremendous influence. As long as Mbeki and Tshabalala-Msimang continued to play a dominant role in policymaking, the AIDS dissidents could influence the policy debates.

Neither Mlambo-Ngcuka nor Madlala-Routledge subscribes to the dissident position on AIDS. Mlambo-Ngcuka has taken steps throughout the year to distance herself and the South African government from AIDS dissidents. At a September 2006 meeting with TAC activists, she told Zackie Achmat that the increasing death rates among young adults was "plausibly explained only by an increase in AIDS-related deaths." She continued, "There are difficulties and misunderstandings that we need to deal with to improve the climate for practical joint action" (UNIRIN 2006). Madlala-Routledge has been even more outspoken. In an interview with a

British newspaper, she commented, "What has happened in South Africa, which is sad and tragic … people are confused about treatment … and this has come about because of the confusing messages coming from the very top." Asked later in the interview if that included President Mbeki and Health Minister Tshabalala-Msimang, she said yes. Madlala-Routledge also indicated that she had previously been gagged from speaking publicly about HIV and AIDS because she disagreed with Tshabalala-Msimang (Bevan 2006).

What does this changing of AIDS policy guard mean for the dissidents? It appears likely that their influence will wane. This does not mean that the dissidents will disappear; rather, it means they will no longer have direct access to the most important policymakers on AIDS. Any epistemic community only plays a significant role in policy debates if it has access to the important policymakers. AIDS dissidents influenced South Africa's debate over AIDS not on the basis of their science itself, but because they had champions in the policymaking process who could promote their science. If Mlambo-Ngcuka and Madlala-Routledge do truly disagree with the AIDS dissident position, then it is entirely conceivable that the AIDS dissidents will lose their ability to influence the AIDS policy debate in South Africa.

Does that mean that South African history and identity have changed? Absolutely not. The important thing to keep in mind about a counter-epistemic community's influence (or any epistemic community), though, is that it depends crucially on access to the important policymakers. No access means no influence. Mbeki and Tshabalala-Msimang may not change their minds about the relationship between HIV and AIDS or whether ARVs are toxic, but the fact that they are no longer the dominant players in AIDS policymaking in South Africa changes the parameters of the debate. AIDS dissidents are losing their 'in' in the policy process.

Conclusion

The counter-epistemic community on AIDS in South Africa translates the country's negative history with public health interventions and its desire to create a new, empowered identity into actual policy decisions. The dissident scientists and experts in this counter-epistemic community share causal beliefs, and have access to policymakers who put their views into action. They offer members of the South African government the expertise and opinions necessary to challenge the dominant epistemic community associated with the international AIDS control regime.

If we compare the traditional experience of epistemic communities with the role and work of AIDS dissidents in South Africa, it becomes apparent that the AIDS dissidents do in fact function as a counter-epistemic community. Members of an epistemic community share similar beliefs about the scope of a particular problem, the appropriate policy responses to alleviate that problem, and the future research needs to address the problem. They share a "core set of beliefs about cause-and-effect relationships" (Haas 1989, 385). Because of their shared knowledge and beliefs, the members of an epistemic community gain a significant amount of involvement in policymaking (Haas 1989, 388). These factors are clearly at play in South Africa's AIDS policies. The AIDS dissidents share similar beliefs about AIDS being a political creation, rather than an actual infectious disease. Further, the

AIDS dissidents agree that governments should not endeavor to provide anti-AIDS drugs as a state policy, as that only causes more illness. Through their work on the Presidential AIDS Advisory Panel, the dissidents have agitated for new research projects to demonstrate the validity of their views.

The counter-epistemic community of AIDS dissidents provides a means by which the South African history with public health interventions and the country's attempts to foster a new, African Renaissance-inspired identity can be translated into actual policy outcomes. Members of this counter-epistemic community share causal beliefs and have access to policymakers, just like members of any other epistemic community. The words and beliefs of this counter-epistemic community resonate with South Africa's history and identity.

Chapter 7

Conclusions and Implications

Of all the countries in the world that would seemingly have a rational basis to cooperate with the international community to combat the AIDS epidemic, South Africa would surely be at the top of that list. It is the dominant political and economic player in sub-Saharan Africa and an increasingly important actor on the international diplomatic stage. With apartheid's end in 1994, the world eagerly anticipated South Africa's reintegration into the international community. Its inspiring story of overcoming racial prejudice, its charismatic leadership, and its promise for the future excited many.

Unfortunately, AIDS has hampered its ambitions. The country is burdened with over 20 percent of its adult population infected with HIV and holds the dubious distinction of having the largest number of HIV-positive adults. The country faces the loss of a generation, and its high hopes have been tempered by this infectious disease.

Given the incredible burdens the country faced in light of the AIDS epidemic, we would expect South Africa to embrace the international community to gain assistance. The world stood at the ready to assist South Africa (and other countries), and numerous governmental and nongovernmental organizations had developed a wide array of public health interventions to combat AIDS. These programs all started from the basic premise that HIV causes AIDS. By the 1990s, international scientific opinion had generally coalesced around the HIV-causes-AIDS hypothesis, and AIDS treatment and prevention programs started from this foundation.

Instead, the country that would logically have the most to gain from collaborating with the international community has failed to do so. Rather than embracing the mainstream orthodoxy about HIV and AIDS, the South African government actively challenged this position. It challenged the international experts who promoted the HIV-causes-AIDS hypothesis, publicly doubting the wisdom, knowledge, and policy prescriptions of this mainstream AIDS epistemic community. It turned instead to a group of dissident scientists, widely discredited by the international community, who approached AIDS from a fundamentally different perspective. This counter-epistemic community shared common causal beliefs about AIDS and how best to treat it, but from a fundamentally different perspective than the mainstream AIDS epistemic community. This counter-epistemic community draws on and reinforces South Africa's negative past experiences with public health interventions and its desire to foster an African Renaissance-inspired identity, providing the government with the information and policy suggestions that it needs to challenge the advice of the mainstream international AIDS control regime.

The disjuncture between the South African government's AIDS policies and the international AIDS control regime presents a paradox to many researchers. Popular press accounts accuse Mbeki of essentially playing politics with a deadly disease

(Beinart 2002; *Economist* 2002, 2004; Masland and King 2000; Noah 2003). They focus on Mbeki's personal characteristics to explain why he steadfastly refuses to follow the mandates of the international community. Mbeki is cast as a pariah and an outlier, operating with no basis in fact.

The reality is considerably more complicated. It is not my aim to champion the views of Mbeki and the AIDS dissidents. To understand what is happening between the South African government and the international AIDS control regime, though, one must move beyond such animosities in order to understand why this situation persists. I have argued that one must understand the crucial roles played by history and identity in shaping the South African government's response to the mainstream AIDS epistemic community. Recognizing the existence and importance of the counter-epistemic community gives us the tools necessary to understand why the South African government would challenge the international community on a seemingly settled matter of science. The counter-epistemic community, approaching the issue with fundamentally different causal beliefs and advocating quite different policy responses, translates the South African government's historical and ideational grievances into real-world, observable policy outcomes.

Review of Previous Chapters

The first chapter laid out the basic paradox guiding this research: why would the state with the highest number of HIV-infected persons in the world not only reject the international AIDS control regime, but actively challenge its epistemological bases? After offering basic facts about the scope and severity of the AIDS epidemic in South Africa, I hypothesized that the roots of the problem lie in the existence of a policy-relevant counter-epistemic community. This approach placed particular emphasis on historical experiences and identity issues, showing how these could give rise to such a group. This counter-epistemic community translates the nebulous notions of history and identity into concrete policy outcomes. It also provided some basic information about the scope of the AIDS epidemic in the world, sub-Saharan Africa, and South Africa.

Chapter 2 examined the state of current knowledge about international regimes and epistemic communities. After explaining the basic contours of the main schools of thought, I explained the limitations in using these theories to explain the South African case. Research on epistemic communities fails to pay attention to discourse, takes a largely functionalist view of international cooperation, and contradicts its epistemological heritage by assuming that only one epistemic community will emerge on a given issue.

Chapter 3 developed the concept of the counter-epistemic community. It showed how a focus on issues of history and identity yielded greater explanatory power and leverage than an emphasis on power, interests, or domestic political concerns. It showed this new concept reflects the epistemological heritage of the epistemic communities literature and better explains how science operates within the international political arena.

Chapter 4 examined South Africa's history of public health interventions. Throughout the past 150 years, government officials and outsiders have used public health policies to undermine African wealth and impose racist policies. Under the guise of offering a helping hand, government public health policies have worked against the interests of Africans. Apartheid itself found justification in public health; segregation was necessary, its proponents argued, to keep both Whites and Blacks healthy. The apartheid government chronically underfunded health infrastructure for Africans, and the health programs they did fund often had nefarious motivations behind them. When AIDS first emerged in South Africa, some conservatives seized on it as proof that Africans were less civilized than whites and that apartheid should be maintained. This history made the South African government wary of outside groups coming into the country and warning of a massive calamity unless it implemented certain programs immediately.

Chapter 5 considered the role of Mbeki's attempts to craft a new, African Renaissance-inspired identity on his AIDS policies. He has championed finding African solutions to African problems in a whole host of areas – economic development, political accountability, and AIDS policies. It has also vigorously promoted locally-crafted AIDS treatments, even after they have been found to be ineffective, because these treatments showed the abilities of African science. By the same token, members of the government have publicly chastised the mainstream international AIDS control regime and world leaders for assuming that treatments that worked in the West would automatically work in Africa. The contours of the AIDS epidemic in Africa, government officials have argued, are fundamentally different than those in the West, and therefore South Africa cannot impose Western experience and expect it to work effectively.

Finally, Chapter 6 offered an in-depth examination of the AIDS counter-epistemic community and its ability to influence the South African government. It addresses the origins a nd membership of this group, its beliefs, and its ability to connect with the country's policymakers. Its beliefs about the profit motivations of international pharmaceutical companies, the uniqueness of the epidemic in Africa, and the role of underdevelopment resonate with South Africa's historical experiences and identity commitments. The counter-epistemic community of AIDS dissidents frames the AIDS epidemic in a manner that connects with the government's interpretations.

These chapters, taken together, tell the story of how a seemingly non-political issue like public health is actually imbued with all sorts of political ramifications. These ramifications significantly affect the prospects for international cooperation – even in the face of an overwhelming 'rational' interest in combating an epidemic. This research has also shown how scientists and experts compete with one another to gain influence and leverage among policymakers, and how their successes with different constituencies can have a dramatic impact on a state's response to an emergent issue.

Counter-epistemic Communities and Policy Relevance

Counter-epistemic communities are more than just a theoretical innovation useful for academic study. They also have real world significance for national foreign policies. By understanding the role that counter-epistemic communities can play and how competing epistemic communities frame discussions about a particular issue in fundamentally different ways, policymakers can take steps to avoid getting bogged down in international deadlock and create constructive foreign policies that prove useful to the international community.

Embracing the concept of counter-epistemic communities forces us to examine the underlying causes of foreign policy disagreements among states. Members of the South African government is not simply being intransigent; it is not out to thumb its nose at the rest of the world. Such a strategy would get the government nowhere, and the AIDS epidemic in South Africa would only continue to get worse. At the same time, the international AIDS control regime cannot simply repeat that it knows best and expect the South African government to suddenly embrace its recommendations.

When the conflicts between states are rooted in fundamentally opposed bases of knowledge, finding any sort of common ground is difficult. The two sides cannot even argue *with* each other; they argue *past* each other. In such a case, persuasion and coercion are unlikely to be effective. As the South African case demonstrates, states will reject regimes – even when those regimes are supported by the strongest states and control necessary financial resources.

Unfortunately, knowledge-based theories of international regimes (into which counter-epistemic communities largely fall) have done little work on compliance and persuasion. Most work assumes that changes occur when policymakers come to embody the norms within the international community, usually due to prodding by domestic or non-state actors (Risse et al. 1999). Such internalization of new norms seemed to occur in an almost organic, natural fashion; certain actors "softened up" policymakers, and then the policymakers eventually accepted the norm. Checkel argues that this line of research

> bracket[s] the process of reaching this end state [adopting the norm]. At this late stage, though, compliance was not an issue of choice in any meaningful sense ... The result was a somewhat static portrayal of social interaction, coupled with correlational and structural arguments built on 'as if' assumptions at the level of agents (Checkel 2001, 557).

Instead, Checkel advocates a theory of social learning, whereby actors change their beliefs through argument and principled debates rather than coercion. He lays out five hypotheses about the conditions under which such social learning may occur: when the situation presents a new and uncertain environment; when the persuadee has few prior beliefs on the situation; the persuader is part of an in-group to which the persuadee aspires; when persuasion occurs through deliberative argument and not lecturing; and when the interaction occurs in private, less-politicized environments (Checkel 2001, 562–563).

By the time a counter-epistemic community emerges, it is likely too late for most of Checkel's hypotheses. The existence of a counter-epistemic community shows that strong beliefs have been established, and it is doubtful that members of the counter-epistemic community would want to be a part of the competing epistemic community's in-group. Further, Checkel's hypotheses imply that one side must necessarily change its beliefs. If the two sides are already so entrenched, it will be difficult to get one to simply change its beliefs.

The last two hypotheses, though, suggest a blueprint for constructing foreign policies that bridge the causal beliefs of competing epistemic communities. Principled discussions between leading members of the international AIDS control regime and the South African government are far more likely to result in a positive outcome than perceived lecturing by the regime. This would be facilitated by taking any discussions out of the highly-politicized realm of formal diplomatic negotiations. Not only would such a depoliticized setting increase the chances that principled discussions could occur, but the lower-stakes nature would encourage each side to respect the beliefs of the other because neither side would be seen as being overly aggressive toward the other. Issue ownership is crucial for all sides of the issue (Piot et al. 2004), and principled discussions could engender such ownership.

The question becomes, how would such discussions look in the real world? It is easy to discuss depoliticized, principled discussions in the abstract, but it can be difficult to envision how these discussions would actually take place in a productive manner. Let us consider the 13th International AIDS Conference in Durban in 2000. This conference, the world's largest on the issue, is supposed to be a coming-together of scientists and policymakers to exchange ideas and information in a non-political and objective forum. Instead, in 2000, the conference quickly devolved into accusations of ignorance and racism. The coverage of the controversy over Mbeki's statements in his opening address overwhelmed much of the coverage of the actual conference itself. Participants quickly seized upon Mbeki's expressed doubts about the conventional AIDS wisdom, drawing up international declarations that demonstrated allegiance to the mainstream scientific consensus. In reaction, the South African government dismissed the Durban Declaration, making the battle lines between the two sides stark.

This outcome was not inevitable. Using Checkel's last two hypotheses about social learning, we can envision alternate reactions to Mbeki's 2000 speech in Durban. Private discussions about Mbeki's socioeconomic framing of AIDS could have encouraged the international AIDS control regime to understand the connections between poverty and disease. Many commentators have noted that higher rates of poverty tend to lead to higher rates of disease because of a lack of access to health care, proper nutrition, and sanitation. Poverty also provides an alternate context in which decisions are made. If the choice is between being a sex worker and not being able to afford food, a seemingly irrational decision suddenly becomes much more understandable. Mbeki's comments about poverty being a great killer also call attention to the health problems that have persisted in sub-Saharan Africa. The region lacks the resources to construct an adequate health care infrastructure. This prevents people from receiving treatment for treatable ailments or learning about health promotion strategies. Poverty, then, is one of the world's great killers in a very real way. Private discussions about these realities as understood by the leader of one of the most prominent developing nations could have infused the international regime's response to AIDS (and other diseases, for that matter) with sensitivity to the meanings and contextual elements of South Africa's response to AIDS.

By the same token, private depoliticized conversations could have offered the South African government the opportunity to understand the international AIDS control regime's emphasis on behavioral changes. The regime has largely moved past discussion about AIDS' origins and its chastisement of Africa for 'unleashing' the disease on the world. Its programs to counter the spread of AIDS do not represent an attempt to recolonize the continent or unnecessarily control the actions of others. It is not out to denigrate African knowledge. Instead, the regime reflects the realities that Western states do in fact have greater resources available for scientific research on AIDS, and that the international community has a vested economic and political interest in stemming the spread of this disease.

Circulating a petition with over 5000 signatures that essentially chastise the South African government cannot achieve this. It instead immediately politicizes the issue, further entrenching the government in its position and making it unwilling to come to the table with the international AIDS control regime. In return, the international AIDS control regime looks upon South Africa as a rogue state and ostracizes all South Africans – including those that want and need treatment – because of the government's position. Neither side wins, and the epidemic continues unabated.

I do not intend to paint an overly optimistic picture of international cooperation. Constructivists have long been criticized for being too optimistic and focusing too much on the good (Checkel 1998, 2004; Kowert and Legro 1996; Palan 2000). At first glance, the discussion presented here about social learning and its possible applications to South Africa and the international AIDS control regime seems to justify that negative stereotype of constructivist analyses. It is important, therefore, to reiterate that this is not an easy process, and no one should be under any illusions that the two sides could come to some sort of understanding, let alone even come to sit across the proverbial table from each other. This presentation does not suggest that an easy solution exists.

The insights of social learning do suggest, though, that the situation is not completely hopeless. Avenues do exist that would permit not only the creation of mutually acceptable prevention programming, but also avoid the necessity of assigning blame or ridiculing away the beliefs of one side. Fundamental causal beliefs may not change, but both parties can discover that such divergence does not automatically rule out cooperation. Neither the international AIDS control regime, nor the South African government and its counter-epistemic community of AIDS dissidents, deny that massive health problems plague South Africa and that action must be taken to alleviate these problems as quickly as possible. The discursive frames used by the two sides need not be mutually exclusive; we can coherently believe both that AIDS is a disease of poverty and underdevelopment *and* that behavioral changes are necessary to stem its further spread. This understanding is unlikely to emerge in a highly politicized, public debate.

Conclusion

New issues frequently emerge on the international political agenda. When this occurs, policymakers frequently turn to an epistemic community of recognized experts on a given issue to understand the issue and policy recommendations. Members of the epistemic community share basic causal beliefs about the origins of the problem and present policy suggestions based on those beliefs.

Most analyses have assumed that an epistemic community will provide objective advice based on neutral facts. They also start from the premise that government policymakers will all essentially recognize the same group of experts as *the* experts on a given issue. In reality, science's role in policymaking is not so linear. Despite common perceptions that science provides neutral facts, it is actually a site of much contestation. An epistemic community's experts necessarily frame an issue in a particular manner, which then influences how (or whether) governments implement policy. This framing is incredibly powerful, and reflects historical experiences and identity commitments. Policymakers and scientists debate the meaning of facts, their interpretation, and their implications. Different opinions emerge. Groups disagree about the basic causal facts of certain scientific processes. These debates can lead to incoherent policymaking or intense international disagreements over the appropriateness of a given course of action.

This is where counter-epistemic communities enter the picture. The experts who populate a counter-epistemic community also share basic causal beliefs and offer policy recommendations stemming from these causal beliefs – but they operate from a fundamentally different vantage point from the main epistemic community. They are recognized by certain policymakers for their expertise, though that does not mean that *all* policymakers will recognize their expertise. The counter-epistemic community draws on a country's history and identity to provide what they view as appropriate policy recommendations.

In the case of AIDS, the majority of the international community embraced an epistemic community of experts who believe that HIV causes AIDS. They then fashioned policy responses appropriate for those causal beliefs. Most governments came to rely on the experts in this epistemic community – but not all. The South African government expressed skepticism about the ideas of this epistemic community. Because of its past experiences with public health interventions and its focus on finding African solutions for African problems, it questioned the causal beliefs and policy recommendations of the AIDS epistemic community. It instead turned to a counter-epistemic community of AIDS dissidents who approached the issue from a fundamentally different perspective. They cast doubt on the connections between HIV and AIDS, and they offered radically different policy responses. Their understanding resonated with South Africa's historical experiences and identity commitments. They provided the South African government with the intellectual ammunition it needed to confront and challenge the mainstream international AIDS control regime.

Five million South Africans will die within the next decade from an incurable disease – despite the availability of drug regimens that could prolong their lives, despite the best intentions of the international AIDS control regime to introduce programs to decrease the disease's spread, and despite the seemingly resolved controversy over the cause of AIDS. Is this state of affairs simply the result of an uncaring, callous group of government officials? Why would a state challenge the very international regime dedicated to combating the greatest scourge that state faces? It is too simplistic to say that South Africa simply does not care about AIDS sufferers or that the international community has shown no inclination to involve itself on this issue. There must be something more at work, some other process that leads to the current paradoxical situation.

AIDS is poised to have devastating consequences for countries with high rates of infection. The hard-won gains for many countries are severely threatened. "Education suffers. Development suffers. It could be argued that where HIV has affected the educated and the mobile ... democratic trends are weakened" (Beyrer 1998, 12). Mbeki's quixotic embrace of AIDS dissidents threatens to wash out the gains South Africa has made in numerous areas since the end of apartheid.

AIDS also impacts the international community. It disrupts the political, economic, social, and military relations among states. It requires large amounts of international aid. It necessitates an unprecedented level of international cooperation and collaboration. Because of these immense impacts, it is crucially important that scholars understand the nature of the challenge AIDS poses to the international community. This book has focused on the epidemic's impact on one arena in the international community – the exchange and creation of knowledge. Knowledge is a unique currency in the international community, yet the mechanisms by which it operates are not fully understood. Research on counter-epistemic communities helps illuminate why the creation and sharing of knowledge is so crucially important for understanding how the international community operates.

When the histories of South Africa about Mbeki and democratic governance are written, AIDS will surely be at the forefront – and AIDS dissidents will play a large role in that story. This book offers us insight into why those dissidents play such a role.

Works Cited

Adler, E. (1997), 'Seizing the Middle Ground: Constructivism in World Politics', *European Journal of International Relations* 3, 319–363.

Adler, E. and P. Haas (1992), 'Conclusion: Epistemic Communities, World Order, and the Creation of a Reflective Research Program', *International Organization* 46, 367–390.

Afrobarometer (2004), 'Public Opinion and HIV/AIDS: Facing Up to the Future?' Afrobarometer Briefing Paper No. 12 (April). <http://www.afrobarometer.org> Accessed 12 March 2006.

Agence France-Presse (2000), 'AIDS declaration fit for dustbin: Mbeki's spokesman' (4 July) <http://www.aegis.com/news/afp/2000/AF000712.html>, accessed 27 May 2004.

Altman, D. (1999), 'Globalization, Political Economy, and HIV/AIDS', *Theory and Society* 28, 559–584.

ANC Today (2004), 'Nevirapine, drugs, and African guinea pigs' (17 December) <http://www.anc.org.za/ancdocs/anctoday/2004/at50.htm#art1>, accessed 13 March 2006.

ANC Today. (2006), 'Understanding South Africa's approach to AIDS' (1 September) <http://www.anc.org.za/ancdocs/anctoday/2006/at34.htm#art1>, accessed 1 September 2006.

Andersson, N. and S. Marks (1988), 'Apartheid and Health in the 1980s', *Social Science and Medicine* 27, 667–681.

Arnold, M. (ed.) (1988), *Imperial Medicine and Indigenous Societies* (Manchester: Manchester University Press).

Arts, B. (2000), 'Regimes, Non-State Actors, and the State System: a "Structurational" Regime Model', *European Journal of International Relations* 6, 513–542.

Associated Press (2001), 'AIDS drugs remain unaffordable, says South Africa's health minister' (13 September). <http://www.hivdent.org/publicp/inter/ppinadrs092001.htm>, accessed 28 September 2003.

AVERT (n.d.), 'AIDS Treatment: Targets and Results', <http://www.avert.org/aidstarget.htm>, accessed 10 April 2006.

Bacsktränd, K. (2003), 'Civic Science for Sustainability: Reframing the Role of Experts, Policymakers, and Citizens in Environmental Governance', *Global Environmental Politics* 3, 24–41.

Barber, B. (1984), *Strong Democracy: Participatory Politics for a New Age* (Berkeley: University of California Press).

Barker, A. and B. Peters (1993a), 'Introduction: Science Policy and Government', in A. Barker and B. Peters (eds).

Barker, A. and B. Peters (eds) (1993b), *The Politics of Expert Advice: Creating, Using, and Manipulating Scientific Knowledge for Public Policy* (Pittsburgh: University of Pittsburgh Press).

Barnes, B. (1985), *About Science* (Oxford: Basil Blackwell).

Barnett, T. and A. Whiteside (2002), *AIDS in the Twenty-First Century: Disease and Globalization* (Houndmills, Basingstoke, Hampshire: Palgrave Macmillan).

Behrman, G. (2004), *The Invisible People: How the US Slept Through the Global AIDS Pandemic, the Greatest Humanitarian Catastrophe of Our Time* (New York: Free Press).

Beinart, P. (2002), 'Social Disease', *New Republic* (21 January), 6.

Benatar, S. (2002), 'The HIV/AIDS Pandemic: a Sign of Instability in a Complex Global System', *Journal of Medicine and Philosophy* 27, 163–177.

Bernstein, S. (2001), *The Compromise of Liberal Environmentalism* (New York: Columbia University Press).

Bevan, S. (2006), 'AIDS confusion catches up to Manto and Mbeki', *Independent Online* (11 December). <http://www.int.iol.co.za/index.php?set_id=1&click_id=13&art_id=vn20061210103826675C682909>, accessed 20 December 2006.

Beyrer, C. (1998), *War in the Blood: Sex, Politics, and AIDS in Southeast Asia* (London: Zed Books).

Bialy, H. (2004), *Oncogenes, Aneuploidy, and AIDS: the Scientific Life and Times of Peter H. Duesberg* (Berkeley: North Atlantic Books).

Bohman, J. (1999), 'Democracy as Inquiry, Inquiry as Democratic: Pragmatism, Social Science, and the Cognitive Division of Labor', *American Journal of Political Science* 43, 590–607.

Boone, C. and J. Batsell (2001), 'Politics and AIDS in Africa: Research Agendas in Political Science and International Relations', *Africa Today* 48, 3–35.

Boseley, S. (2005), 'AIDS groups condemn South Africa's 'Dr. Garlic'', *The Guardian (London)* (6 May): 16.

Bosia, M. (2005), '"*Assassin!*" AIDS and Neoliberal Reform in France', *New Political Science* 27, 291–308.

Bridgland, F. (2004), 'Mbeki accused of AIDS "murder"', *Sunday Herald* (18 July). <http://www.sundayherald.com/43479>, accessed 15 October 2004.

Brink, A. (1999), *Debating AZT*. <http://www.aidsinfobbs.org/debate.html>, accessed 12 December 2006.

Broderick, J. (2001), 'Searching for the "New" in South African Foreign Policy?' In Broderick et al. (eds).

Broderick, J., G. Burford, and G. Freer (eds) (2001), *South Africa's Foreign Policy: Dilemmas of a New Democracy* (Houndsmill, Basingstoke, Hampshire: Palgrave Macmillan).

Brown, B. (1987), 'Facing the "Black Peril": the Politics of Population Control in South Africa', *Journal of Southern African Studies* 13, 256–273.

Bull, H. (1977), *The Anarchical Society: A Study of Order in World Politics* (London: Macmillan).

Butler, A. (2003), 'South Africa's Political Futures', *Government and Opposition* 38, 93–112.

Butler, A. (2005), 'South Africa's HIV/AIDS Policy, 1994–2004: How Can It Be Explained?' *African Affairs* 104, 591–614.

Cairns, G. (2005), 'The Rath of Con', *POZ* 114 (July). <http://www.poz.com/ articles/264_1871.shtml>, accessed 13 March 2006.

Caldwell, J., I. Orubulye, and P. Caldwell (1992), 'Underreaction to AIDS in Sub-Saharan Africa', *Social Science and Medicine* 34, 1169–1182.

Cameron, E. (2003), 'The Dead Hand of Denialism.' Speech given at Harvard Law School. 8 April. <http://www.aegis.com/news/dmg/2003/MG030410.html>, accessed 28 February 2006.

Carolan, M. (2006), 'Do You See What I See? Examining the Epistemic Barriers to Sustainable Agriculture', *Rural Sociology* 71, 232–260.

Carolan, M. and M. Bell. (2003), 'In Truth We Trust: Discourse, Phenomenology, and the Social Relations of Knowledge in an Environmental Dispute', *Environmental Values* 12, 225–245.

Carton, B. (2003), 'The Forgotten Compass of Death: Apocalypse Then and Now in the Social History of South Africa', *Journal of World History* 37, 199–218.

Checkel, J. (1998), 'The Constructivist Turn in International Relations Theory', *World Politics* 50, 324–348.

Checkel, J. (2001), 'Why Comply? Social Learning and European Identity Change', *International Organization* 55, 553–588.

Checkel, J. (2004), 'Social Constructivisms in Global and European Politics: a Review Essay', *Review of International Studies* 30, 229–244.

Cherry, M. (1999), 'South Africa Says AIDS Drug "Toxic"', *Nature* 402, 3.

Cherry, M. (2005), Personal communication with author, 4 August.

Chirimuuta, R. and R. Chirimuuta (1989), *AIDS, Africa, and Racism* (London: Free Association Books).

Christy, J. (2000), Testimony before U.S. Senate Committee on Commerce, Science, and Transportation. 17 May. <http://www.gcrio.org/OnLnDoc/pdf/pdf/ christy000517.pdf>, accessed 15 September 2004.

Cohen, J. (1994), 'The Duesberg Phenomenon', *Science* 266, 1642–1649.

Cohen, J. (1996), 'The Changing of the Guard', *Science* 272, 1876–1879.

Cohen, J. (2000), 'AIDS Researchers Decry Mbeki's Views on HIV', *Science* 288, 590.

Cohen, M. (2004), 'George W. Bush and the Environmental Protection Agency: a Midterm Appraisal', *Society and Natural Resources* 17, 69–88.

Coile, Z. (2006), 'Senator fights the tide, calls global warming by humans a hoax', *San Francisco Chronicle* (11 October), A1.

Colgrove, J. (2005), '"Science in a Democracy": the Contested Status of Vaccination in the Progressive Era and the 1920s', *Isis* 96, 167–191.

Conlan, M. (1998), 'Interview: David Rasnick, a Real Scientist', *Zenger's Magazine.* <http://www.virusmyth.net/aids/data/mcinterviewdr.htm>, accessed 16 July 2004.

Copson, R. (2003), 'IB10050: AIDS in Africa', *CRS Issue Brief for Congress.* Washington, DC.

Corrigan, T. (1999), *Mbeki: His Time Has Come – an Introduction to South Africa's New President* (Johannesburg: South African Institute on Race Relations).

Cox, R. (1996), *Approaches to World Order* (Cambridge: Cambridge University Press).

Crewe, M. (1992), *AIDS in South Africa: The Myth and the Reality* (London: Penguin Books).

Crosby, A. (1986), *Ecological Imperialism: The Biological Expansion of Europe, 900–1900* (Cambridge: Cambridge University Press).

Daalder, I. and J. Goldgeier (2006), 'Global NATO', *Foreign Affairs* (September/October), 105–113.

Daley, S. (2000), 'AIDS in South Africa: A president misapprehends a killer', *New York Times* (14 May): 4.

Dawkins, R. (2003), *A Devil's Chaplain* (Boston: Houghton Mifflin).

Democratic Alliance (2004), 'Putting Patients First'. <http://www.da.org.za/da/Site/Eng/Policies/Downloads/Health.asp>, accessed 13 October 2004.

Diamond, J. (1999), *Guns, Germs and Steel* (New York: W.W. Norton).

Dimitrov, R. (2003), 'Knowledge, Power, and Interests in Environmental Regime Formation', *International Studies Quarterly* 47, 123–150.

Dorrington, R., L. Johnson, D. Bradshaw, and T.-J. Daniel (2006), *The Demographic Impact of HIV/AIDS on South Africa: National and Provincial Indicators for 2006* (Cape Town: Centre for Actuarial Research, South African Medical Research Council, and Actuarial Society of South Africa).

Doyal, L. (1981), *The Political Economy of Health* (Boston: South End Press).

Dr. Rath Foundation (n.d.) <http://www.dr-rath-foundation.org.za>, accessed 29 March 2006.

Dr. Rath Health Foundation (2003), '"A people's agenda": an interview with Dr. Matthias Rath, April 2003', <http://www4.dr-rath-foundation.org/pdf-files/interview/interview_english.pdf>, accessed 13 March 2006.

Dr. Rath Health Foundation (2005), 'Stop AIDS genocide by the drug cartel!' <http://www4.dr-rath-foundation.org/open_letters/img-nyt0506/NYT280203FinalC.pdf>, accessed 13 March 2006.

Dr. Rath Foundation (2006), 'High Court ruling exposes TAC!' <http://www.dr-rath-foundation.org.za/thetruthabouttac/pdf-files/High_Court_20060309.pdf>, accessed 13 March 2006.

Dubow, S. (1995), *Scientific Racism in South Africa* (Cambridge: Cambridge University Press).

Dubow, S. (1998), 'Placing "Race" in South African History', in Lamont (ed.).

Duesberg, P. (1992), 'AIDS Acquired by Drug Consumption and Other Noncontagious Risk Factors', *Pharmacology and Therapeutics* 55, 201–277.

Duesberg, P. (1997), *Inventing the AIDS Virus* (New York: Regnery Publishing).

Duesberg, P. (2000), 'The African AIDS Epidemic: New and Contagious, or Old Under a New Name?' Comments to the President's AIDS Advisory Panel, Pretoria, South Africa. 22 June. <http://www.duesberg.com/subject/africa2.html>, accessed 27 May 2004.

Duesberg, P., C. Koehnlein, and D. Rasnick (2003), 'The Chemical Bases of the Various AIDS Epidemics: Recreational Drugs, Anti-Viral Chemotherapy and Malnutrition', *Journal of Bioscience* 28, 383–412.

Duesberg, P. and D. Rasnick (1998), 'The AIDS Dilemma: Drug Diseases Blamed on a Passenger Virus', *Genetica* 104, 85–132.

Dunn, K. (2001), 'MadLib #32: the (Blank) African State: Rethinking the Sovereign State in International Relations Theory', in K. Dunn and T. Shaw (eds).

Dunn, K. (2003), *Imagining the Congo: the International Relations of Identity* (New York: Palgrave Macmillan).

Dunn, K. and T. Shaw (eds) (2001), *Africa's Challenge to International Relations Theory* (Houndsmill, Basingstoke, Hampshire: Palgrave).

Dunton, C. (2003), 'Pixley KaIsaka and the African Renaissance debate', *African Affairs* 102, 555–573.

'Durban Delcaration' (2000), *Nature* 406, 15–16.

Durodie, B. (2003), 'Limitations of Public Dialogue in Science and the Rise of New "Experts"', *Critical Review of International Social and Political Philosophy* 6, 82–92.

Echenberg, M. (2002), 'Pestis Redux: the Initial Years of the Third Bubonic Plague Pandemic, 1894–1901', *Journal of World History* 13, 429–449.

Economist (1999), 'Mbeki's Words of Website Wisdom' (13 November), 46.

Economist (2002), 'In Mandela's Shadow' (14 December), 22–23.

Economist (2004), 'The Party of Apartheid Departs' (14 August), 44.

Economist (2006), 'Beetroot But No Blushes' (26 August), 39.

Elbe, S. (2005), 'AIDS, Security, Biopolitics', *International Relations* 19, 403–420.

Ellis, J. (2002), 'International Regimes and the Legitimacy of Rules: a Discourse-Ethical Approach', *Alternatives* 27, 273–300.

Epstein, H. (2001), 'The Mystery of AIDS in South Africa', in Ferris (ed.).

Epstein, S. (1991), 'Democratic Science? AIDS Activism and the Contested Construction of Knowledge', *Socialist Review* 21, 35–54.

Epstein, S. (1996), *Impure Science: AIDS, Activism, and the Politics of Knowledge* (Berkeley: University of California Press).

Epstein, S. (1997), 'Activism, Drug Regulation, and the Politics of Therapeutic Evaluation in the AIDS Era: a Case Study of ddC and the "Surrogate Markers" Debate', *Social Studies of Science* 27, 691–726.

Epstein, S. (2000), 'Why Science Can't Cope with Mbeki', *Washington Post* (4 June), B05.

Evans, T. and P. Wilson (1992), 'Regime Theory and the English School of International Relations: a Comparison', *Millennium: Journal of International Studies* 21, 329–352.

Ezrahi, Y. (1990), *The Descent of Icarus: Science and the Transformation of Contemporary Democracy* (Cambridge: Harvard University Press).

Farber, C. (1992), 'Fatal Distraction', *Spin* (June). <http://www.virusmyth.net/aids/data/cffatal.htm>, accessed 3 March 2006.

Farber, C. (2006), 'Out of Control: AIDS and the Corruption of Medical Science', *Harper's Magazine* (March), 37–52.

Farmer, P. (2003), *The Uses of Haiti* (Monroe, ME: Common Courage Press).

Farmer, P. (2005), *Pathologies of Power: Health, Human Rights, and the New War on the Poor* (Berkeley: University of California Press).

Fassin, D. (2002), 'Embodied History: Uniqueness and Exemplarity of South African AIDS', *African Journal of AIDS Research* 1, 65–70.

Fassin, D. (2003), 'The Embodiment of Inequality', *EMBO Reports* 4, 34–39.

Fassin, D. and H. Schneider (2003), 'The Politics of AIDS in South Africa: Beyond the Controversies', *British Medical Journal* 326, 495–497.

Feldman, D. (ed.) (1994), *Global AIDS Policy* (Westport, CT: Bergin and Garvey).

Ferris, T. (ed.) (2001), *The Best American Science Writing 2001* (New York: Harper Collins).

Fidler, D. (1998), 'Microbialpolitik: Infectious Diseases and International Relations', *American University International Law Journal* 14, 1–53.

Forrest, D. and B. Streek (2001), 'Mbeki in bizarre AIDS outburst', *Mail and Guardian* (26 October). <http://www.aegis.com/news/DMG/2001/MG011021. html>, accessed 14 March 2006.

Fortin, A. (1989), 'AIDS and the Third World: The Politics of International Discourse', *Alternatives* 14, 195–214.

Fourie, P. (2006), *The Political Management of HIV and AIDS in South Africa: One Burden Too Many?* (New York: Palgrave).

Frank, D. (1995), 'The Social Bases of Environmental Treaty Ratification, 1900–1990', *Sociological Inquiry* 69, 523–550.

Fredland, R. (1998), 'AIDS and Development: an Inverse Correlation?', *Journal of Modern African Studies* 36, 547–568.

Friedland, W. and C. Rosberg (eds) (1964), *African Socialism* (Stanford, CA: Stanford University Press).

Furlong, P. and K. Ball. (1999), 'From Apartheid to Development: Science Policy and the Politics of Race in South Africa', *New Contree* 45, 117–133.

Garrett, L. (1992), 'Panel: AIDS drug Kemron ineffective', *Newsday* (28 April). <http://www.aegis.com/news/newsday/1992/ND920412.html>, accessed 14 March 2006.

Geshekter, C. (1997), 'Reappraising AIDS in Africa: Underdevelopment and Racial Stereotypes', *Reappraising AIDS* (September/October). <http://www.virusmyth. net/aids/data/cgreappraising.htm>, accessed 27 May 2004.

Gilpin, R. (1981), *War and Change in World Politics* (Cambridge: Cambridge University Press).

Glenn, B. (2004), 'God and the Red Umbrella: Risk, Responsibility, and the Politics of Mutual Assistance in America', *Connecticut Insurance Law Journal* 10, 277–307.

Global Fund to Fight AIDS, Tuberculosis, and Malaria (n.d.), <http://www. theglobalfund.org/en>, accessed 30 March 2004.

Gmax.org.za (2004), 'Treatment Action Campaign contender for Nobel Prize' (8 October), <http://www.gmax.co.za/look04/10/08-SAtacachmat.html>, accessed 13 October 2004.

Gough, C., E. Darier, B. de Marchi, S. Funtowicz, R. Grove-White, A. Guimaraes Pereira, S. Shackley, and B. Wynne (2003), 'Context of Citizen Participation', in Kasemir, Jäger, Jaeger, and Gardner (eds).

Gough, C. and S. Shackley (2001), 'The Respectable Politics of Climate Change: the Epistemic Communities and NGOs', *International Affairs* 77, 329–345.

Government of South Africa (2002), 'Statement of Cabinet on HIV/AIDS', <http:// www.polity.org.za/html/govdocs/pr/2002/pr0417c.html?rebookmark=1>, accessed 6 December 2006.

Government of South Africa (2004), 'Key issues', <http://www.gov.za/issues/index. html>, accessed 22 April 2004.

Green, D. (ed.) (2002), *Constructivism and Comparative Politics* (Armonk, NY: M.E. Sharpe).

Green, D. (2002), 'Constructivist Comparative Politics: Foundations and Framework', in Green (ed.).

Guccione, B. (1993), 'AIDS: Words from the Front', *Spin* (September). <www. virusmyth.net/aids/data/bginterview.htm>, accessed 1 June 2004.

Gumede, W. (2005), *Thabo Mbeki and the Battle for the Soul of the ANC* (Cape Town: Zebra Press).

Guthrie, T. and A. Hickey (2004), *Funding the Fight: Budgeting for HIV/AIDS in Developing Countries* (Cape Town: IDASA).

Haas, P. (1989), 'Do Regimes Matter? Epistemic Communities and Mediterranean Pollution Control', *International Organization* 43, 377–403.

Haas, P. (1992), 'Introduction: Epistemic Communities and International Policy Coordination', *International Organization* 46, 1–35.

Haas, P. (2000), 'International Institutions and Social Learning in the Management of Global Environmental Risks', *Policy Studies Journal* 28, 558–575.

Haas, P. (2001), 'Policy Knowledge: Epistemic Communities', in Smelser and Baltes (eds).

Haas, P. (2004), 'When Does Power Listen to Truth? A Constructivist Approach to the Policy Process', *Journal of European Public Policy* 11, 569–592.

Haas, P. and E. Haas (2002), 'Pragmatic Constructivism and the Study of International Institutions', *Millennium: Journal of International Studies* 31, 572–601.

Hall, R. (1999), *National Collective Identity: Social Constructs and International Systems* (New York: Columbia University Press.)

Hall, R. (2003), 'The Discursive Demolition of the Asian Development Model', *International Studies Quarterly* 47, 71–99.

Hamill, J. and D. Lee (2001), 'A Middle Power Paradox? South African Diplomacy in the Post-Apartheid Era', *International Relations* 15, 33–59.

Hasenclever, A., P. Mayer and V. Rittberger (1997), *Theories of International Regimes* (Cambridge: Cambridge University Press).

Hassan, F. (2004), 'Updated First Report on the Implementation of the Operational Plan for Comprehensive HIV/AIDS Care, Management, and Treatment for South Africa (Operational Plan)', July. <http://www.tac.org.za/Documents/ARVRollout/ FinalFirstARVRolloutReport.pdf>, accessed 12 June 2006.

HIV Prevention Trials Network (2005), 'HIVNET012', <http://www.hptn.org/ research_studies/hivnet012.asp>, accessed 12 December 2006.

Hodgkinson, N. (1993), 'The Plague that Never Was', *Sunday Times of London* (3 October). <http://www.virusmyth.net/aids/data/nhplague.htm>, accessed 19 December 2006.

Hopf, T. (1998), 'The Promise of Constructivism in International Relations Theory', *International Security* 23, 171–200.

Howard-Jones, N. (1975), *The Scientific Background of the International Sanitary Conferences, 1851–1938* (Geneva: World Health Organization).

Human Sciences Research Council (2002), *Nelson Mandela/HSRC Study of HIV/AIDS: Household Survey, 2002* (Cape Town: Human Science Research Council).

Hyden, G. and K. Lanegran (1993), 'Mapping the Politics of AIDS: Illustration from East Africa', *Population and Environment* 14, 245–263.

Iliffe, J. (2006), *The African AIDS Epidemic: A History* (Athens: Ohio University Press).

Independent Online (2005), 'Harvard researchers tear into Rath' (10 May), <http://www.iol.co.za/index.php?set_id=1&click_id=13&art_id=qw1115720462822B232>, accessed 22 June 2006.

Ingham, R. (2004), 'UN Envoy Blasts US for "Ideological Agenda" on Abstinence to Combat AIDS', Agence France Presse (15 July). <http://www.aegis.com/news/afp/2004/AF0407E4.html>, accessed 12 March 2005.

Innocenti, N. and J. Reed (2004), 'Facing up to AIDS', *Financial Times (London)* (21 January), 17.

Institute of Medicine (2005), *Review of the HIVNET012 Perinatal HIV Prevention Study* (Washington: National Academies Press).

Irwin, A. and B. Wynne (1996a), 'Introduction', in Irwin and Wynne (eds).

Irwin, A. and B. Wynne (eds) (1996b), *Misunderstanding Science? The Public Reconstruction of Science and Technology* (Cambridge: Cambridge University Press).

Jacoby, H. and D. Reiner (2001), 'Getting Climate Policy on Track after The Hague', *International Affairs* 77, 297–312.

Jasanoff, S. (2004a), 'The Idiom of Co-Production', in Jasanoff (ed.).

Jasanoff, S. (ed.) (2004b), *States of Knowledge: the Co-Production of Science and the Social Order* (London: Routledge).

Jasanoff, S. (2004c), 'What Enquiring Minds *Should* Want to Know', *Studies in the History and Philosophy of Science* 35, 149–157.

Jasanoff, S. (2005), *Designs on Nature: Science and Democracy in Europe and the United States* (Princeton: Princeton University Press).

Jochelson, K. (2001), *The Colour of Disease: Syphilis and Racism in South Africa, 1800–1950* (New York: Palgrave).

Johnson, K. (2005), 'Globalization, Social Policy, and the State: an Analysis of HIV/AIDS in South Africa', *New Political Science* 27, 309–329.

Johnston, R., M. Irwin, and D. Crowe (2001), 'Durban Declaration Rebuttal', <http://www.healtoronto.com/durban>, accessed 14 March 2006.

Johnston, R., M. Irwin, and D. Crowe (n.d.), *NIAID/NIH "Evidence" Rebuttal* <http://www.rethinkaids.info/documents/Specialist%20Literature/NIH%20Rebuttal.pdf>, accessed 13 April 2006.

Jones, P. (2005), '"A Test of Governance": Rights-Based Struggles and the Politics of HIV/AIDS Policy in South Africa', *Political Geography* 24, 419–447.

Kaiser Network (2004), 'ANC criticizes nevirapine trials in US' (20 December). <http://www.kaisernetwork.org>, accessed 3 January 2005.

Kaiser Network (2005), 'HIV/AIDS could reduce life expectancy in South Africa to 46 years, experts say' (published 11 October 2005) <http://www.kaisernetwork.org/daily_reports/rep_index.cfm?DR_ID=33014>, accessed 10 April 2006.

Kapp, C. (2005a), 'SA Health Minister Urged to Stop Vitamin-Peddling Doctor', *Lancet* 366, 1837–1838.

Kapp, C. (2005b), 'Court Case Shines Spotlight on South African AIDS Policy', *Lancet* 365, 1910–1911.

Kasemir, B., C. Jaeger, and J. Jäger (2003), 'Citizen Participation in Sustainability Assessments', in Kasemir, Jäger, Jaeger, and Gardner (eds).

Kasemir, B., J. Jäger, C. Jaeger, and M. Gardner (eds) (2003), *Public Participation in Sustainability Science: a Handbook* (Cambridge: Cambridge University Press).

Katzenstein, P. (ed.) (1996), *The Culture of National Security* (New York: Columbia University Press).

Kauffman, K. and D. Lindauer (ed.) (2004), *AIDS and South Africa: the Social Expression of a Pandemic* (Houndsmill, Basingstoke, Hampshire: Palgrave Macmillan).

Keck, M. and K. Sikkink (1999), 'Transnational Advocacy Networks in National and International Politics', *International Social Science Journal* 51, 89–101.

Keeley, J. and I. Scoones (2003), *Understanding Environmental Policy Processes: Cases from Africa* (London: Earthscan Publications).

Keeton, C. (2006), '"Yes men" undermine SA medical institutions', *Sunday Times* (7 May). <http://www.sundaytimes.co.za/Articles/TarkArticle.aspx?ID=2030798>, accessed 3 July 2006.

Keohane, R. (1984), *After Hegemony: Cooperation and Discord in the World Political Economy* (New York: Columbia University Press).

Kistner, U. (2002), 'Necessity and Sufficiency in the Aetiology of HIV/AIDS: the Science, History, and Politics of the Causal Link', *African Journal of AIDS Research* 1, 51–61.

Klotz, A. (2002), 'Transnational Activism and Global Transformations: the Anti-Apartheid and Abolitionist Experiences', *European Journal of International Relations* 8, 49–76.

Klotz, A. (2004), 'State Identity in South African Foreign Policy', Paper presented at the 45th Annual International Studies Association Convention, Montreal, Quebec.

Knopf, J. (2003), 'The Importance of International Learning', *Review of International Studies* 29, 185–207.

Kotwal, G., J. Kaczmarek, S. Leivers, Y. Ghebremariam, A. Kulkarni, G. Bauer, C. de Beer, W. Preiser, and A. Mohamed (2006), 'Anti-HIV, Anti-Poxvirus, and Anti-SARS Activity of a Nontoxic, Acidic Plant Extract from the *Trifollium* Species Secomet-V/anti-Vac Suggests That It Contains a Novel Broad-Spectrum Antiviral', *Annals of the New York Academy of Sciences* 1056, 293–302.

Kowert, P. and J. Legro (1996), 'Norms, Identity, and Their Limits: a Theoretical Reprise', in Katzenstein (ed.).

Krasner, S. (1983), *International Regimes* (Ithaca: Cornell University Press).

Kratochwil, F. (1989), *Rules, Norms, and Decisions: On the Conditions of Practical and Legal Reasoning in International Relations and Domestic Affairs* (Cambridge: Cambridge University Press).

LaFraniere, S. (2004), 'Minister who balked on AIDS is reappointed', *New York Times* (29 April), 12.

Lamont, W. (ed.) (1998), *Historical Controversies and Historians* (London: UCL Press).

Latour, B. (1987), *Science in Action* (Cambridge: Harvard University Press).

Lee, K. and A. Zwi (1996), 'The Global Political Economy Approach to AIDS: Ideology, Interests, and Implications', *New Political Economy* 1, 355–373.

Legro, J. (1997), 'Which Norms Matter? Revisiting the "Failure" of Internationalism', *International Organization* 51, 31–63.

Leonard, T. (2006), 'Scientists rip S. African AIDS policies', *Washington Post* (6 September), <http://www.washingtonpost.com/wp-dyn/content/article/2006/09/06/AR2006090600586.html>, accessed 6 December 2006.

Lewis, J. (2004), 'Assessing the Demographic and Economic Impact of HIV/AIDS', in Kyle D. Kauffman and David L. Lindauer (eds).

Lidskog, R. and G. Sundqvist (2002), 'The Role of Science in Environmental Regimes: the Case of LRTAP', *European Journal of International Relations* 8, 77–101.

Litfin, K. (1994), *Ozone Discourses: Science and Politics in Global Environmental Cooperation* (New York: Columbia University Press).

Litfin, K. (1995), 'Framing Science: Precautionary Discourse and the Ozone Treaties', *Millennium: Journal of International Studies* 24, 251–277.

Lund, G. (2003), '"Healing the Nation": Medicolonial Discourse and the State of Emergency from Apartheid to Truth and Reconciliation', *Cultural Critique* 54, 88–119.

Maclennan, B. (2004), 'What Has Happened to Thabo's AIDS Panel?' *Independent Online* (9 May). <hhtp://www.iol.co.za>, accessed 20 May 2004.

Mahoney, G. (n.d.), 'An Interview with Dr. David Rasnick', *Pure Water Gazette*. <http://www.purewatergazette.net/rasnickinterview.htm>, accessed 30 March 2006.

Mail and Guardian (2005), 'Mbeki dismisses Rath' (25 March). <http://www.aegis.com/news/dmg/2005/MG050306.html>, accessed 13 March 2006.

Mail and Guardian (2006a), 'UCT acts against academic associated with AIDS tonic' (3 July). <http://www.mg.co.za/articlePage.aspx?articleid=276134&area=/breaking_news/breaking_news__national/#>, accessed 3 July 2006.

Mail and Guardian (2006b), 'Manto says she won't resign' (25 August). <http://www.mg.co.za/articlePage.aspx?articleid=281912&area=/breaking_news/breaking_news__national/>, accessed 1 September 2006.

Mail and Guardian (2006c), 'Manto's AIDS claims "breaking the laws of the country"' (29 August). <http://www.mg.co.za/articlePage.aspx?articleid=282394&area=/breaking_news/breaking_news__national/>, accessed 1 September 2006.

Mail and Guardian (2006d), 'SA unveils ambitious new AIDS plan' (1 December). <http://www.mg.co.za/articlePage.aspx?articleid=292000&area=/breaking_news/breaking_news__national/>, accessed 4 December 2006.

Makgoba, W. (ed.) (1999), *African Renaissance: The New Struggle* (Cape Town: Mafube Publishing).

Makhanya, M. (2002), 'Mbeki shuns AIDS dissidents', *Sunday Times* (21 April). <http://ww4.aegis.org/news/suntimes/2002/ST020407.html>, accessed 13 February 2006.

Mallaby, S. (2005), 'Zimbabwe's enabler', *Washington Post* (4 April), A21.

Mann, C. (2005), *1491: New Revelations of the Americas Before Columbus* (New York: Vintage).

Marks, S. and N. Andersson (1984), 'Epidemics and Social Control in Twentieth-Century South Africa', *Society for the Social History of Medicine Bulletin* 34, 32–34.

Marks, S. and N. Andersson (1987), 'Issues in the Political Economy of Health in Southern Africa', *Journal of Southern African Studies* 13, 177–185.

Masland, T. and P. King (2000), 'Flirting with Strange Ideas', *Newsweek* (17 April), 36.

Mattes, R. (2004), 'Understanding Identity in Africa: a First Cut', Afrobaromter Working Paper No. 38. (Cape Town: IDASA).

Mbali, M. (2004), 'AIDS Discourses and the South African State: Government Denialism and Post-Apartheid AIDS Policy-Making', *Transformation* 54, 104–122.

Mbeki, T. (1997), 'Address by Executive Deputy President Thabo Mbeki to Corporate Council on Africa's "Attracting Capital to Africa" Summit', Chantilly, Virginia (19–22 April).

Mbeki, T. (2000a), 'State of the Nation Address at the Opening of Parliament' (4 February). <http://www.anc.org.za/ancdocs/history/mbeki/2000/tm0204.html>, accessed 31 March 2004.

Mbeki, T. (2000b), 'Speech at the Opening Session of the 13th International AIDS Conference' (9 July). <http://www.anc.org.za/ancdocs/history/mbeki/2000/tm0709.html>, accessed 31 March 2004.

Mbeki, T. (2000c), 'S. African addresses AIDS in Africa' (19 April). <http://www.washingtonpost.com/ac2/wp-dyn?pagename=article&contentId=A40387-2000Apr18&notFound=true>, accessed 11 January 2005.

Mbeki, T. (ed.) (2001), *Africa: Define Yourself* (Cape Town: Tafelberg).

Mbeki, T. (2001a), 'The African Renaissance: Africans defining themselves', Address at the University of Havana, Cuba. 27 March. In Mbeki (ed.).

Mbeki, T. (2001b), 'State of the Nation address of the President of South Africa at the Opening of Parliament' (9 February). <http://www.anc.org.za/ancdocs/history/mbeki/2001/tm0209.html>, accessed 31 March 2004.

Mbeki, T. (2001c), 'Towards an African Renaissance', Address at the 25th meeting of the Association of African Central Bank Governors, Sandton, South Africa (16 August). In Mbeki (ed.).

Mbeki, T. (2002), 'State of the Nation Address to the Joint Sitting of the Houses of Parliament' (8 February). <http://www.anc.org.za/ancdocs/history/mbeki/2002/tm0208.html>, accessed 31 March 2004.

Mbeki, T. (2003), 'State of the Nation Address' (14 February). <http://www.anc.org.za/ancdocs/history/mbeki/2003/tm0214.html>, accessed 31 March 2004.

Mbeki, T. (2004a), 'Building a better Africa', *Washington Post* (10 June), A19.

Mbeki, T. (2004b), 'State of the Nation Address' (6 February). <http://www.anc.org.za/ancdocs/history/mbeki/2004/tm0206.html>, accessed 31 March 2004.

Mbeki, T. (2005), 'State of the Nation Address' (11 February). <http://www.info.gov.za/speeches/2005/05021110501001.htm>, accessed 23 June 2006.

Mbeki, T. (2006), 'State of the Nation Address' (3 February). <http://www.info.gov.
    za/speeches/2006/06020310531001.htm>, accessed 23 June 2006.

McFadden, D. (1995), *International Cooperation and Pandemic Diseases: Regimes
    and the Role of Epistemic Communities in Combating Cholera, Smallpox, and
    AIDS* (Ph.D. dissertation, Claremont Graduate University).

McGreal, C. (2000), 'Friends deserting Mandela's heir: the fire ignited by President
    Mbeki's dismissive views on AIDS is spreading', *Guardian (London)* (23
    September), 19.

McGreal, C. (2006), 'South Africa ends long denial over AIDS crisis', *Guardian
    (London)* (30 November). <http://www.guardian.co.uk/international/story/
    0,,1961143,00.html>, accessed 4 December 2006.

McNeill, W. (1976), *Plagues and Peoples* (Garden City, NY: Anchor Books).

Mearsheimer, J. (1994/95), 'The False Promise of International Institutions',
    International Security 19, 5–49.

Miller, H. and C. Fox. (2001), 'The Epistemic Community', *Administration and
    Society* 32, 668–685.

Milner, H. (1997), *Interests, Institutions, and Information: Domestic Politics and
    International Relations* (Princeton: Princeton University Press).

Miyagawa, M. (2005), 'Integrating Asia Through Free Trade', *Far Eastern Economic
    Review* 168, 45–49.

Mooney, C. (2004), 'Blinded by Science: How "Balanced" Coverage Lets the
    Scientific Fringe Hijack Reality', *Columbia Journalism Review* (Nov/Dec).
    <http://www.cjr.org/issues/2004/6/mooney-science.asp>, accessed 1 June 2005.

Mooney, C. (2005), *The Republican War on Science* (New York: Basic Books).

Moore, B. (1966), *Social Origins of Dictatorship and Democracy: Lord and Peasant
    in the Making of the Modern World* (Boston: Beacon Press).

Muleme, G. (2004), 'Doctors, AIDS activists in Africa worry governments may halt
    drug's use amid concerns about effect on pregnant women', *Associated Press* (16
    December).

Munusamy, R. (2002), '"Stop AIDS nonsense": Mandela tells Mbeki's government
    to halt debates and fight the war', *Sunday Times (Johannesburg)* (17 February).
    <http://www.aegis.com/news/suntimes/2002/ST020208.html>, accessed 15 October
    2004.

Murphy, C. (2001), 'Foreword', in Dunn and Shaw (eds).

Mzala (1988), 'AIDS and the Imperialist Connection', *Sechaba*, 23–27.

National Catholic Reporter (1997), 'S. African murder called a religious act: Derby-
    Lewis planned murder of anti-apartheid Chris Hani' (12 September). <http://
    www.highbeam.com/library/docFree.asp?DOCID=1G1:19804271>, accessed 28
    June 2006.

National Institutes of Allergy and Infectious Diseases/National Institutes of Health
    (2003), *The Evidence That HIV Causes AIDS*. <http://www.niaid.nih.gov/
    factsheets/evidhiv.htm>, accessed 13 April 2006.

Nattrass, N. (2004), *The Moral Economy of AIDS in South Africa* (Cambridge:
    Cambridge University Press).

Nel, P. (1999), 'Foreign Policy Beliefs of South Africans: a First Cut', *Journal of
    Continental African Studies* 17, 123–146.

Noah, B. (2003), 'AIDS and Antiretroviral Drugs in South Africa: Public Health, Politics, and Individual Suffering: a Review of Brian Tilley's "It's My Life"', *Journal of Law, Medicine, and Ethics* 31, 144–148.

Nyerere, J. (1964), 'Ujamaa: the Basis of African Socialism', in Friedland and Rosberg (eds).

Okumu, W. (2002), *The African Renaissance: History, Significance, and Strategy* (Trenton, NJ: Africa World Press).

Oreskes, N. (2004), 'The Scientific Consensus on Climate Change', *Science* 5702, 1686.

Packard, R. (1989), *White Plague, Black Labor: Tuberculosis and the Political Economy of Health and Disease in South Africa* (Berkeley: University of California Press).

Packard, R. and P. Epstein (1991), 'Epidemiologists, Social Scientists, and the Structure of Medical Research on AIDS in Africa', *Social Science and Medicine* 33, 771–783.

Palan, R. (2000), 'A World of Their Making: an Evaluation of the Constructivist Critique of International Relations', *Review of International Studies* 26, 575–598.

Pao, M. (2006), 'Q&A: Access to HIV/AIDS Care in South Africa', National Public Radio, 19 April. <http://www.npr.org/templates/story/story.php?storyId=5349660>, accessed 2 December 2006.

Papadopulos-Eleopulos, E., V. Turner, J. Papadimitrou, and H. Bialy (1995), 'AIDS in Africa: Distinguishing Fact from Fiction', *World Journal of Microbiology and Biotechnology* 11, 135–143.

Peterson, M. (1992), 'Whalers, Cetologists, Environmentalists, and the International Management of Whaling', *International Organization* 46, 147–186.

Phillips, H. (1990), *'Black October': the Impact of the Spanish Influenza Epidemic of 1918 on South Africa* (Pretoria: Government Printer).

Phillips, H. (2004), 'HIV/AIDS in the Context of South Africa's Epidemic History', in Kauffman and Lindauer (eds).

Phillips, N. (2005), 'US Power and the Politics of Economic Governance in the Americas', *Latin American Politics and Society* 47, 1–25.

Piot, P., R. Feachem, J. Lee, and J. Wolfensohn (2004), 'A Global Response to AIDS: Lessons Learned, Next Steps', *Science* 304, 1909–1910.

Pope, J. (2006), 'Mother Nature's little helpers', *Annals of the New York Academy of Sciences Extra.* <http://www.nyas.org/annals/annalsExtra.asp?annalID=31>, accessed 3 July 2006.

Population and Development Review (2000), 'The United Nations on the Demographic Impact of AIDS', Vol. 26, 629–634.

Power, S. (2003), 'The AIDS Rebel', *New Yorker* (19 May), 54–68.

Presidential AIDS Advisory Panel (2001), *A Synthesis of the Deliberations by a Panel of Experts Invited by the President of the Republic of South Africa, the Honourable Thabo Mbeki* (Pretoria: Government Printer).

Pressly, D. (2005), 'Manto "doesn't recall" endorsing Rath', *Mail and Guardian* (5 May). <http://www.mg.co.za/articlePage.aspx?articleid=237103&area=/breaking_news/breaking_news__national/>, accessed 13 March 2006.

Radaelli, C. (1995), 'The Role of Knowledge in the Policy Process', *Journal of European Public Policy* 2, 159–183.

Ranger, T. (1988), 'The Influenza Pandemic in Southern Rhodesia: a Crisis of Comprehension', in Arnold (ed.).

Rasnick, D. (1996), 'Inhibitors of HIV Protease Are Useless Against AIDS Because HIV Doesn't Cause AIDS', *Reappraising AIDS* (August). <http://www.virusmyth. net/aids/data/drinhibit.htm>, accessed 16 July 2004.

Rasnick, D. (2000), 'David Rasnick's Contributions to Mbeki's Expert AIDS Panel', <http://www.healtoronto.com/rasnick_mbeki.html>, accessed 20 April 2006.

Rasnick, D. (2001), 'The AIDS Blunder', *Mail and Guardian* (24 January). <http:// www.virusmyth.net/aids/data/drblunder.htm>, accessed 27 May 2004.

Reader, J. (1999), *Africa: a Biography of the Continent* (New York: Knopf).

Regush, N. (1999), 'No AZT for my baby, please', ABCnews.com (15 September). <http://www.virusmyth.net/aids/data/nrsecop54.htm>, accessed 12 April 2006.

Republic of South Africa (1990), *Debates of Parliament* (Cape Town: Government Printer).

Reuters (2006), 'S. Africa AIDS activists win defamation case' (3 March). <http:// www.alertnet.org/thenews/newsdesk/L03761424.htm>, accessed 13 March 2006.

Risse, T., S. Ropp, and K. Sikkink (eds) (1999), *The Power of Principles: International Human Rights Norms and Domestic Change.* (Cambridge: Cambridge University Press).

Roberts, J. (2006), 'There is no AIDS virus, says HIV-positive accused', *Townsville Bulletin* (26 October). <http://townsvillebulletin.news.com.au/common/story_ page/0,7034,20645649%255E421,00.html>, accessed 19 December 2006.

Robins, S. (2004), '"Long Live, Zackie, Long Live": AIDS Activism, Science, and Citizenship After Apartheid', *Journal of Southern African Studies* 30, 651–672.

Robins, S. (2005), 'AIDS, Science, and Citizenship After Apartheid', in Scoones and Wynne (eds).

Robinson, A. and Z. Robinson (1997), 'Science has spoken: global warming is a myth', *Wall Street Journal* (4 December).

Rosamond, B. (2000), *Theories of European Integration* (Houndmills, Basingstoke, Hampshire: Palgrave).

Rosen, S., J. Vincent, W. MacLeod, M. Fox, D. Thea, and J. Simon (2004), 'The Cost of HIV/AIDS to Businesses in Southern Africa', *AIDS* 18, 317–324.

Rüdig, W. (1993), 'Sources of Technological Controversy: Proximity to or Alienation from Technology?', in Barker and Peters (eds).

Sabatier, R. (1988), *Blaming Others: Prejudice, Race, and Worldwide AIDS* (Philadelphia: New Society Publishers).

Salomon, J. (2000), 'Science, Technology, and Democracy', *Minerva* 38, 33–51.

Schlemmer, L. (2004), 'Whatever Happened to the Opposition?', *Focus* 34 (June), 5–9.

Schmandt, J. (1998), 'Civic Science', *Science Communication* 20, 62–69.

Schneider, A. and H. Ingram (1993), 'Social Construction of Target Populations: Implications for Politics and Policy', *American Political Science Review* 87, 334–347.

Schneider, H. (2002), 'On the Fault-Line: the Politics of AIDS Policy in Contemporary South Africa', *African Studies* 61, 145–167.

Schneider, H. and D. Fassin (2002), 'Denial and Defiance: a Socio-Political Analysis of AIDS in South Africa', *AIDS* 16, S45-S51.

Schneider, H. and J. Stein (2001), 'Implementing AIDS Policy in Post-Apartheid South Africa', *Social Science and Medicine* 52, 723–731.

Schoofs, M. (2000), 'Debating the obvious', *Village Voice* (5 July). <http://www.thebody.com/schoofs/obvious.html>, accessed 15 March 2006.

Scoones, I. and B. Wynne (eds) (2005), *Science and Citizens: Globalization and the Challenge of Engagement* (London: Zed Books).

Seepe, J. and M. Sibanda (2006) 'No AIDS death crisis: Mbeki', *City Press* (26 February).

Shapin, S. (1994), *A Social History of Truth: Civility and Science in Seventeenth-Century England* (Chicago: University of Chicago Press).

Shaw, G. (2002), 'Peter Mokaba', *Guardian Unlimited* (12 July). <http://www.guardian.co.uk/aids/story/0,7369,753812,00.html>, accessed 23 June 2006.

Shilts, R. (1987), *And the Band Played On: Politics, People, and the AIDS Epidemic* (New York: St. Martin's Press).

Shlensky, A. (2006), 'Rath paid R200,000 to MRC for workshops', *Cape Times* (7 June). <http://www.int.iol.co.za/index.php?set_id=1&click_id=125&art_id=vn20060607015709357C273582>, accessed 3 July 2006.

Sidley, P. (2000), 'Mbeki Dismisses "Durban Declaration"', *British Medical Journal* 321, 67.

Silverstein, K. (1997), 'Hello. I'm calling this evening to mislead you', *Mother Jones* (November/December). <http://www.motherjones.com/news/feature/1997/11/silverstein.html>, accessed 5 May 2006.

Sitze, A. (2004), 'Denialism', *South Atlantic Quarterly* 103, 769–811.

Smelser, N. and P. Baltes (eds) (2001), *International Encyclopedia of the Social and Behavioral Sciences* (New York: Elsevier).

Snidal, D. (1985), 'The Limits of Hegemonic Stability Theory', *International Organization* 39, 579–614.

Solomon, J. (2004), 'Research flawed on key AIDS medicine', *Washington Post* (14 December), A14.

Sontag, D. (2004), 'Early tests for U.S. in its global fight on AIDS', *New York Times* (14 July): A1.

South African Department of Health (2004), *National HIV and Syphilis Antenatal Sero-Prevalence Survey in South Africa 2004* (Pretoria: Department of Health). <http://www.doh.gov.za/docs/reports/2004/hiv-syphilis.pdf>, accessed 25 April 2006.

South African Department of Health (2006), *National HIV and Syphilis Antenatal Sero-Prevalence Survey in South Africa 2005* (Pretoria: Department of Health).

South African Press Association (2005), 'MCC to probe Virodene relaunch', *iAfrica* (7 September). <http://iafrica.com/aidswise/news/481982.htm>, accessed 12 December 2006.

Sparks, A. (2003), *Beyond the Miracle: Inside the New South Africa* (Chicago: University of Chicago Press).

Stine, G. (2005), *AIDS Update 2005* (San Francisco: Benjamin Cummings/Pearson Education).

Strand, P., K. Matlose, and A. Strode (2005), *Democratic Governance in a Time of AIDS: Exploring the Impact of the HIV and AIDS Epidemic on the 2004 Electoral Process in South Africa* (Pretoria: IDASA).

Stremlau, J. (1999), 'African Renaissance and International Relations', in Makgoba (ed.).

Swanson, M. (1977), 'The Sanitation Syndrome: Bubonic Plague and Urban Native Policy in the Cape Colony, 1900–1909', *Journal of African History* 18, 387–410.

Swarns, R. (2000), 'Dissent on AIDS by South Africa's president: thoughtfulness or folly?', *New York Times* (8 July), A5.

Terreblanche, C. and J. Battersby (2003), 'Anti-retrovirals do not cure, says Manto', Independent Online, 20 March. < http://www.int.iol.co.za/index.php?sf=2901&set_id=&sf=2901&click_id=13&art_id=vn20030320150316507C744577&set_id=1>, accessed 2 January 2007.

Tesh, S. (1988), *Hidden Arguments: Political Ideology and Disease Prevention Policy* (New Brunswick, NJ: Rutgers University Press).

Thom, A. (2005), 'Eastern Cape struggling to cope with AIDS', *Health-E* (6 December). <http://www.health-e.org.za/news/article.php?uid=20031346>, accessed 3 July 2006.

Thompson, L. (1995), *A History of South Africa* (New Haven: Yale University Press).

Thucydides (1982), *The Peloponnesian War.* T.E. Wick (ed.) (New York: Random House).

Timberg, C. (2005), 'Mandela says AIDS led to death of son', *Washington Post* (7 January), A10.

Tomkins, S. (1994), 'Colonial Administration in British Africa during the Influenza Epidemic of 1918–19', *Canadian Journal of African Studies* 28, 60–83.

Treatment Action Campaign (2006a), *TAC Electronic Newsletter* (9 May). <http://www.tac.org.za/newsletter/2006/ns09_05_2006.html>, accessed 19 December 2006.

Treatment Action Campaign (2006b), 'TAC Wins Court Case against Rath', 3 March. <http://www.tac.org.za>, accessed 4 March 2006.

Treichler, P. (1999), *How to Have Theory in an Epidemic: Cultural Chronicles of AIDS* (Durham: Duke University Press).

Tshabalala-Msimang, M. (2003), 'Cabinet Statement on Comprehensive Treatment Plan for HIV/AIDS' (19 November). <http://www.gov.za/issues/hiv/careplan19nov03.htm>, accessed 31 March 2004.

UNAIDS (2004), *HIV/AIDS, Human Rights, and Law.* <http://www.unaids.org/en/in+focus/hiv_aids_human_rights.asp>, accessed 27 February 2004.

UNAIDS (2006a), 'South Africa', <http://www.unaids.org/en/Regions_Countries/Countries/south_africa.asp>, accessed 18 December 2006.

UNAIDS (2006b), *AIDS Epidemic Update, December 2006* (Geneva: UNAIDS).

UNICEF (2005), 'Zimbabwe's HIV infection rate falls, but much still to be done', 10 October. <http://www.unicef.org/media/media_28660.html>, accessed 2 January 2007.

United Nations Integrated Regional Information Networks (2004c), 'TAC slams government on nevirapine safety claims', 20 December.

United Nations Integrated Regional Information Networks (2006), 'South Africa: Labour urged to demand sacking of health minister', 19 September.

Vale, P. and S. Maseko (1998), 'South Africa and the African Renaissance', *International Affairs* 74, 271–287.

Van der Vliet, V. (1994), 'Apartheid and the Politics of AIDS', in Feldman (ed.).

Van der Vliet, V. (1996), *The Politics of AIDS* (London: Bowerdean Publishing Company).

Van der Vliet, V. (2001), 'AIDS: Losing "the New Struggle"?', *Daedalus* 130, 151–184.

Van Onselen, C. (1972), 'Reaction to Rinderpest in Southern Africa', *Journal of African History* 13, 473–488.

Vaughan, M. (1991), *Curing Their Ills: Colonial Power and African Illness* (Stanford: Stanford University Press).

Ventura, A. (2001), 'Science and Technology: Vital Correlates of Democracy', *Interciencia* 26, 81–84.

Vogel, S. and H. Heyne (1996), 'Rinderpest in South Africa – 100 Years Ago', *Journal of the South African Veterinary Association* 67, 164–170.

Waltz, K. (1979), *Theory of International Politics* (Reading, MA: Addison-Wesley).

Weldes, J. and D. Saco (1996), 'Making State Action Possible: the United States and the Discursive Construction of "the Cuban Problem," 1960–1994', *Millennium* 25, 361–380.

Wendt, A. (1999), *Social Theory of International Politics* (Cambridge: Cambridge University Press).

Whiteside, A. and A. de Waal (2004), '"That's Resources You See!": Political Economy, Ethics, and the HIV/AIDS epidemic', *New Political Economy* 9, 581–594.

Whiteside, A., R. Mattes, S. Willan and R. Manning (2002), 'Examining HIV/AIDS in Southern Africa Through the Eyes of Ordinary Southern Africans', Afrobarometer Working Paper No. 21. <http://www.afrobarometer.org>, accessed 16 October 2005.

Whiteside, A. and C. Sunter (2000), *AIDS: the Challenge for South Africa* (Cape Town: Human and Rousseau).

Willan, S. (2004), 'Briefing: Recent Changes in the South African Government's HIV/AIDS Policy and Its Implementation', *African Affairs* 103, 109–117.

Wilson, B. (2005), 'U.N. urges use of AIDS drug in Africa', *All Things Considered* (6 March). <http://www.npr.org/templates/story/story.php?storyId=4524736&sourceCode=RSS>, accessed 13 March 2006.

Wines, M. (2004), 'South Africa: Minister defends garlic AIDS diet', *New York Times* (10 February). <http://query.nytimes.com/gst/fullpage.html?res=9802E2DB143AF933A25751C0A9629C8B63>, accessed 15 March 2006.

World Health Organization (1983), *Apartheid and Health* (Geneva: World Health Organization).

Wynne, B. (1991), 'Knowledge in Context', *Science, Technology, and Human Values* 16, 111–121.

Wynne, B. (1996), 'Misunderstood Misunderstandings: Social Identities and Public Uptake of Science', in A. Irwin and B. Wynne (eds).

Young, O. (1999), *Governance in World Affairs* (Ithaca: Cornell University Press).

Zaba, B., A. Whiteside, and J. Boerma (2004), 'Demographic and Socioeconomic Impact of AIDS: Taking Stock of the Empirical Evidence', *AIDS* 18, S1–S7.

Zito, A. (2001), 'Epistemic Communities, Collective Entrepreneurship, and European Integration', *Journal of European Public Policy* 8, 585–603.

Zwi, A. and D. Bachmayer (1990), 'HIV and AIDS in South Africa: What is an Appropriate Public Health Response?', *Health Policy and Planning* 5, 316–326.

Index

history 38–9
identity 38–9
learning 28
oversights in 4, 40–41
policymakers 44
politicization 54
trust 38–9
truth 38–9
eugenics 33, 63
negative 63
positive 63

family planning 71–2
forced sterilization 72
feudalism 60
Food and Drug Administration (US) 37

Gallo, Robert 47
Gay Related Immune Deficiency (GRID) 44
Glaxo Wellcome 82–3, 109
Global Fund to Fight AIDS, Tuberculosis, and Malaria 18
contributions from United States 18
Global Program on AIDS 46

Haitians
as AIDS risk group 77
Heckler, Margaret 47
HIV infection rates
Caribbean 6
differences among South African provinces 7
South Africa 1, 6–9
sub-Saharan Africa 6
women 6
worldwide 5–6
HIVNET012 83–4
reaction by AIDS dissidents 84
Hodgkinson, Neville 101–2

identity
AIDS 94
public 93
South Africa 92–5
Incas 60
influenza 65–7
blame for 65–6
drugs 66
germ theory 66–7
inoculation 66
segregation 66–7
Inhofe, James 52

interest groups 53–4
transnational 54
International AIDS Conference (Durban) 20, 88–90, 127–8
Inventing the AIDS Virus 104

Kemron 53, 82fn4
Kenya 54, 62
knowledge
boundaries of 30
co-production with science 30
democratic theory 32
depoliticization 33
"foreign science" 118
networks 30
recognition of expertise 32
social and political processes 31–2
Koch, Robert 65
Koch's postulates 98–9
Krynen, Philippe and Evelyne 101–2
Kyoto Accord 51–2

Mandela, Nelson 10, 11
criticism of Mbeki 22–3
Madlala-Routledge, Nozizwe 12, 119–20
Mankhlana, Parks 82–3, 90, 91
Massasoit 61
Mbeki, Thabo 1, 4–5, 20–25
African Renaissance 78–80, 91–2
Afro-pessimism 92
AIDS dissidents 87, 109–11, 116–19
Brink, Anthony 110
critique of Western scientific knowledge 112
concern about AZT 82–3
demonization of 24
denialism 113–15
letter to world leaders 88–9
comparisons with apartheid 89
defense of AIDS dissidents 89
national AIDS policy 8, 10–12, 20, 81–3
political views 79–80
popular portrayal 123–4
Rath, Matthias 87
speech to International AIDS Conference 89–90
outcry to 89–90
State of the Nation Addresses 20
Tshabalala-Msimang, Manto 80
views on AIDS 80–81, 88–9
poverty 89
racism 90